Fatal Desire

Fatal Desire

Women, Sexuality, and the

English Stage, 1660–1720

 JEAN I. MARSDEN

Cornell University Press

ITHACA AND LONDON

First published 2006 by Cornell University Press

Printed in the United States of America

Library of Congress Cataloging-in-Publication Data
Marsden, Jean I.
  Fatal desire : women, sexuality, and the English stage, 1660–1720 / Jean I. Marsden.
      p. cm.
  Includes bibliographical references and index.
  ISBN-13: 978-0-8014-4447-0 (cloth : alk. paper)
  ISBN-10: 0-8014-4447-0 (cloth : alk. paper)
    1. English drama—Restoration, 1660–1700—History and criticism.
2. Women in the theater—England—History—17th century.   3. English drama (Tragedy)—History and criticism.   4. Women and literature—England—History—17th century.   5. Literature and society—England—History—17th century.   6. Sex role in literature.   I. Title.
  PR698.W6M27 2006
  822'.3093522—dc22   2005027429

Cornell University Press strives to use environmentally responsible suppliers and materials to the fullest extent possible in the publishing of its books. Such materials include vegetable-based, low-VOC inks and acid-free papers that are recycled, totally chlorine-free, or partly composed of nonwood fibers. For further information, visit our website at www.cornellpress.cornell.edu.

Cloth printing   10 9 8 7 6 5 4 3 2 1

Contents

For Lane

Acknowledgments

I thank a variety of people and institutions who helped make this book possible. Release time provided by a University of Connecticut Provost's Fellowship enabled me to begin writing the project, and the University of Connecticut Research Foundation has been generous in its provision of travel and research monies. My Department Head, Bob Tilton, and Dean, Ross MacKinnon, have also provided invaluable support, and I would have been lost without the assistance of the English Department staff, in particular the cheerful help and friendship of Mary Udal. More recently the University of Connecticut Humanities Institute has assisted me with final preparations of the manuscript. I owe Richard Bleiler of the Homer Babbidge Library a special note of thanks for his tireless work on behalf of all of us in the Humanities; his expertise has aided not only this project but those of many of my colleagues.

I have benefited from the learning of many in the field of eighteenth-century studies. I am deeply grateful to my two readers for Cornell University Press, Lisa A. Freeman and Cynthia Lowenthal: their generous comments proved invaluable in revising the manuscript. I also offer my thanks to the many scholars whose work and conversation have shaped my thought about Restoration and eighteenth-century drama: Helen Burke, Deborah Payne Fisk, Pat Gill, Peter Holland, Clare Kinney, Robert Markley, Jessica Munns, Bridget Orr, Katherine Quinsey, Laura Rosenthal, and Kristina Straub. Sadly, one name is missing from this list as all of us who work in the field of Restoration and eighteenth-century drama mourn the passing of J. Douglas Canfield.

Over the years, my colleagues at the University of Connecticut have furnished me with intellectual and moral support. In particular, Raymond Anselment, Margaret Higonnet, Jerry Phillips, and Hans Turley have read portions of the manuscript and provided much needed advice. I am also grateful for the input of numerous classes of graduate students and for the efforts of my research assistants Aparna Gollapudi, Dawn Goode, and Jeff Roberts. Farther afield, I have been fortunate in the friendship of Anne Goldgar, Michael Dobson, and Sue Stacey and in the hospitality of David Lee, which allowed me to conduct so much of my research at the British Library.

Finally, I thank my family who have put up with me during the duration of this project. I only wish that my uncle, David M. Pletcher, had lived to see its completion. My greatest debt is and always will be to my husband Lane Barrow, who has provided both moral support and invaluable editorial commentary throughout the life of this project. It is dedicated to him.

Portions of this book have appeared in earlier publications. Chapter 1 appeared as "Female Spectatorship, Jeremy Collier, and the Antitheatrical Debate," *ELH* 65 (1998): 851–72; and segments of chapters 3 and 5 appeared as "Sex, Politics, and She-Tragedy: Reconfiguring Lady Jane Grey," *SEL* (summer 2002): 501–22. I am grateful to these publications for permission to reprint this material.

JEAN I. MARSDEN

Storrs, Connecticut

Introduction

Commissioned by Thomas Killigrew and the King's Men, minor poet Thomas Jordan wrote a special prologue for a performance of *Othello* on December 8, 1660. The new prologue stressed the importance and novelty of the day's production, with an actor coming forward to announce:

> I come unknown to any of the rest,
> To tell you news; I saw the Lady drest;
> The Woman plays to day: mistake me not
> No Man in Gown, or Page in Petty-Coat.[1]

In the guise of a backstage spy, Jordan's speaker comes to let the audience in on his secret: the role of Desdemona will be played by a woman, not by a boy, as had been the case when the play was last publicly staged. His words draw attention to one of the most important developments in the history of English drama, the advent of the actress on the public stage. For the first time, female characters were represented by female actors. Although actresses were common elsewhere in Europe during the sixteenth and seventeenth centuries, in England the only women actors had been those visiting with foreign theater companies or ladies who participated in private theatricals. Although there is no question that the boy actors of the Renaissance stage were effective, this practice of an earlier generation must have seemed decidedly old-fashioned to Charles II and his court after their years in exile on the continent.

---

1. Thomas Jordan, Prologue to *Othello*, in *A Nursery of Novelties in Variety of Poetry. Planted for the delightful leisures of Nobility and Ingenuity* (1665), 22.

The very existence of women representing women on the stage, of an actual female presence displayed in public, was to alter the world of English theater. It provided playwrights with a new group of professionals for whom to write and created the opportunity for new literary and dramatic effects. The presence of actresses also provided theater managers with a potent new marketing tool; as the prologue to *Othello* demonstrates, the audience is expected to share the speaker's excitement at the innovation to follow. The implication suggested by the speaker, by Thomas Jordan, and by the management of the King's Men is that a woman in gown and petticoat represents a great improvement in theatrical spectacle over the cross-dressed "man in gown" or "page in petticoat."

And spectacle the actress undoubtedly was. As the speaker in the prologue emphasizes, he "*saw* the lady drest" and thus can assure the audience that what they will be seeing is the real thing: a woman, corporeal and recognizably female. Because he saw the lady "drest" he has ocular proof of exactly what is—and is not—underneath the gown and petticoats. That visible sexual difference is touted as the most noteworthy element of the day's entertainment, and this early prologue makes clear the central importance of looking at the actress, of observing sexual difference. Acknowledging that the actress will "Play upon the Stage, where all eyes are upon her," Jordan praises this change in English theatrical tradition:

> And let this be our custom I advise,
> I'm sure this Custom's better then [*sic*] th' Excise,
> And may procure us custom, hearts of flint
> Will melt in passion when a woman's in't.
>
> (22)

Jordan's multiple pun on "custom" links the sight of the woman to both theatrical innovation and cold, hard cash. Not only will the actress be a pleasant addition to the theater, but her presence on the stage will "procure" "custom," primarily, Jordan suggests, through the erotic component her presence will bring to the theater. When a (male) audience has a woman to lay eyes upon, even "hearts of flint / will melt in passion."[2] That passion, Jordan reminds us, generated by the sight of the actress, represents financial gain to the fledgling theaters.

---

2. While I certainly do not wish to deny the possibility of same-sex desire excited by the spectacle of the actress, the prologues and epilogues of the later seventeenth century display an overwhelming emphasis on male desire for the female image of the actress.

Jordan ignores and even downplays the potential verisimilitude of having a woman play a woman, describing the actress's visual impact almost exclusively in terms of her sexual appeal to the audience. So strong was this erotic element, that it even overrode attempts to eliminate the obscene or lascivious. Although Jordan promises to "purge every thing that is unclean" (22), he does not expect this cleansing process to negate the financially profitable arousal of passion stimulated by the presence of the actress. Her appearance made possible the use of female sexuality not simply as discourse but as genuine spectacle, and playwrights and theater managers were quick to take advantage of this new opportunity. Plays written and adapted for the new theaters were to reflect the new female presence within the formulas of the dramatic text, as playwrights created scenes and characters that allowed the actresses to display their sexual difference and to demonstrate that they were much more than a page in petticoats. At the same time, the staging of Restoration drama emphasized the presence of the female body on the stage by producing tableaux that revealed this sexualized body to the audience's gaze. Sexual titillation was certainly nothing new to the English stage—it is a staple of much Jacobean tragedy—but titillation focused on the spectacle of an actual female body was a new development.

Fatal Desire explores the impact of the theatrical spectacle of female sexuality on the world of Restoration and early-eighteenth-century theater. I do not intend to examine individual actresses, their lives, and professional appearances, nor do I wish to focus exclusively on the literary texts of the Restoration. Too often, studies of Restoration and eighteenth-century theater have tended to splinter into one or the other of these camps, either focusing intensively on historical detail or downplaying the historical context of performance in favor of textual exegesis. Instead, this book focuses on the impact of women on the stage and in the theater, examining the ways in which their material presence altered the representation of women in drama and even reshaped dramatic form at a time when theater was the most public and most debated literary venue. Using the upsurge of female-centered tragedy as a lens, *Fatal Desire* examines the implications of both the real and symbolic representation of women on our understanding of the construction of gender during this pivotal time in English history. Moving beyond the confines of the stage and exploring critical and moral debates as well as play texts, I consider how the theater of the late seventeenth and early eighteenth centuries reflected and informed the changing sexual roles women played in society. Through this approach, I bring together text and context, the fact of a woman's presence and the ways in which its effect was assessed and exploited.

IN his landmark *History of Sexuality,* Michel Foucault defines sexuality as "the name that can be given a historical construct,"[3] an argument that today has become almost a truism in literary studies. Nancy Armstrong likewise emphasizes the term's temporal connections, describing sexuality as "the cultural dimension of sex."[4] Even though both Foucault and Armstrong link sexuality and its consequences specifically to language, even more relevant for the study of drama is the sexual "discourse" created not only verbally but visually. While the relationship between the performance of sexuality and its role on the stage has been considered in recent studies of the boy actors of the Renaissance,[5] these issues have had less impact on studies of the Restoration and eighteenth-century theater, although Elizabeth Howe and Deborah Payne Fisk have written fine studies of early actresses.[6] The actress was recognizably female, with her breasts, loosened hair, and frequently revealed legs, all signs of womanhood emphasized in the roles she played. These physical signs not only established the actress's sex, but also linked her to other women, especially those sitting in the theater. This seeming equation between the image of woman on the stage and the woman in the audience becomes a source of cultural anxiety, especially, I would suggest, because the representation of women cannot be separated from a representation of their sexuality. To understand the effect of the actress as emblem of female sexuality, we must situate her presence within a cultural context that incor-

3. Michel Foucault, *History of Sexuality,* vol. 1, *An Introduction,* trans. Robert Hurley (1976), 105.

4. Nancy Armstrong, *Desire and Domestic Fiction: A Political History of the Novel* (1987), 11.

5. See for example Lisa Jardine, *Still Harping on Daughters: Women and Drama in the Age of Shakespeare* (1983); Michael Shapiro, *Gender in Play on the Shakespearean Stage: Boy Heroines and Female Pages* (1994); and Stephen Orgel's numerous publications on the subject, including "Nobody's Perfect; or, Why Did the English Stage Take Boys for Women," *Southern Atlantic Quarterly* 88 (1989): 7–30, and *Impersonations: The Performance of Gender in Shakespeare's England* (1996).

6. Elizabeth Howe, *The First English Actresses: Women and Drama 1660–1700* (1992); Deborah Payne Fisk, "Reified Object or Emergent Professional? Retheorizing the Restoration Actress," in *Cultural Readings of Restoration and Eighteenth-Century Theater,* ed. J. Douglas Canfield and Deborah Payne, 13–38 (1995). For other considerations of women in the theater see also *Broken Boundaries: Women and Feminism in Restoration Drama,* ed. Katherine M. Quinsey (1996), and the work of Pat Gill, Cynthia Lowenthal, and Laura J. Rosenthal. Jacqueline Pearson's useful book *The Prostitute Muse: Images of Women and Women Dramatists, 1642–1737* (1988), focuses largely on women playwrights.

porates both the stage and its patrons. Only then can we, like Thomas Jordan, *see* the performative nature of gender and sexuality on the Restoration and eighteenth-century stage.

In studying Restoration and eighteenth-century theater, we find that discussions of the female image quickly become discussions of sexuality. Not only the drama of the period, but the extradramatic material, pamphlets, poems, prefaces, and reviews, focus incessantly on the sexual nature and behavior of women in the theaters, both those represented on the stage and those present in the audience. With concepts of femininity linked inextricably with sexual behavior, the representation of women became of necessity a representation of sexuality. How this sexuality should be depicted was a topic of debate, with female sexual desire a contested site/sight in both comedy and tragedy. Although the presence of the actress provided theater managers and playwrights with a means to market sexuality, this salable commodity could also be dangerous. The sight of the lady rather than the page in petticoats might be a theatrical boon and a sexual turn-on, but the representation of this image had serious social and political implications to late-seventeenth- and early-eighteenth-century audiences. Female sexuality was the means by which power and property were handed down from generation to generation; women were the vessel not simply for the male seed but for the legitimate lines of inheritance. Properly managed, their fecundity ensured the orderly succession of property and power from father to son, reinforcing the patrilinear structures underlying early modern English society. Thus sociopolitical stability was dependent on patrilinear control of female sexuality.

Even representing a woman's desires could have profound political implications. As some observers warned, uncontrolled female appetites could result in the downfall of the emerging British Empire. Dramatic representation of transgressive sexual behavior could, it was feared, set a bad example and influence otherwise virtuous women in the theater audience, in effect shattering national security. When Drury Lane chose to stage *All for Love* rather than his version of Shakespeare's *Coriolanus*, playwright and critic John Dennis used precisely this reasoning to object to the staging of Dryden's play:

> Is not the Chastity of the Marriage Bed one of the chief Incendiaries of Publick Spirit, and the Frequency of Adulteries one of the chief Extinguishers of it? . . . For when Adultery's become so frequent, especially among Persons of Condition, upon whose Sentiments all Publick Spirit chiefly depends, that a great many Husbands begin to believe, or perhaps

but to suspect, that they who are called their Children are not their own; I appeal to you, Sir, if that Belief or that Suspicion must not exceedingly cool their Zeal for the Welfare of those Children, and consequently for the Welfare of Posterity.[7]

For Dennis, as for many moralists of the Restoration and eighteenth century, married chastity represents the foundation of public spirit and ultimately patriotism, because by being unchaste a woman can destroy the structure of inheritance ("posterity") on which the nation is built. Allowing the theater to represent displays of unlicensed desire such as that depicted in *All for Love* could lead, as Dennis asserts, to the destruction of the aristocracy and through it the state itself. Thus, uncontrolled female desire can result not only in illegitimate children but, by extension, illegitimate governments.

Female sexuality also becomes the focus of nascent class conflict as members of the growing merchant class voice their resentment at upper-class cultural hegemony in terms of the image of women they see on the stage. Writing in opposition to the building of a theater in Goodman's Fields, one merchant asks why *any* man of his class would want to attend the theater. "For what?" he inquires,

Not to see what may improve themselves in their *Business,* or teach them how to regulate their *Lives,* govern their *Families,* or educate their *Children* to honest Labour and Industry; for all this Sort of Instruction is beneath the Scope of all the Plays that have hitherto been represented on the *British* stage . . . but to see how the People in *high Life* confound all Distinction of Right and Wrong; how the Men of *Taste* intrigue and form Plots upon the *Wives* and *Daughters* of the *honest* Citizens in particular; how they run out their Fortunes, pay nobody, and make a Jest of this Class of Men, who are to be tempted to come and see acted in Representation, what they have found too much of before in fact.[8]

As the writer observes, these plays present the sight of aristocratic "Men of *Taste*" seducing the wives and daughters of honest citizens, "in particular." Although his argument is with rakes who "make a Jest" of him and his fellow citizens, his complaint is voiced in terms of a woman's bed. The fears articulated in this pamphlet can be seen as harbingers of a shift in

7. John Dennis, from a letter to Sir Richard Steele (1719), *The Critical Works of John Dennis,* ed. Edward Niles Hooker, (1943), 2:163–64.

8. *A Seasonal Examination of the Pleas and Pretensions of the Proprietors of, and Subscribers to, Play-Houses, Erected in Defiance of the Royal Licence. With Some Brief Observations on the Printed Case of the* Players *belonging to* Drury-Lane *and* Covent-Garden *Theatres* (1735), 15.

cultural control as "honest citizens" gain political and economic power and become more than mere butts of the aristocratic "Jest." This shift in cultural control is represented symbolically through the female image. By the mid eighteenth century, new drama would project a decidedly less sensuous vision of female sexuality where chastity on all social levels becomes an expected virtue.[9] In the process, older plays would be carefully edited to remove offending passages, as if eliminating the representation would eliminate the actuality.

As Dennis and the author of *A Seasonal Examination* indicate, spectatorship becomes the means by which to articulate social and political concerns. Dennis distrusts the staging of *All for Love*, the author of *A Seasonal Examination* the staging of any British play, because of what the audience will see. What they will see is indeed the actress, if not the lady, dressed. This repeatedly articulated concern with the role of the spectator and the function of the female image prompts me to turn to film studies as a means of bringing together text and performance in Restoration and eighteenth-century theater. Despite a gap of nearly three hundred years, the issues central to much recent work on film are strikingly analogous to those expressed centuries earlier, especially in regard to the consideration of women's role as spectacle. In the past two decades, film theory has focused increasingly on what Teresa de Lauretis describes as "cinematic codes that construct woman as image, as the object of the spectator's voyeuristic gaze."[10] Strongly influenced by the work of Freud and Lacan, these studies probe the workings of these codes and the ways in which they affect the spectator, much as early writings on the theater probed the effect of theater on its audience.

The genesis of this psychoanalytic and semiotic approach was Laura Mulvey's influential 1975 article, "Visual Pleasure and Narrative Cinema." Basing her argument on Freud's discussion of scopophilia, Mulvey examined the sources of scopic pleasure in cinema, finding them located in the display of the female figure:

> In their traditional exhibitionist role women are simultaneously looked at and displayed, with their appearance coded for strong visual and erotic impact so that they can be said to connote *to-be-looked-at-ness*. Woman displayed as sexual object is the leitmotif of erotic spectacle: from pin-ups to

---

9. To see the shift in attitudes, one need only compare George Lillo's *The London Merchant* (1731), written shortly before this pamphlet, with Thomas Shadwell's *The Squire of Alsatia* (1688). In Shadwell's play, a middle-class character (Lucia, daughter of an attorney) is seduced by the hero of the play while in Lillo's the saintly Maria, daughter of a wealthy tradesman, does not even admit her love for Barnwell until he is condemned to death.

10. Teresa de Lauretis, *Technologies of Gender: Essays on Theory, Film, and Fiction* (1987), 13.

striptease, from Ziegfeld to Busby Berkeley, she holds the look, plays to and signifies male desire.[11]

The important component here is Mulvey's concept of "to-be-looked-at-ness," the cultural construction of the woman as object of the gaze. Although the male controls the gaze, the woman becomes its object, a commodity to be displayed for its erotic impact. Her figure thus becomes "erotic spectacle," the desired object for both the characters within the film (or drama) and in the auditorium. Mulvey suggests that cinematic and cultural codes establish the woman as icon, the passive object of the gaze, and the man as active subject, the "figure in the landscape" whose adventures constitute narrative.

Most work in film theory since Mulvey has wrestled with these basic elements: the spectator, the object, and the nature of scopic pleasure. Such studies are perhaps most useful in their exploration of the connection between sight and desire. In the system they describe, the gaze creates desire within the subject and establishes the person gazed on as object so that as a corollary, the act of gazing objectifies the other person. Scopophilia's crucial distinction thus lies between the desiring subject and the desired object, the gazer and the gazed on. The paradigm with which we are most familiar has consisted of a male spectator gazing on a female object, and it is this scenario that has formed the basis for most discussions of spectatorship and cinema. In conventional film, Mulvey and de Lauretis argue, the audience is invited to play the voyeur and gaze at the body of the actress—a spectacle presented for public consumption.

These theories have obvious resonance for Restoration and eighteenth-century theater. Like twentieth-century film, theater after 1660 was a highly visual medium, using spectacle of all kinds to attract audiences. Although observers mentioned the auditory effects of the theater, most writers, like those cited above, focused on the visual; even though a reader might be affected by reading a play, written text lacked the power of visual representation. (Authors of antitheatrical tracts argued that because of its linked visual and sensual qualities, the event of theater was morally debased and even dangerous.)[12] In their emphasis on theater's iniquity, even writers

11. Laura Mulvey, "Visual Pleasure and Narrative Cinema," *Screen* 16, no. 3 (autumn 1975): 6–18; reprinted in *The Sexual Subject: A Screen Reader in Sexuality* (1992), 27.

12. See for example, Anthony Horneck, D.D., *Delight and Judgment; or, A Prospect of the Great Day of Judgment, and its Power to damp, and imbitter Sensual Delights, Sports and Recreations* (1684): "There is a great difference between reading of a thing and seeing it acted with all the vanity and boldness, that usually attend it. In reading, a mans serious thoughts are not dispersed or scattered, but keep within the balance of modesty, and weigh things in the ballance of reason, whereas being Acted to the life, they naturally strike vanity into the mind,

such as Jeremy Collier relied on theories of spectatorship in order to bolster their claims regarding the noxious effects of theater. Although positive in their approach, dramatists were equally dependent on these concepts. Because of the importance placed on spectacle in seventeenth- and eighteenth-century theater, theories of spectatorship and the gaze provide a powerful tool with which to examine the role the new female presence on the stage played in this realm of the visual. Her "to-be-looked-at-ness" is repeatedly exploited for dramatic effect, especially in the she-tragedies that dominated the stage during these years. As this book will show, much Restoration and early-eighteenth-century drama depended on a display of the eroticized woman for its visual and emotional effect.

Perhaps most important, the work of Mulvey, de Lauretis, and other film theorists provides a means for considering Restoration drama not simply as text but as text in performance. It was on the stage, not on the page, that drama's potential to sway public emotion could be realized. Not merely the by-product of postmodern theorizing, these concerns with gazing and with the power of that gaze were also current in the Restoration and eighteenth century. Throughout that period, the issues of vision permeated drama, while the language of sight defined much of the contemporary discussion of drama, a fact recognized and exploited by writers, dramatists, and theatergoers. Restoration and eighteenth-century playwrights, critics, and moralists were well acquainted with the power of the gaze and its ability to arouse desire and even shape political and gender ideology. In a social system that had already identified women as commodities for homosocial exchange, the advent of the actress presented an opportunity for visual representation of this exchange. At the same time, plays such as Nicholas Rowe's *Tragedy of Lady Jane Gray* repeatedly code political subtexts in terms of female display.

However, the application of film studies to theater has important limitations. Most important, despite sharing the common components of spectator and event, cinema and theater are two distinctly different mediums. Where film depends on an image frozen in time and space, controlled and endlessly repeatable, the theater spectator gazes on a living image. This distinction has significant implications. Mulvey's description of how spectatorship functions within the movie theater underscores the lack of a one-to-one correspondence between film and theater, a correspondence that some critics have been too willing to make. Most mainstream films, she suggests,

---

affect the sensual part, drive away seriousness, and leave an unhappy tincture behind them" (221).

portray a hermetically sealed world which unwinds magically, indifferent to the presence of the audience, producing for them a sense of separation and playing on their voyeuristic phantasy [*sic*]. Moreover, the extreme contrast between the darkness in the auditorium (which also isolates the spectators from one another) and the brilliance of the shifting patterns of light and shade on the screen helps to promote the illusion of voyeuristic separation.[13]

But the world of Restoration theater was not hermetically sealed, nor was it indifferent to the presence of the audience. Not only did members of the audience sit on the stage, but in some cases they became part of the action and objects of the gaze, a gaze which could be wielded by the actress herself, as demonstrated in numerous prologues and epilogues. Spectatorship operated differently in this different environment; not only was the contrast between darkness and light largely nonexistent, making the "illusion of voyeuristic separation" more difficult, but the audience's gaze could wander between several images on the stage and within the audience itself. In general, the intimate character of Restoration and early-eighteenth-century playhouses made attendance a communal event. Under these circumstances, to what degree could the audience's experience be said to be voyeuristic? Although characters on stage might—and did—play the voyeur, their counterparts in the audience would have had more difficulty participating in this "voyeuristic phantasy." Faced with an audience whose gaze was easily fragmented, playwrights had to employ a variety of techniques to direct the eyes of their audience. Theatrical spectacle was one such technique, and as in film, the source of this spectacle was often the female image, sexualized and objectified.

Although I have drawn from the Lacanian-inspired work of Mulvey and de Lauretis, my incorporation of the concepts generated by work in film theory diverges from theirs, just as the different media of film and theater diverge. One significant difference appears in my use of key concepts, in particular two terms central to my discussion of the representation of women: desire and agency. In keeping with *Fatal Desire*'s emphasis on historical context, my use of the term *desire* is narrowly focused to mean a woman's specifically *sexual* feelings, thus incorporating the Restoration and eighteenth century's deep anxiety over women's sexual behavior. Much of the drama of this period hinges on questions involving whether women felt these urges, and crucially, in what context? Most

---

13. Mulvey, "Visual Pleasure and Narrative Cinema," 25. Other critics such as Mary Ann Doane also stress the importance of the separation between spectator and image. See "Film and Masquerade: Theorizing the Female Spectator," *Screen* 23, nos. 3–4 (1982): 74–87.

important of all, did they act on their sexual feelings? This introduces the concept of "agency," the degree to which a woman actively rather than passively participates in her sexual activity. The distinction between active and passive sexuality becomes increasingly important as the eighteenth century progresses. Where earlier dramas tend to consider a woman's sexual experiences more generally, for later writers and audiences, the central point becomes the degree to which the woman *acted* on these urges—even if her action consisted of no more than articulating her feelings. By the end of the period I examine, the expression of desire itself becomes a questionable act, even within the sanctity of the marriage bed. The ultimate illustration of this sexually mute woman becomes the mother rather than the wife or lover and, later in the century, the faithful daughter.

As a theoretical model, film theory provokes a variety of useful questions for feminist studies of Restoration and eighteenth-century theater, questions that have also surfaced in recent debates over the direction of feminist film studies. Perhaps the most central and problematic questions have concerned the function of the female spectator. By assuming that the dominant or "normal" spectator is male, Lacanian film theory, particularly that written during the 1970s and early 1980s, privileged the male gaze, resulting in the virtual exclusion of the female gaze. Although this approach has been reconsidered, determining a methodology that can accommodate the woman as spectator has proved to be difficult.[14] The problem of theorizing a female spectator prompted Mulvey to revisit her argument in "Visual Pleasure and Narrative Cinema" years later.[15] Mary Ann Doane, author of "Film and the Masquerade: Theorizing the Female Spectator," an early and influential essay on the mechanism of female spectatorship, has also returned to the topic several times in subsequent articles and books.[16] No consensus on female response has emerged out of these considerations and reconsiderations.

As Jackie Stacey observes in her study of women cinemagoers, some of

14. *Camera Obscura* devoted an entire special issue to differing formulations of the female spectator (20/21, 1989).

15. "Afterthoughts on 'Visual Pleasure and Narrative Cinema' inspired by *Duel in the Sun*," *Framework* 6, nos. 15–17 (1981): 12–15; reprinted in *Feminism and Film Theory*, ed. Constance Penley (1988), 69–79. The opening of this essay addresses the issue directly: "So many times over years since my article 'Visual Pleasure and Narrative Cinema,' was published in *Screen*, I have been asked why I only used the male third person singular to stand in for the spectator" (69).

16. "Film and Masquerade: Theorizing the Female Spectator," *Screen* 23, nos. 3–4 (1982): 74–87; "Masquerade Reconsidered: Further Thoughts on the Female Spectator," *Discourse* 11, no. 1 (1988–89): 42–54. Both essays are reprinted in *Femmes Fatales: Feminism, Film Theory, Psychoanalysis* (1991); several other essays in this volume also touch on the question of the female spectator.

the difficulty with the female spectator has arisen out of theory itself. Calling for a more historical approach to the "woman in the audience," she notes that "instead of the textual spectator within feminist theory, much recent cultural studies work has argued for a model of the spectator as a social subject, who is herself inscribed by various and competing discursive formations (such as gender, class, ethnicity and sexuality)."[17] Like Stacey, I am interested in the historical and cultural context of the woman in the audience. However, scholars of late-seventeenth- and early-eighteenth-century theater are faced with the additional difficulty that very few documents survive (if indeed they ever existed) which provide a firsthand account of a woman's response to the theater. Thus, although the female spectator played a pivotal role in the theater[18] and in writings about the theater, she herself remains a cipher. In light of this, my comments on the female spectator focus more on how she was constructed by playwrights, critics, and moralists than on the historical entity of the woman in the audience. Although historical records of women's response to the theater may not exist, the nature of this response was discussed as much by her contemporaries as by scholars today. It was to many a source of anxiety even greater than the female image represented on the stage— if the theatrical image was supposed to raise "passion" in a male viewer, what effect would this image have on a woman?

As responses such as those by Dennis and the author of *A Seasonal Examination* reveal, early modern theatergoers and theater critics tended to view the stage in relation to its social impact. Their concern with the sociopolitical effect of the female image presented on the audience and especially on the female audience suggests that the historical scholar must balance any theoretical model with a careful consideration of the cultural context in which a play was staged. Because of the importance of this context to those who wrote both for and about the theater, studying the drama of the Restoration and early eighteenth century requires a balance between text and performance. There, the image of woman's sexuality was both exciting and frightening, but more a source of social rather than individual anxiety.[19] With the preservation of property and privilege de-

17. Jackie Stacey, *Star Gazing: Hollywood Cinema and Female Spectatorship* (1994), 47. For an lucid discussion of arguments regarding the female spectator in feminist theory, see chap. 2, "From the Male Gaze to the Female Spectator," especially 22–30.

18. See David Roberts, *The Ladies: Female Patronage of Restoration Drama, 1660–1700* (1989), for a discussion of the female audience and the effect of their patronage of the theater.

19. Because of its foundations in psychoanalysis, much film theory has been inclined to read the cinematic representation of woman and her image as the cue for individual anxiety. To the male spectator, the female image represents castration while the female spectator is in essence erased. Mulvey, for example, claims that woman is seen as "the bearer of the

pendent on male control of female sexuality, unrestrained women represented the potential for complete social disintegration. Tantalizing, destructive, possibly even liberating, female sexuality was inevitably recognized as a paramount social issue (even though it might have important individual ramifications). In order to explore the representation of sexuality, we must incorporate its cultural context, which is radically different from that of the late twentieth century. If we reject essentialism, we must consider reception. Remembering that drama functions as a technology of gender, we must examine sexuality both as it was constructed for and perceived by its audience: How were the plays, and the images of women within them, received by the spectators and by the culture at large? In what ways were these images designed to elicit a specific response? In addition, because culture is not static, we need to consider the ways in which these responses change over time. Thus theory intersects with culture, bringing us back to the historical imperative with which I began my discussion of the issue of sexuality.

Although these musings may seem a simultaneous demand for and rejection of a theoretical reading of drama, they are meant as a call for an approach both informed by theory and yet not driven by that theory, rigorous in examination of historical context and yet willing to transcend detail. Such a balanced approach accommodates the abstract concepts of spectatorship employed by Restoration and eighteenth-century writers, as I explore in my opening chapter. It also provides an effective context for considering the woman-centered drama of this period, a time when the erotic spectacle of the suffering woman dominated the stage.

USING serious drama as a focal point, *Fatal Desire* examines the representation of women from the Restoration into the early eighteenth century, concentrating on the ways in which the dramatic depiction of female sexuality functions to promote a broader gender ideology. Post-Restoration tragedy, particularly that of the last decade of the seventeenth century and the first two decades of the eighteenth century, has long been overlooked or denigrated largely because of its emphasis on pathos and a general sense that such an overt emotional appeal is unliterary. There has been strangely little interest in the drama that not only dominated the

bleeding wound; she can exist only in relation to castration and cannot transcend it" ("Visual Pleasure and Narrative Cinema," 22). In such a biologically determined system, spectator response becomes a feature of universal psychological principles dependent on sex, principles which, according to psychoanalytic theory, remain constant through time rather than culturally determined qualities such as gender, class, or politics.

stage at the time it was written but which remained in theaters throughout the eighteenth century, second in popularity only to Shakespeare.[20] I
argue that the feminization of serious drama during this period is tied to
the cultural function of theater. Because of women's function as symbols
of both domestic and imperial propriety, any consideration of women in
drama must link the representation of women on the stage to the social
context in which they appeared and to the moral and often political
lessons they presented to the men and women in the audience. These
lessons are especially evident in the tragedies that are the main subject of
Fatal Desire; although the witty heroines of comedies were usually ab-
sorbed into the social fabric via proper marriages with witty gentlemen,
the heroines of tragedy suffer for their sins, real or perceived. Their suffering serves the dual purpose of pleasing and educating the theater
audience.

The book opens with an exploration of seventeenth- and eighteenth-
century assumptions concerning the female spectator and the effect,
both good and bad, of theatergoing on women. These assumptions appear most strikingly in the antitheatrical debate that raged at the turn of
the eighteenth century in the wake of Jeremy Collier's argument that not
only was England's theater immoral and profane but that this model of
immodesty would have deleterious effects on the women who viewed
it. The second chapter expands this discussion of female spectatorship
into an examination of two comedies, William Wycherley's *The Plain
Dealer* (1676) and John Vanbrugh's *The Prokov'd Wife* (1697), which directly confront the problem of the woman as spectator. The two plays
reach very different conclusions about the relationship between the female gaze and a woman's virtue. Although Wycherley's hard-edged
comedy attacks women who stray from the feminine ideal, the under-
current of sympathy for the abused wife in Vanbrugh's comedy corre-

---

20. Notable exceptions to this tendency include the work of J. Douglas Canfield, in his
early monograph *Nicholas Rowe and Christian Tragedy* (1977) and more recently in his study
of Restoration and early-eighteenth-century serious drama, *Heroes and States: On the Ideology
of Restoration Tragedy* (2000). Derek Hughes gives a thorough overview of the tragedies of the
period in *English Drama, 1660–1700* (1996), frequently bringing in issues of gender, although
his preference lies with the comedies of the post-Otway era. While in *The Development of English Drama in the Late Seventeenth Century* (1976) Robert D. Hume extends his discussion of
later-seventeenth-century drama into the early eighteenth century, his assessment of the
affective tragedies of this period is frequently scathing. Eric Rothstein is more forgiving;
however his discussion of post-Otway tragedy focuses largely on the heroes rather than
the heroines of late-seventeenth-century drama (*Restoration Tragedy: Form and the Process of
Change* [1967]). Recently the plays of female playwrights such as Delarivier Manley, Mary
Pix, and Catharine Trotter have attracted renewed attention; however, much of this scholarship has focused on comedy rather than tragedy.

sponds to the broader focus on female distress prevalent in the tragedies of Vanbrugh's contemporaries.

As plays such as *The Provok'd Wife* demonstrate, by the end of the seventeenth century drama took on a female face, and in serious drama the shift was profound as the representation of women became the primary source of emotional response. Using the discussion of female sexual agency and spectatorship explored in the opening chapter as a foundation, the remainder of the book examines the growing use of female suffering for spectacular effect. In the so-called "she-tragedies" of the later seventeenth and early eighteenth centuries, audience members were invited to watch female characters in erotic situations that led to their suffering and eventual death. As Kristina Straub notes in her discussion of sexuality and the eighteenth-century actor, "the assumption that the structure of the gaze empowers the spectator over the spectacle is a historical construction, probably just emerging in the eighteenth century," arising out of "a consciousness that the spectator's gaze is enacted within a power differential between the watcher and the watched."[21] She-tragedy provides one of the clearest examples of this power dynamic at work on the stage, a dynamic manipulated for the benefit of the theater audience. The third chapter examines the mechanics of sight and gender as articulated by writers of the time and as embodied in she-tragedy, exploring works such as Thomas Otway's *The Orphan* (1680), Thomas Southerne's *The Fatal Marriage; or, The Innocent Adultery* (1694), and William Congreve's *The Mourning Bride* (1697). The most popular tragedies of their time, these plays present women who have been tainted by a sexual sin, usually performed unwittingly, and whose suffering becomes the play's visual and emotional center. In an age of cynicism and political turmoil, such suffering provided a kind of authenticity that the fate of kings and empires no longer possessed.

Subsequent chapters address important variations on this theme. For example, when female suffering has become the raison d'être of tragedy, the question arises of how women playwrights deal with such a potentially problematic literary form. The fourth chapter considers tragedies written by three female playwrights, the so-called "Female Wits," and explores the ways in which women writers adopt and, in the case of Catharine Trotter, challenge the prevailing ethos of female desire and its link to suffering and death. The fifth and sixth chapters contextualize the tragedies of Nicholas Rowe in order to address developments both in drama and in gender ideology. As the eighteenth century began, she-tragedy

---

21. Kristina Straub, *Sexual Suspects: Eighteenth-Century Players and Sexual Ideology* (1992), 5.

moved away from the lurid plots of the final years of the seventeenth century into more decorous forms of spectacle. Women still form the centerpiece of drama, but the plays express increasing anxiety over female agency, as demonstrated not only in Rowe's two great she-tragedies, *The Fair Penitent* (1703) and *Jane Shore* (1714), but in a variety of less celebrated works. I conclude by examining the obsession with Lady Jane Grey that accompanied the Hanoverian succession; the emphasis on Jane's chastity as well as her role as a Protestant martyr heralds later developments in drama as depictions of female eroticism became unacceptable to audiences in the later eighteenth century. Using Nicholas Rowe's *The Tragedy of Lady Jane Gray* (1715) as its focal point, this final chapter examines the interplay between female desire and political ideology, a dynamic that led to the collapse of she-tragedy. In order to make his political argument successful, Rowe establishes his heroine as an icon of political and sexual virtue rather than a titillating spectacle. As responses to the play indicate, without the familiar spectacle of female distress, she-tragedy fails.

The conjunction of *Lady Jane Gray* and the Hanoverian succession brings to a close an unusual period in English theater, a time when women rather than men dominated the stage and when the heroine rather than the hero defined tragedy. At this time, drama was both a social and a literary form, the only major literature that was publicly presented; the events and figures represented therefore took on symbolic importance. *Fatal Desire* explores how the heroines of these plays were constructed, staged, and received. Why did playwrights turn to women as the embodiments of tragic meaning and what did these images of female suffering teach their audience? Because she-tragedy was public theater not closet drama, we need to approach these questions by considering the spectator as well as the actress, as did critics and playwrights both in theory and in practice. The female image was both actress and character, a socially charged emblem comprised of flesh and blood.

CHAPTER 1

Female Spectatorship, Jeremy Collier, and the Antitheatrical Debate

In 1662, Richard Baker defended the stage by protesting, "Indeed, it is not so much the Player, that makes the Obscenity, as the Spectator himself."[1] Baker's words, written in response to William Prynne's massive diatribe against the theater, *Histrio-Mastix, the Players Scovrge; or, Actors Tragaedy* (1633), express the shift in emphasis from actor to spectator that was to become the central focus of late-seventeenth- and early-eighteenth-century writing for and about the stage. Taking issue with Prynne's description of the actor as not only obscene but hypocritical, Baker represents theater as the interaction of spectator and spectacle, a communal experience in which the audience plays a crucial role in interpreting the representation. This emphasis on audience response is a critical component in the many discussions of the theater published during the next fifty years. Although Baker's own work deals more with exposing the fallacies of a previous generation of antitheatrical prejudices, its emphasis on theater as representation and on the dynamics of audience response is important to the Restoration and eighteenth-century understanding of drama. His book represents the first of a series of often sophisticated discussions of the complex relationship between visual representation and the spectator and between spectatorship and desire.

These commentaries, most notably those in opposition to the theater, articulate a complex concept of spectatorship, prefiguring by several cen-

---

1. Richard Baker, *Theatrum Redivivum; or, The Theatre Vindicated, in Answer to Mr. Pryn's Histrio-mastix: Wherein his groundless Assertions against Stage-Plays are discovered, his miss-taken Allegations of the Fathers manifested, as also what he calls his Reasons, to be nothing but his Passions* (1662), 31.

turies Lacan and an entire generation of film theorists. The system they describe involves an image (here a living image), an audience which watches that image, and a reflexive gaze that excites desire. As Baker explains, it is the spectator who makes the "obscenity," who creates the erotic context for what he—or she—sees. In addition, as revealed by attacks on the theater such as Jeremy Collier's *Short View of the Immorality and Profaneness of the English Stage* (1698), concerns of spectatorship cannot be separated from sexuality, particularly female sexuality. Although critics had attacked the immorality of the stage for more than a millennium, among English writers the link between spectatorship and female sexuality can be traced to the explosion of publications that followed Collier. Earlier writers, such as Prynne or Stephen Gosson,[2] had focused their arguments on issues such as the corruptness of actors or the hypocrisy involved in acting, and in particular on the evils of dressing men in women's clothing.[3] This late-seventeenth-century concern with spectatorship appears to be an English phenomenon; continental writers express little interest in the dynamics of audience response.[4]

It is only in the late seventeenth century that attacks on the stage begin to focus directly and repeatedly on the effect of theater on the audience, and in particular on the female members of the audience. The sexuality of the female spectator and the sexuality of the female image that she watches becomes a vital issue in this controversy. Specifically, the antitheatrical writers express an unconcealed fear of the female gaze and its ramifications. How will women respond to what they see on the stage— and how will their reaction affect family and state? Interestingly, these opponents of the stage take women more seriously than those who defend it, admitting the consequences as well as the potency of the female gaze, which they link inexorably to a woman's sexuality. Defenders of the stage not only downplay any potential danger, but frequently ignore the female spectator altogether.

Ironically, there is no female voice in this debate. Despite the widespread concern about the effect of theater on women, and the emphasis on the female spectator that appears in prologues and epilogues, few

2. *Plays Confuted in Five Actions* (1582).

3. Thus violating the edict in Deuteronomy against cross-dressing: "The woman shall not wear that which pertaineth unto a man, neither shall a man put on a woman's garment," 22:5.

4. As Jonas Barish notes, in the seventeenth century "the French writers . . . began to probe the nature of the actor's psychic life," seeing in some cases "an unholy pact between [the actor's] conscious self and his own darkest impulses. *The Antitheatrical Prejudice* (1981), 196–97. Jacques Benigne Bossuet represents perhaps one exception to the rule in his discussion of the spectator in *Maximes et reflexions sur la comedie* (1694).

women actually recorded their responses to the theater. For us, they remain a silent and mysterious presence on whom a generation of moralists projected their own fears. We know they were capable of expressing both displeasure and pleasure; as Wycherley's bitterly witty "Epistle Dedicatory" to *The Plain Dealer* makes clear, the ladies in the London audiences plainly objected to the obscenity of *The Country Wife* and were adept at communicating their objections.[5] Nonetheless, no woman published her views, leaving us without a firsthand account of theatergoing in the Restoration and early eighteenth century. As a result, we find ourselves confronted with a theorized spectator, a woman constructed through the writings of men.[6] Unlike recent work by scholars such as David Roberts and Laura Rosenthal, which focuses on actual women in the theater,[7] my interest in this chapter is this phantom woman, that figure whose shadowy existence and dangerous gaze, it was argued, could lead to moral corruption and social catastrophe.

Jeremy Collier and the "Inclination of Ladies"

Jeremy Collier was neither the first nor the most extreme of the antitheatrical polemicists. The first two decades of Charles II's reign saw little in the way of actual publication against the theater, but by the end of the century even this tacit support had eroded. Although Anthony Horneck's treatise *Delight and Judgment; or, A Prospect of the Great Day of Judgment, And its Power to damp, and imbitter Sensual Delights, Sports and Recreations* appeared in 1684, it was not until the last decade of the seventeenth century that the great wave of antitheatrical books and pamphlets appeared. The timing of this onslaught is not surprising; in the 1680s, London's playhouses had struggled, reduced to a single company

5. See 2.1.390–462 of *The Plain Dealer* in which Wycherley satirizes the "modest" woman's response to *The Country Wife* as well as the sardonic "Epistle Dedicatory" addressed to "Lady B—" (Mother Bennett, a well-known bawd) in which he rails at the women who object to his plays.

6. In this they are not much different from current film theorists who also have a difficult time accommodating the female spectator to their theories of spectatorship. See Stacey on the problems of contemporary film criticism, *Star Gazing*, especially chap. 2: "From the Male Gaze to the Female Spectator."

7. David Roberts, *The Ladies: Female Patronage of Restoration Drama, 1660–1700* (1989), and Laura Rosenthal, "'Counterfeith Scrubbado': Women Actors in the Restoration," *The Eighteenth Century: Theory and Interpretation* 34, no. 1 (1993): 3–22. See also Harold Love, "Who Were the Restoration Audience?" and Arthur H. Scouten and Robert D. Hume, "'Restoration Comedy' and Its Audiences, 1660–1776," both in *The Yearbook of English Studies* 10 (1980): 21–44 and 45–69, for more general accounts of the Restoration theater audience.

by poor audiences and political unrest. After 1695, when audiences were once again sufficient to support two licensed playhouses, theaters rebounded and the number of new plays increased. However, times and audiences had changed. Charles II and James II were gone, and the new monarchs were supported by a Whig government with ties to those very merchants and citizens who had been the object of ridicule in much Restoration comedy. To this contingent, reforming manners was a national concern, and the often bawdy drama popular during Charles II's reign was openly opposed, if not by audiences themselves, then by a growing faction of clergymen, both Anglicans and Dissenters.[8] The first flood of print lasted into 1699, followed by a second burst in 1704.[9] Similar attacks continued to be published through much of the eighteenth century, mostly, however, in the years prior to the passage of the Licensing Act in 1737. Although it is simplistic to link changes in drama to Collier's works alone, Collier's popularity suggests that his ideas had widespread support.[10]

The authors of the earliest attacks were most often churchmen, such as Horneck, Collier, and Arthur Bedford who wrote books and pamphlets, letters, and sermons; Collier himself contributed five books and pamphlets to the growing mass of publications.[11] From the publication of Collier's work onward, the pernicious influence of theater on women became a central feature of these works, and by the eighteenth century, attacks on the theater were often designed for a female audience. Whether sermons, learned treatises, or letters to "Ladies of Quality," these works share a common anxiety regarding the effect of women watching dramatic representations. For the authors, the danger of theater lies in its ability to excite the passions and "fasten upon the Memory"[12] through the medium of sight. Even concerns over profanity or blasphemy wane in comparison

8. The antitheatrical writers were not necessarily "Puritans"; Collier himself had Jacobite sympathies.

9. For a useful summary of the antitheatrical debate see Sister Rose Anthony, *The Jeremy Collier Stage Controversy, 1698–1726* (1937).

10. The best recent assessment of the impact (or lack thereof) of Collier's reform movement is Robert D. Hume, "Jeremy Collier and the Future of the London Theater in 1698," *Studies in Philology* 96, no. 4 (fall 1999): 480–511.

11. In addition to *A Short View* (1698), Collier wrote four additional treatises on the theater: *A Defence of the Short View* (1699); *A Second Defence of the Short View* (1700); *Mr. Collier's Dissuasive from the Playhouse* (1703); and *A Farther Vindication of the Short View* (1708). The second edition of the *Dissuasive from the Playhouse* is much expanded and contains additional responses to his opponents. References to the stage and drama appear in many of Collier's other works.

12. *A Representation of the Impiety and Immorality of the English Stage, With Reasons for putting a Stop thereto: and some Questions Addrest to those who frequent the Play-Houses* (1704), 22.

to the corruption that can result from watching actors and actresses represent "Love Intrigues" and "all Manner of Lewdness." Thus, Horneck claims, spectators see acts performed which in turn prompt them to similar actions: "Here all the wanton looks, and gestures, and postures that be in the mode, are practiced according to art, and you may remember, you have seen people when dismist from a play, strive and labour to get that grace and antick meen [*sic*], they saw in the mimick on the stage."[13] The theaters, in essence, become schools of immodesty as the audience seeks to reproduce what it saw represented so that sight leads inevitably to sin. The only way to fight against such corruption, Horneck notes, is to reject sight entirely, to withdraw the eye from that object completely, "as if it were actually pluck'd out, or were of no use in the body."[14] The physicality of Horneck's image graphically illustrates the physicality of the concern; for him and for the writers who follow him, the gaze is no abstraction but an entity capable of producing a dangerously sensual response.

The erotic link between sight and body is intrinsic to these antitheatrical arguments, and their descriptions of the carnality of the gaze are explicit and even violent. Like Horneck, the anonymous author of *The Conduct of the Stage Consider'd. Being a Short Historical Account of its Original, Progress, various Aspects, and Treatment in the Pagan, Jewish and Christian World* (1721) focuses directly on the eye as a conduit for sin.[15] Citing St. Chrysostom, an early Christian opponent of the stage, the writer uses a biblical example of sexual transgression as his analogy for the dangers of the theater:

> SPEAKING of *David* and *Bathsheba*, he says *David* saw her, and was wounded in his Eye. Let those who hear this who contemplate the beauty of others, and who are possess'd with an unruly Desire after Stage-Plays, who say, we behold them without hurt. What hear I? *David* is hurt, and art not thou? He is wounded, and can I trust to thy Strength? Did he fall who had so great a measure of the Spirit? And canst thou stand? Yet he beheld not an Harlot, but an honest Woman, and that not in the Theatre, but at home; but thou beholdest an Harlot in the Playhouse, where even the very Place itself makes the Soul liable to Punishment.[16]

13. Anthony Horneck, *Delight and Judgment*, 214.
14. Ibid., 217.
15. Complete title: *The Conduct of the Stage Consider'd. Being a Short Historical Account of its Original, Progress, various Aspects, and Treatment in the Pagan, Jewish and Christian World. Together with the Arguments urg'd against it, by Learned Heathens, and by Christians, both Antient and Modern. With Short Remarks upon the Original and Pernicious Consequences of Masquerades.*
16. Ibid., 14–15.

In this passage, the author makes clear the associations between spectatorship and sexuality. The "unruly Desire after Stage-Plays" is translated into a more specific sexual desire mediated through the gaze. Like David, the spectator at the playhouse will be "wounded in his Eye," in other words overcome with desire, through the simple act of gazing on a female image represented by the actress on the stage. The danger lies not in the Harlot/actress, but in the act of looking itself.

Although references to church fathers such as Chrysostom and Cyprian were also common in earlier centuries (Prynne cites them extensively), by the end of the seventeenth century the polemicists focus more definitively on passages that stress the role of the spectator rather than, as in the past, those citing the evils of cross-dressing or the sinful nature of pleasure itself.[17] Citing Salvian, the author of *The Stage Condemn'd* (1698) equates the spectator with what he or she sees because "the Pollution of the Theatre and Stage-Plays are such, as make the Actors and Spectators equally guilty; for whilst they willingly look on, and by that means approve them, they become Actors themselves by Sight and Assent."[18] Sight creates a bond between spectator and event, which of necessity implicates the observer. Because of the link between sight and desire, the nature of this guilt is always distinctly sexual, so that "the Pleasures that are reap'd from the Stage must needs be sensual."[19]

Through their reiteration of the sensual pleasures of the stage, these works establish a dynamic of spectatorship that links the gaze inevitably with the sexuality not only of the object gazed on but of the spectators themselves. Theater thus becomes dangerous not merely as representation in itself but as representation before an audience. Through the medium of sight, theater excites the passions of viewers and encourages them to imitate the passions they see enacted before them. Ultimately, concerns of spectatorship underlie almost every argument against the immorality of the stage. This link between sight and sex becomes of primary

17. Such references are common in the more theologically oriented of the treatises such as in *The Conduct of the Stage Consider'd*. Figures cited most commonly include St. Chrysostom, St. Cyprian, Salvian, Tertullian, and Lactanius.

18. *The Stage Condemn'd, and The Encouragement given to the Immoralities and Profaneness of the Theatre, by the English Schools, Universitys and Pulpits, Censur'd. King Charles I. Sundays Mask and Declaration for Sports and Pastimes on the Sabbath, Largely Related and Animadvertsed upon. The Arguments of all the Authors that have Writ in Defence of the Stage against Mr. Collier, Consider'd. And the Sense of the Fathers, Councils, Antient Philosophers and Poets, and of the Greek and Roman Stages, and of the First Christian Emperours concerning the DRAMA Faithfully Deliver'd. Together with the Censure of the English State and of several Antient and Modern Divines of the Church of England upon the STAGE. And Remarks on diverse late Plays, as also on those presented by the two UNIVERSITIES to King Charles I* (1698), 69.

19. Ibid., 172.

importance with regard to the female spectator, whose gaze becomes the true source of anxiety for Jeremy Collier and his followers.

Collier's popular and controversial *Short View of the Immorality and Profaneness of the English Stage* articulates the problem of the female gaze more cogently than either those who supported him or those who attempted to refute his arguments. As the title indicates, Collier has two main concerns, immorality and profanity; what is less clear is that the immorality he cites is almost entirely directed toward women: the roles they represent on the stage and their experience as members of the audience. After a short introduction, he begins his book with a lengthy chapter on the "Immodesty of the Stage," the immodesty, that is, of its female creations (of the nine characters he cites specifically for immodesty, eight are women).[20] For Collier, "immodesty" connotes openly sexual behavior, whether in speech or action; as modesty characterizes the female sex, "immodesty" represents something gone badly awry, something unnatural, in the behavior of a woman. He returns to this topic throughout the remaining chapters of his diatribe. Even within his discussion of "immodesty" he raises only two topics unrelated to women.[21] These pale beside the potential danger of Restoration drama's sexualization of "Ladies of Quality" and the damaging effect these characters have on the women who watch them.

Like his contemporaries, Collier couches his argument in terms of spectatorship. He claims that theater itself is not an evil thing; however, when it has been abused, it can provoke an evil response.[22] He compares watching drama to looking on a "Lewd Picture," well drawn by a "Masterly Hand" (5). Gazing on a sexualized image creates desire, "rais[ing] those Passions which can neither be discharged without Trouble, nor satisfyed without a Crime" (5). In the theater, these dangerous images are represented by actresses playing the roles of women who take sexual "liberties"; the end result of such representation is to "Tincture the Audience" leading them to "make Lewdness a Diversion" (5). Again, the event of spectatorship is crucial; Collier's emphasis on audience response, particularly that of the women in the audience, suggests that plays become dangerous only in representation. When staged, a play puts into effect a

---

20. The only male character is Horner in Wycherley's *The Country Wife. A Short View of the Immorality, and Profaneness of the English Stage, together With the Sense of Antiquity upon his Argument* (1698), 3–4. All further references cited in the text.

21. Collier's other concerns are the obviousness of the bawdry—it is not even masked by double entendre—and the disrespect such bawdry displays toward religion.

22. Collier would later deny theater even this limited good. See *A Farther Vindication of the Short View.*

complex network of cause and effect in the audience, beginning with sight and leading to general moral debasement characterized by desire and from there to "lewd" action. Physical representation before the eyes of an audience is an imperative. Collier reiterates his interpretation of drama as performance later in the work when he describes language as heard rather than read. Even here, however, the auditor becomes an observer as Collier explains that *"Words* are a Picture to the Ear" (204).

The emphasis on spectatorship becomes central to Collier's attack on the representation of women in late-seventeenth-century drama. His objections to these representations are threefold. First, he complains that the women in these plays "speak Smuttily," expressing without constraint their sexual desires. Collier's concern here is less with the language itself than it is with connection between words and action. He uses Euripides' Phaedra as an example of a woman possessed by an "infamous Passion" who nonetheless concealed her desire, remaining "regular and reserv'd in her Language" and thus managed to retain her modesty (9–10). For him, Phaedra's chaste language represents a deeper sexual virtue. She feels an "infamous Passion," but because she does not express it, it remains cloaked and ultimately destroyed. In contrast, openly sexual language not only expresses improper appetites but in itself engenders these appetites. Here Collier turns quickly from language to action, arguing that playwrights deliberately depict women as mad or silly in order to "enlarge their Liberty" (10), to allow them to behave in an openly sexual manner. Speech thus provides the opportunity for action.

Collier's second objection develops directly out of his apprehension that smuttiness is an expression of deeper desires, desires which have grave social consequences. Playwrights not only allow their female characters to talk of sex and behave in an openly sexual manner, but they "Represent their single Ladys, and Persons of Condition, under these Disorders of Liberty" (12). "Disorders of Liberty," unnatural states of sexual freedom unrestrained by patriarchal control, are reprehensible in English drama not simply in themselves but because of the high rank of those who embody these immodest desires. Collier's emphasis on "single Ladys" and "Persons of Condition" indicates the key role class plays in his concerns over sexuality. Although immodesty is never fitting, it becomes a disorder when women "of condition" engage in it. Single ladies should not acknowledge desire, and when such behavior occurs in the upper classes, the danger increases. Not only should persons of quality represent models of virtue, but their failure to do so—when female—could upset the lines of patrilinear succession. Such behavior threatens the social fabric by making the lady of quality no better than a whore, an erasure of social distinction which Collier deems a "monstrous" irregularity.

Collier's final protest against the improper depiction of women on the English stage again interweaves class and sexuality as he objects to prologues and epilogues, citing them as "Lewdness without Shame or Example" (13). "Here," he continues, "are such Strains as would turn the Stomach of an ordinary Debauchee, and be almost nauseous in the *Stews*. And to make it the more agreeable, Women are Commonly pick'd out for this Service" (13). Although we might expect Collier to decry the use of women for such a "nauseous" duty, his argument quickly turns from the sexualized woman who speaks the prologue to the woman who hears it as Collier voices his objection in terms of the woman in the audience rather than on the stage. The reason behind such a shift in focus is founded in Collier's careful differentiation between the illusory and the real, a distinction based on the principle of identification. When delivering a prologue or epilogue, the actress "quit[s] the *Stage*, and remove[s] from Fiction into Life" (13), speaking in her own voice rather than that of a fictional lady of quality. The social distinction that made the representation of "liberty" in the character of the lady a "Contradiction to Nature" (12) here compels Collier to censure playwrights less for making women speak indecently than for allowing an upper-class female audience to hear such indecent words. Collier suggests that the erotic behavior of a lower-class woman, the actress, *in her own character*, is of little moment. It has no natural or political implications and does not threaten the structure of society. It is the fictional representation that constitutes the danger because, he fears, ladies in the audience will identify with the character on the stage, not with the actual actress herself.

Searching for a more decorous model for staging female behavior, Collier turns to Roman and Greek playwrights, most notably Plautus, Terence, and Sophocles. Using a profusion of examples, he argues that, in contrast to modern plays, classical playwrights properly depicted the behavior of women. In these plays, only "prostituted and Vulgar People" indulge in sexual liberties (15). Women of quality are by contrast both silent and modest. Terence, as he notes, "is Extreamly careful in the Behavior of his Women," rarely allowing them "any Share of Conversation upon the *Stage*" (20). Sophocles does not allow his lovers appear on stage together, "for fear," Collier suggests, "they might prove unmanagable" (29). Collier's reading of the classics provides a curious model of female behavior. Although female sexuality seems a province only of the lowest classes, prostitutes and the vulgar, Collier's emphasis on the careful corralling of women, silencing them, and keeping them isolated lest they spontaneously engage in an immodest act, reveals it to be latent in his mind if not in the plays of Plautus, Terence, and Sophocles. His argument that a pair of lovers could prove "unmanageable" tells us more about his views of sexuality than those of Sophocles; sexuality, particularly female sexuality, is always latent and apt to explode into "liberties" if not rigidly controlled.

This fear of latent unmanagability provides the key to one of Collier's deepest concerns, the effect that watching libertine plays will have upon the female spectator. As he comments frequently, "the *Ladies*" make up a considerable part of the audience, and it is the response of this audience to the immodest representations of the seventeenth century which troubles him. The male audience is virtually ignored throughout *A Short View*. At the very best, Collier argues, late-seventeenth-century drama presents a confusing contradiction for women. Such drama assumes that ladies have vicious imaginations and are "pleased with Scenes of Brutishness." At the same time, he notes, conduct books and the "Customs of Education" (7) require women to behave in a very different fashion, with meekness and chaste modesty. In essence, the plays leave women in an untenable position; on the one hand, the plays themselves are immodest, on the other, a truly virtuous woman should not be able to recognize this immodesty: "'tis almost a Fault for them to Understand they are ill Used. They can't discover their Disgust without disadvantage, nor Blush without disservice to their Modesty" (7–8). Recognizing that the plays are indecent, not to mention laughing at the lewd jests, incriminates a woman because it indicates that she is familiar, in theory if not in practice, with such indecency and thus that her understanding and hence her virtue is tainted. Following this logic, however, an indecent play should not trouble the truly modest woman as she would not know that she had been "ill used."

The inherent contradiction becomes even more problematic, for as Collier argues, such tainted understanding goes against all the manifestations of female modesty, a quality which is at the core of a woman's nature. Citing Rapin, he notes that modesty "is the *Character* of Women. To represent them without this Quality; is to make Monsters of them, and throw them out of their Kind" (9). Declaring that modesty was "design'd by Providence as a Guard to Virtue," Collier goes on to describe it as an almost physical entity, "wrought into the Mechanism of the Body" (11), a theory which was promptly attacked by his detractors.[23] Reading the de-

---

23. See, for example, Edward Filmer: "I ever look upon the great Modesty of the generality of our Women, to have been the happy Effect rather of a pious, careful, and wary Edu-

scription of how this mechanism operates, however, reveals an acutely sensual apparatus that seems to parallel closely the operation of the passions themselves:

> [Modesty is] proportion'd to the occasions of Life, and strongest in Youth when Passion is so too. 'Tis a Quality as true to Innocence, as the Sences are to Health; whatever is ungrateful to the first, is prejudicial to the latter. The Enemy no sooner approaches, but the Blood rises in Opposition, and looks Defyance to an Indecency. It supplys the room of Reason, and Collection: Intuitive Knowledge can scarcely make a quicker Impression; And what then can be a surer Guide to the Unexperienced? It teaches by suddain Instinct and Aversion; This is both a ready and a powerful Method of Instruction. The Tumult of the Blood and Spirits, and the Uneasiness of the Sensation, are of singular Use. (11)

In this schema, modesty is instinctive, characterized by physical manifestations such as blushes and a "tumult of Blood and Spirits." By the end of this passage, as Collier describes the result of modesty as tumultuous "Sensation," modesty seems almost indistinguishable from the youthful passion it is supposed to protect against.

Despite or perhaps because of the tumultuous nature of feminine modesty, Collier finds it severely threatened by the "liberty" of stage representations. Somehow the mechanism fails to work once a woman steps inside a playhouse. Instead, like his contemporaries, he finds the stage dangerous because of its ability to strike through the eye and excite the passions, encouraging the spectator to imitate what she sees before her. He proposes a theory of identification in which the female spectator equates herself with the female character she sees on the stage, although not the actual actress. Thus, when replaying the scene in her mind, she enacts it herself, so that the erotic conduct becomes her own. In this manner, he explains, "Love-representations oftentimes call up the Spirits, and set them on work. The *Play* is acted over again in the *Scene* of Fancy, and the first Imagination becomes a Model . . . thus the Disease of the *Stage* grows catching" (281). The scene represented in the theater is internalized, so that the mind's eye replays the picture, creating a spectator within as well as without. When the subject is love or the sexual liberty that Collier claims disfigures so much contemporary drama, the internal spectator creates an endless cycle of contagion.

---

cation, than of any thing extraordinary in the Contexture of their Bodies." *A defence of Plays; or, The Stage Vindicated, From several Passages in* Mr. Collier's Short View, *&c. Wherein is offer'd The most Probable Method of Reforming our* PLAYS. *With a Consideration How far Vicious Characters may be allow'd on the* STAGE (1707), 16.

Lurking behind Collier's fear of female spectatorship and his outrage over the stage depictions of women is the figure of the prostitute, the overtly sexual woman in the audience and the potential alter ego to the ladies Collier addresses. The third part of a female sisterhood that also comprises the actress and the lady, she becomes the locus of Collier's sexual and social fears. Citing the character of Leonora in Dryden's *The Spanish Friar*, he protests her "lascivious" raptures and questions sarcastically, "Are these the *Tender Things* Mr. Dryden says the Ladys call on him for? I suppose he means the *Ladys* that are too Modest to show their Faces in the *Pit*" (9). Only such "ladies" of the galleries, their faces hidden "modestly" behind the vizard masks that advertised their trade, can enjoy such entertainment: "it regales their Lewdness, graces their Character, and keeps up their Spirits for their Vocation" (9). But if only prostitutes can gaze on these stage representations of sexual liberty with pleasure, what does that say about the ladies of quality, those virgins and matrons who continue to frequent the theaters? This question becomes key to the anxieties underlying Collier's attack on the immodesty and immorality of the stage. Haunted by the specter of the immodest woman, he questions, "Do Women leave all the regards to Decency and Conscience behind them when they come to the *Play-House*? Or does the Place transform their Inclinations and turn their former Aversions into Pleasure?" (7). What does happen to ladies when they act as spectators? As Collier asks, "Can this Stuff be the Inclination of *Ladies*?" (284). If it is, then the lady has the proclivities of a whore. Unlike ancient Roman and Greek drama (excepting of course Aristophanes) where sexuality is restricted to slaves and prostitutes and where these class distinctions prevent the mirror effect of theater, in England a woman can go to theater and see versions of herself represented onstage. Responding to these images, her gaze excites desires that can perhaps be too easily satisfied. Thus, through the visual medium of the playhouse, the lady is transformed into the whore. Collier links such catastrophic behavior with leveling classes and destroying English society. If the ladies in the theater begin behaving like the ladies on the stage, the consequences for society are disastrous, no less than "Poverty and Disease, the Dishonour of Families, and the Debauchery of Kingdoms" (55).

Collier's followers go even further and make the connection between the lady and the prostitute explicit. The author of *The Stage Condemn'd* first cites the ladies as the chief supporters of theater (their "*Encouragement and Presence is the most powerful argument (after all) for the* Defence *of the Stage*"),[24] and thus indirectly the instigators of the lewdness that char-

24. "Epistle Dedicatory," *The Stage Condemn'd.*

acterizes the stage. Using classical sources, he then articulates what Collier left implicit, that the sight of the stage play would result in uncontrolled sexual behavior on the part of the female spectator:

> *It were to be wished that our English Ladies and* Gentlewomen, *would be pleased to consider, 'That the wise* Roman Senate *approv'd the Divorce which* Sepronius Sophus *gave to his Wife for no other Reason,* but that she resorted to the Cirques *and* Playhouses *without his Consent; the* Sight *of which might make her an* Adultress, *and cause her to defile his Bed. And the Christian Emperor* Justinian *made the following Constitution, That a Man might lawfully put away his Wife, if she resort to* Cirques, *to* Play-houses *or* Stage-Plays *without his* Privity *and Consent, because her* Chastity *might thereby be endangered.*[25]

Citing St. Cyprian, he later adds, "Thus is Adultery learned whilst it is beheld."[26] Women, it seems, are peculiarly susceptible to visual stimulation. The author charts a direct cause and effect relation between the female gaze and the excitation of desire, desire which is seemingly impossible to control once it has been raised. Thus a man is justified in divorcing his wife simply because she watches a play; her gaze sets in motion a chain of events that results inevitably in promiscuity.

With increasing anxiety *The Stage Condemn'd* paints a lurid picture of women driven mad with desire by stage representations, claiming "it is a Miracle if there be found any Woman or Maid, which with those Spectacles of strange Lust, is not frequently inflam'd to down right Fury."[27] The real threat posed by these representations of sexual behavior is that the control that a patriarchal society must have over female sexuality will vanish, and with it the entire structure of society. Virginity as well as the chastity of the marriage bed will be lost, leaving chaos in its wake.[28] This paradigm establishes a firm link between female spectatorship and female promiscuity so that by definition the only woman who can attend the theater is the whore. Fifty years later, the author of the anonymous *An Address to the Ladies on the indecency of appearing at Immodest Plays* (1756) indicts the entire female (but not the male) audience, complaining "when I hear of Plays which are big with obscenity, being performed Night after

---

25. Ibid.

26. Ibid., 66. He continues his cause and effect argument, adding, "she who at first came perchance a chast Matron to the Play, returns unchast from the Playhouse."

27. Ibid., 106. In this passage the author cites Salvian's *Third Blast of Retreat from Plays and Theatres*.

28. Almost every attack on the theater uses this argument for the regulation or outlawing of theater.

Night, to crowded Houses, I am almost tempted to suspect that the whole Female World, either are or would be Prostitutes."[29]

Linked by their sex with the characters represented on the stage, at the very least the female audience pays their "sisters" to prostitute themselves on the stage. At the worst, inflamed by a gaze which supposedly filled even the chastest woman with uncontrollable desire, they became the third part of the sisterhood, the whores who lined the galleries or walked the streets outside Drury Lane. The potential for such sexual transgression on the stage or off raises the horrifying specter of uncontrolled female sexuality, a prospect with grave consequences for both the domestic circle and the state. In their discussions of female spectatorship, the antitheatrical writers envision a world in which families are ruined by female license. Innocent virgins are seduced by villains once they have witnessed amorous interludes, chaste matrons return adulteresses from the theaters, and ladies make up for the "deficiencies" of their lords with footmen.[30] Simple theatergoing has larger implications, as the author of *An Address to the Ladies* reminds his female readers: "A Nation's Taste Depends on you. / —Perhaps a Nation's Virtue too."[31] For these writers, female spectatorship leads to the breakup of the family, the corruption of lines of lineage, and the resultant dismantling of hereditary lines of wealth and power—in effect shattering the social structures on which national security depends.

The Lady Vanishes: Defenses of the Theater

Whereas the attacks on the theater show a certain uniformity of method and philosophy, the defenses of the stage which sprang up shortly after the publication of *A Short View* were disparate and often misdirected. Playwrights such as Congreve, Dryden, D'Urfey, and Vanbrugh responded directly to Collier's complaints, often refuting his arguments against their plays point by point. Other critics and playwrights responded more generally, often admitting that stage representations were immodest or even perverse, but defending the stage in general for its abil-

---

29. *An Address to the Ladies on the indecency of Appearing at Immodest Plays* (1756), 10.

30. "And how would many *noble Families* be lineally descended down, if the Stage did not teach *Ladies*, that the *Footman* can amply make up the Deficiency of *my Lord*." *A Letter to a Noble Lord, To whom alone it Belongs. Occasioned by a Representation at the Theatre Royal in Drury-Lane of a Farce, called Miss Lucy in Town* (1742), 4.

31. Quoted in *An Address to the Ladies*, 18. The lines cited are from a poem by William Whitehead.

ity to teach, in particular through the means of satire and caricature. In their accounts, theater acts as a mirror in which human follies are faithfully represented.[32] Where attacks on the theaters saw libertine or foolish characters as potentially dangerous examples, the defenses point to them as instructive, models for how not to behave. In their arguments, the experience of spectatorship is educational, largely because the spectator's identification with the image onstage is rational rather than emotional, providing a sense of distance between spectator and representation. Where the opponents of the stage detail an economy of gaze and desire, most of the defenses assume a link between gaze and reason, so that watching a play becomes an ongoing process of analysis that prevents the onset of desire.

Often contemptuous of Collier and his arguments, the defenses seem to have misjudged the growing opposition to the immorality of late-seventeenth-century comedy that made Collier's works so popular. In addition, most writers misconstrue the nature of the degeneracy Collier feared. Where the attacks on the theater concentrate on the nature of stage representations and the moral effect of those representations on the audience, many defenses of the theaters focus on the morality of the actors and actresses rather than on the morality of the audience.[33] But the antitheatrical writers seem only tangentially concerned with the moral status of the actors (that argument is more characteristic of earlier attacks on the theater such as Prynne's or of the contemporary French antitheatrical writings). Nonetheless, the defenses continue to assure those opposed to the theater that while actresses may triumph on the stage, they do not offstage; young men will not mistake them for ladies and "catch the real Itch of Love from their counterfeit Scrubbado."[34] Likewise, Oldmixon contends that few women have thrown away "favors" on actors and that dancing schools are more dangerous than playhouses.[35] Again, such assurances miss the mark as actors themselves are not a threat in the eyes

32. This argument is most effectively presented in John Dennis's *The Usefulness of the Stage, to the Happiness of Mankind, to Government, and to Religion. Occasioned by a Late Book, Written by Jeremy Collier, M.A.* (1698). See *The Critical Works of John Dennis*, 2 vols., ed. Edward Niles Hooker (1943), 1:146–193. All references to Dennis are from this edition and will be made in the text.

33. John Oldmixon, for example, reminds his readers that actors, "as well as their Fellow Subjects, are liable to the Laws made against Immorality and Profaneness." *Reflections on the Stage, and Mr. Collyer's Defence of the Short View. In Four Dialogues* (1699), 188.

34. [James Drake], *The Antient and Modern Stages Survey'd; or, Mr. Collier's View of the Immorality and Profaneness of the English Stage set in a true light. Wherein some of Mr. Collier's mistakes are rectified, and the comparative Morality of the* English *Stage is asserted upon the Parallel* (1699), 107.

35. Oldmixon, *Reflections on the Stage*, 189.

of the antitheatrical writers; virtually no one expresses concern over the potential for relationships between actors or actresses and members of the audience. The actor/actress becomes dangerous not in him/herself, but as the means of representation, as object of the gaze.

By focusing on the influence of actors, arguments such as those made by Oldmixon and Drake overlook the very real concern expressed by Collier over the moral ramifications of the female gaze. References to women are largely absent from defenses of the stage. By and large, when women are considered, the issue of female spectatorship is subsumed under a general defense of the morality of Englishwomen. Writers argue that Collier's opinion of the ladies is too harsh, that their essential piety and virtue prevents them from being corrupted by a "meer Representation."[36] Although willing to admit that women in other cultures may have been led astray, the defenses argue that English women possess special virtues which protect them against "disorders of Liberty." The anonymous *The Stage Acquitted* argues that, by virtue of the cooler English climate, English women have cooler passions than those of ancient Greece; their sexuality is more under control and can tolerate the temptations of the theater. In other words, Collier misjudged the nature of his countrywomen and thus his arguments have no merit. This ethnocentric argument sidesteps the questions of spectatorship and of character depiction, ultimately conceding that the stage does have the power to corrupt.[37]

Although some critics, such as John Dennis, admit the dubious morality of the female characters in some plays, most choose to ignore the issue. (Congreve even remarks flippantly that "it was a mercy that all four Women [in *Love for Love*] were not naught; for that had been maintaining that there was not one Woman of Quality honest.")[38] But even those playwrights who defended the honor of their female characters, sent mixed messages. In the preface to *The Phaeton* (1698), one of the first responses to Collier to appear after *A Short View,* Charles Gildon describes in great detail the honorable nature of his character Althea, concluding the preface with a paean to the ladies of "Honour, Piety, and Sense" who have

36. Filmer, *A defence of Plays,* 37.

37. A more successful tack is taken by Thomas D'Urfey, who defends the honor of Englishwomen in the theater by reminding his readers that the late Queen Mary attended the theater and remained, of course, morally unscathed. Preface to *The Campaigners; or, The Pleasant Adventures at Brussels. A Comedy. With a Familiar Preface Upon a Late Reformer of the Stage. Ending with a Satyrical Fable of the Dog and the Ottor* (1698), 26.

38. *Memoirs of the Life, Writings, and Amours of William Congreve Esq; Interspersed with Miscellaneous Essays, Letters, and Characters Written by Him. Also some very Curious Memoirs of Mr. Dryden and his Family, with a Character of Him and his Writings by Mr. Congreve. Compiled from their respective Originals, by Charles Wilson, Esq.* (1730), 32–33.

supported the plays to which Collier objects. Yet this defense of the moral uses of drama and Gildon's own virtuous representation of women is followed immediately by a prologue that stresses the visually sensual nature of the actresses who represented these virtuous women. The prologue begins with a male actor pleading for the play, but he is soon elbowed out of the way by "Mrs. Cross and six of the Youngest Actresses" who insist that their pleading will be more effective because they evoke the body: "Pray let us speak—We shall be understood, / We speak the Language of All Flesh and Blood." They explicitly display themselves as sexual objects, claiming that by doing so they arouse support from the (male) audience:

> If then this Charming Tribe shou'd fail to win ye,
> I needs must say some strange dull Devil's in ye.
> Cannot our Eyes, our Youth, our Form appease ye?
> And have we Nothing?—Nothing that can please ye?

Pointing to their sexual attractiveness ("eyes," "youth," and "form"), they suggest there are additional charms they can provide. The prologue concludes with the women making a *Lysistrata*like threat to withhold sexual favors if the play does not receive audience support. While in the prologue the actress has moved, as Collier noted, "from fiction into life" and is thus less dangerous as an example to the women in the audience, prologues such as this display the actress as sexual object and make obvious the erotic overtones of even a "moral" play such as *Phaeton*.

The conflict which Gildon fails to see, but which Collier does, is between the simple morality of a character and the sexual content of that character as represented by the "flesh and blood" actress on the stage. Where Collier does object to the specific words and actions of female characters, he is even more concerned with the effect these representations will have on the women audience members who may identify with the women they see on the stage. Eventually, Collier, like Bedford, Law, and most of the anonymous authors, completely rejects the feasibility of theater as legitimate entertainment. Yet, few of the defenses even consider the issue of female spectatorship and its ramifications. Filmer denies the connection between the gaze and desire (and ignores completely the troublesome issue of the female gaze) central to all attacks on the theater in the late seventeenth and early eighteenth century, contending that "tho the Eye may like and look upon a beautiful Woman, yet the Heart must Lust after her, before that Look becomes Adulterous."[39] He does not con-

39. Filmer, *A defence of Plays*, 32.

sider what happens when a woman looks on a handsome man or watches a tempting seduction.

Those few writers who consider the female spectator envision her mostly as learning from the drama she watches, stressing drama's function as a mirror of society. Such arguments, however, also necessitate admitting the misogyny that underlies much late-seventeenth-century comedy. Vanbrugh, for example, cites *The Relapse* as giving a "homer Check to the Lewdness of Women" when Worthy admits in soliloquy that had Amanda succumbed to his blandishments he would have left her.[40] His argument admits the principle of female identification with the character onstage, but depends on her recognizing the misogyny of the libertine creed in order to control her own desires. Dennis, the most prolific defender of the theater,[41] while avoiding the problem of the female spectator in his original response to Collier, returns to the question twenty years later. In a letter addressed to Judas Iscariot, Esq (Barton Booth), Dennis writes that women are, if anything, too consciously prim in their response to drama, sitting through depictions of rapes and seductions in tragedies while "flinch[ing] back like unback'd Fillies, at the least Approach of *Rem* to *Re* in Comedy."[42] He attributes this skittishness less to the immodest subject matter than to the satiric commentary on women that appears in Restoration comedy. The openly sexual rape fails to insult because "a Rape in Tragedy is a Panegyric upon the Sex . . . for she is to remain Innocent, and to be pleas'd without her Consent; while the Man, who is accounted a damn'd Villain, proclaims the Power of Female Charms, which have the Force to drive him to so horrid a Violence" (2:166).

---

40. Vanbrugh, *A Short Vindication of the Relapse and the Provok'd Wife, from Immorality and Profaneness* (1698), in *Complete Works*, 2 vols., ed. Bonamy Dobree and Geoffrey Webb (1927), 1:76–77. The lines to which Vanbrugh refers are:

> Could women but our secret counsels scan,
> Could they but reach the deep reserves of man,
> They'd wear it [the robe of virtue] on, that love might last;
> For when they throw off one, we soon the other cease. (4.4.24–29)

41. For a complete listing of Dennis's critical works, see *The Critical Works of John Dennis*.

42. "To Judas Iscariot, Esq; On the present State of the Stage," April 3, 1719 (2:166). Dennis continues on to accuse women of being afraid to watch satires on their sex: "I have been sometimes apt to entertain a Suspicion, that 'tis not the luscious Matter which disturbs them in Comedy, but the secret implicite Satire upon the sex. For a Woman in Comedy never grants the last favour to one to whom she is not marry'd, but it proclaims the Man's Triumph and her Shame. It always shews her Weakness and often her Inconstancy, and sometimes her Fraud and Perfidiousness. But a Rape in Tragedy is a Panegyrick upon the sex: For there the Woman has all the Advantage of the Man. For she is suppos'd to remain innocent, and to be pleas'd without her Consent; while the Man, who is accounted a damn'd Villain, proclaims the Power of Female Charms, which have the Force to drive him to so horrid a Violence."

In contrast, comedies present no such "panegyric upon the Sex," and, Dennis claims, any objection to comedy constitutes a refusal to look in the satiric mirror provided by comedy, denying it its role as moral corrective. Thus, the female spectator's "modesty" represents her rejection of the roles staged before her, not her identification with these characters.

Only *The Stage Acquitted* deals with the larger implications of female spectatorship. Admitting like Vanbrugh and Dennis that "bad" women serve as negative examples, the author also proceeds to show the positive consequences of female identification with stage representations:

> I must own, I think there can be no more engaging and pleasing Object in the world, than the Poets draught of a good Wife. *Belvidera,* and *Monimia, Melesinda, Portia* &c. are what all men would desire; they give so taking a Beauty to a Woman, that all the sensible of the Sex must be in Love with it. And on Conjugal Love the Happiness and being of Families and Nations depend, therefore the *Poet* here too is *highly meretorious.* But you say this is sufficiently recommended by the *Pulpit;* I grant 'tis recommended, but a bare Precept is less touching than *Example.* The *Pulpit* gives the *Rule,* the *Stage* the *Example.* This explains that, by this you see what that recommends; and by seeing the Charms of the *Example,* you are struck with the Beauty of the *Precept;* so that here again the *Stage* discovers *Merit* that challenges the *publick protection,* since the *Cement* and *Interest* of all *Families* are *advanced* by it.[43]

The author's argument for the usefulness and morality of the stage depends on mechanisms of spectatorship: visual examples and identification with these examples. Here the gaze constitutes a necessary part of moral instruction; the author repeatedly stresses the necessity of sight: by the stage "you see what [the pulpit] recommends," by "seeing" the "Charms" of "Example" the spectator, if male, is drawn to desire the charming example, and if female, to emulate it. Thus the stage becomes even more powerful as a moral instrument than the pulpit. In this model, however, the possibility of female desire is avoided: men may look upon Belvidera and Monimia with desirous eyes, but the question of women desiring what they see or of having unruly and disastrous desires excited by stage representations is put aside.

The author also evokes the larger concerns raised by Collier: stability of family and nation. Where Dennis addressed the issue of national se-

---

43. *The Stage Acquitted. Being a Full Answer to Mr.* Collier, *and the other Enemies of the Drama. With a Vindication of King* Charles *the Martyr, and The Clergy of the Church of England, From the Abuses of a Scurrilous Book, Called,* The Stage Condemned. *To which is added, the Character of the Animadverter, and the Animadversions on Mr.* Congreve's *Answer to Mr.* Collier (1699), 79.

curity more generally by claiming that drama provides a check to rebellion while exalting the mind of the people, here the writer underscores
the role that controlled female sexuality plays in both the private and
public spheres. "Conjugal love," or the sanctity of the marriage bed represented through the chasteness of the wife, he argues, comprises the
"happiness" and essential being of the domestic unit and the national
unit; that which enhances conjugal love thus constitutes "publick protection" and advances civic interest. Theater contributes to civil order directly by means of visual representation. Rather than being wounded in
the eye and corrupted by desire, the spectator "discovers merit."

Even representations of female lewdness contribute to public protection—at least in the eyes of John Dennis. Dennis argues that one of the
great benefits of the current stage to family and to the state is its function
as an antidote to sodomy. Arguing that "the Corruption of the Nation . . .
partly proceeds from having no Plays at all" (1:155), Dennis divides the
"reigning Vices" into four categories: love of women, drinking, gaming,
and "unnatural sins." He dismisses drinking and gaming as made ridiculous by the stage, but considers the issue of desire, both "natural" and
"unnatural" at some length. Although Dennis never addresses the problem of women's desires, he is seemingly extremely concerned by the dangerous nature of some male desire. He concedes at length that the stage
does foment the "love of women," but that this is if anything a necessary
evil; such lust is completely natural and thus less vicious than drinking,
gambling, or sodomy, and more importantly, it distracts men from their
potential homoerotic desires, "the Restraining of which, the Happiness of
Mankind is, in so evident a Manner, concerned" (1:156). By providing
such a check on dangerous inclinations, Dennis argues, the stage is to be
praised rather than condemned. In contrast to Collier, Dennis sees sexual
and political threat located within the sodomite rather than the promis-
cuous woman. Indeed, throughout his writings, he considers female sexuality almost exclusively as image: the figure on the stage rather than
the woman in the audience. With its actresses depicting scenes of love,
the theater presents appropriate objects for the male gaze. In this sense,
the objectified woman acts as a social safeguard, a means of regulating
unruly male desires for the betterment of society.[44]

Near the end of his life Dennis returned to this theme, defending the
stage once again against charges of immorality, this time from the writings of Law rather than Collier. Notably, the only charge against the stage

---

44. The author of *The Stage Condemn'd* responds to Dennis's argument by using Stubbs's
outdated argument regarding cross-dressing (189); although female cross-dressing was
common in Restoration drama, male cross-dressing was extremely rare.

with which he can agree is that of illicit sexuality, that it may—perhaps—
"excite in Men a Desire to the unlawful Enjoyment of Women" (2:314).
"Unchast and immodest Images" of women ought to be banished, he
agrees, but he finds a moral purpose even in these images:

> And yet I cannot help thinking, that if ever those Passages could be ex-
> cusable, they would be so at this Juncture, when the execrable Sin of
> Sodomy is spread so wide, that the foresaid Passages might be of some
> Use to the reducing Mens Minds to the natural Desire of Women. Let For-
> nication be ever so crying a Sin, yet Sodomy is a Crime of a thousand times
> a deeper Dye . . . I cannot here omit observing one Thing, That this un-
> natural Sin has very much increased since *Collier's* Books were publish'd
> against the Stage. (2:314)

Here as elsewhere, Dennis focuses explicitly on male rather than female
desire, and thus in his eyes the immorality of the playhouse is relative.
Yes, the plays may tempt men into illicit yet "natural" sex, but men will
thus be prevented from performing the "unnatural" act of sodomy. Depicting men as innately—and constantly—desirous, Dennis suggests
that the visual representation of female unchasteness acts to regulate this
desire into proper channels. As support for this claim, he links what he
sees as the rise of sodomy (citing "no less than four Persons condemn'd
for it the last Sessions: The like of which was never heard of in *Great
Britain* before," 2:314) to Collier's attack on the "profaneness" of the stage
and the subsequent popularity of more decorous drama. Deprived of
"unchaste images," men become worse than immoral.

As Dennis's argument suggests, the debate over the immorality/mo-
rality of the stage was founded on two different ways of looking at the
theater—and at women. Collier and his followers consider women as potentially desiring subjects; in their arguments against the theater they
construct a vision of the female spectator predicated on the potential for
uncontrolled sexual desire. By contrast, the defenders of the stage, many
of them playwrights accustomed to constructing stage representations of
women, downplay the possibility of a link between the female gaze and
desire. In this sense, the crucial difference between the opposing arguments is the gendered nature of spectatorship. For the opponents of the
stage, the gaze of both sexes can generate desire, wounding the spectator
in the eye by exciting lust. Those who support the stage construct a gendered theory of the gaze; although the male gaze may excite desire, in
women the gaze operates differently: rather than desire, it leads to education (via satire), or because of the cold and damp English climate, the
female gaze may have no effect whatsoever.

A common tie on both sides of the debate becomes theater's role in the control of society and social hierarchies, an issue strongly linked to sexuality. As seen by the emphasis on female chastity, sexual incontinence, specifically female sexual incontinence, equals social incontinence. Even the defenders of the stage find the regulation of female desire essential; they suggest that the theater provides a public service in this regard. In contrast, the male gaze seems to keep society running—without the male gaze and its corresponding female object, desire runs amuck, threatening both individual and state. While all agree that uncontrolled female sexuality can undermine the foundations of society, the most significant distinction between the antitheatrical polemicists and theater loyalists appears in their construction of both the female spectator and the female image. In their characterization of women as gazing subjects rather than as passive objects of male desire, Collier and his followers articulate an ideology of the female spectator inextricably linked to the female sexual body.

CHAPTER 2

Women Watching: The Female Spectator
in Late-Seventeenth-Century Comedy

If fear of female sexuality lies beneath the attacks on the theater, how does the drama of the later seventeenth century represent this dangerous issue? In turning from the critics to the "New World of Vice" they decried or defended, I want to focus on the link between spectatorship and sexuality developed by Collier and his followers, a link which the playwrights themselves articulated, if not in their responses to Collier, at least in the plays that spurred Collier's antitheatrical diatribes. Certainly the drama of the later seventeenth century is permeated with scenes of men and women watching each other, looking into mirrors, and gazing at portraits. How the female gaze is represented in these scenes is in many cases an issue of genre. Although women with wandering eyes and correspondingly insatiable appetites inevitably represent the villainesses of serious drama, such distinctions are less absolute in the social world of comedy. Because these comedies explore the problem of the female gaze explicitly and because their representations of this contested subject expose larger social assumptions regarding women and sexuality, I want to examine their depictions of spectatorship before turning to the female-centered tragedies that dominated the stage at the very end of the century.

The plays that bracket this consideration of women and desire, Wycherley's *The Plain Dealer* (1676/77) and Vanbrugh's *The Provok'd Wife* (1697), directly address the contested issue of female spectatorship, linking it inexorably to sexuality. These two plays, both controversial because of their overtly sexual content, provide unusually explicit representations of the woman as spectator, specifically within the theater. In addition to reflecting the playwright's view of the female spectator, both plays center on the sexuality of their female characters and through these characters develop an ideology of gaze, gender, and desire. Although the two plays share a focus on women both as sexual subjects and sexual objects, their approach and ultimately their conclusions differ notably. The spectrum of perspectives revealed in this movement from libertine comedy toward problem play sets in relief those attitudes that lie beneath the rise of she-tragedy and its continued popularity through much of the eighteenth century.

In its willingness to present characters actually engaged in fornication, *The Plain Dealer* is recognizable as a sex comedy of the 1670s, although its bitingly satiric tone and avoidance of the conventions of wit set it apart from contemporary works such as *The Man of Mode*. Although less explicit, *The Provok'd Wife* ultimately became the more controversial drama. One of the so-called "marriage plays" of the pre-Collier 1690s, the play provides its audience with a frank examination of sexual relations both inside and outside of marriage. In addition to their focus on women, personal agency, and sexuality, both plays explore in some detail the problem of female spectatorship rather than the more conventional trope of woman as spectacle, which would become so central to the serious drama of the later seventeenth and early eighteenth centuries. These two plays, each focusing on female rather than male sexuality, use female spectatorship and its ultimate lack of power to contain this sexuality. In their discussions of women's response to the theater and the implications of this response for a woman's subsequent attempts to control her own sexuality (a subject which clearly disturbed Collier), these comedies downplay or even reverse the dangerous potential of female spectatorship. In effect, such scenes render female sexuality containable, a commodity accessible not only to the male characters in *The Plain Dealer* and *The Provok'd Wife* but to the audiences who watched each play.

Women and Plain Dealing

First staged in December 1676, *The Plain Dealer* was a critical and eventually a popular success, winning for Wycherley the sobriquet of "the Plain Dealer."[1] While critics such as Dryden and Dennis would

1. When the original response to *The Plain Dealer* was lukewarm, friends of Wycherley organized a "claque" to create applause. As John Dennis notes in *The Causes of the Decay and Defects of Dramatick Poetry, and of the Degeneracy of the Publick Tast* (1725), "And when upon the first representations of the *Plain Dealer*, the Town, as the Authour has often told me, appeard Doubtfull what Judgment to Form of it; the aforemention'd gentlemen [the duke of

praise its "truth" and the soundness of its moral,[2] others found the play offensively libertine and crude. *The Plain Dealer* is one of the first plays mentioned by name in *A Short View;* on the first page of the first chapter ("The Immodesty of the Stage"), Collier refers to the Widow Blackacre and Olivia as examples of immodesty, lamenting that Wycherley "should stoop his Wit thus Low, and use his Understanding so unkindly" (3) as to produce such characters and such a play. Despite Collier's objections, and the play's openly libidinous action, *The Plain Dealer* remained popular throughout much of the first half of the eighteenth century. It then disappeared from the stage for over two decades, only to reappear in shortened and expurgated form as altered by Isaac Bickerstaff, who described the play as "one of the most celebrated productions of the last century" and faulted Wycherley's "tainted" muse for the play's length and "excessive obscenity."[3]

The Plain Dealer has been much discussed in recent decades, with critics questioning the epistemological underpinings of the play, its genre, and even the events within the play.[4] What these various readings sometimes overlook is the way in which Wycherley uses female sexuality to construct ideology, often by means of violence. The play is intensely concerned with the sexuality of its female characters, much more so than that of its male characters. Are they chaste, it asks—or merely pretending? An

---

Buckingham, the earl of Rochester, the earl of Dorset, the earl of Mulgrave, Mr. Savil, Mr. Buckley, Sir John Denham, and Mr. Waller] by their loud aprobation of it, gave it both a sudden and a lasting reputation. *The Critical Works of John Dennis*, 2:277.

2. Dryden frequently praised Wycherley warmly, as in the preface to *The State of Innocence* (1677) where he writes "satire lashes vice into reformation, and humour represents folly so as to render it ridiculous. Many of our present writers are eminent in both these kinds; and particularly the author of the *Plain Dealer*, whom I am proud to call my friend, has obligued all honest and virtuous men by one of the most bold, most general, and most useful satires which has ever been presented on the English Theatre."

3. Isaac Bickerstaff, preface to *The Plain Dealer* (1766), v, vi. In Bickerstaff's adaptation, Manley becomes a gentler hero and Fidelia somewhat more decorous. The play's attempted rape scenes are softened, and the scene in which Manley takes Fidelia's place in Olivia's bedroom is omitted although he does report that he has been to her chambers. In addition, Olivia's discussion with Eliza is greatly shortened and the discussion of *The Country Wife* omitted entirely. Fifty years later, John Kemble would adapt Bickerstaff's adaptation, shortening the play still further and removing additional indecencies.

4. See Richard Braverman, *Plots and Counterplots: Sexual Politics and the Body Politic in English Literature, 1660–1730* (1993); Helen Burke, "'Law Suits,' 'Love Suits,' and the Family Property in Wycherley's *The Plain Dealer*," in *Cultural Readings of Restoration and Eighteenth-Century Theater*, ed. J. Douglas Canfield and Deborah C. Payne, 89–113 (1995); J. Douglas Canfield, *Tricksters and Estates: On the Ideology of Restoration Comedy* (1997); Peter Holland, *The Ornament of Action: Text and Performance in Restoration Comedy* (1979); Derek Hughes, "*The Plain Dealer*: A Reappraisal," *Modern Language Quarterly* 43, no. 4 (1982): 323–24; Robert Markley, *Two-Edg'd Weapons: Style and Ideology in the Comedies of Etherege, Wycherley, and Congreve* (1988).

important component of this exploration of female sexuality is a woman's response to the theater. Although Wycherley's views on female modesty are radically different from those of Collier, like Collier he does see a link between a woman's sexual appetites and her response to theater, an issue articulated first in the "Epistle Dedicatory" and later within the play itself. Smarting from female attacks on the obscenity of *The Country Wife*, he chose to dedicate his final play to "Mother Bennett," a noted bawd who he claimed was less hypocritical than those women who had damned *The Country Wife*.[5] The dedication, with its implicit comparison of fine ladies to whores, initiates a connection that recurs not only in the "Epistle Dedicatory," but throughout the play. The prostitute, a shadowy figure in the arguments against the stage, becomes a central figure in Wycherley's dedication and his play. She represents both the overt sexual object whose function is her sexuality, but she is also the representative of debased sexuality, of uncontrolled female desire. In a world in which both the lady of quality and the prostitute sit in the same theater and, Wycherley claims, wear the same mask, how does one tell the lady from the whore? Where Collier and his followers would worry that women could slip from one category to another, Wycherley suggests that they already have.

The "Epistle" begins with mock praise of "Lady B—," as Wycherley claims he must turn to her because his plays have lost reputation "with the ladies of stricter lives in the playhouse." But he quickly moves from praise of Lady B—'s discernment to an assault on the minds of those women who condemn his plays:

> *Nay, nothing is secure from the power of their imaginations; no, not their Husbands, whom they Cuckold with themselves, by thinking of other men, and so make the lawful matrimonial embraces Adultery; wrong Husbands and Poets in thought and word, to keep their own Reputations; but your Ladyship's justice, I know, wou'd think a Woman's Arraigning and Damning a Poet for her own obscenity like her crying out a Rape, and hanging a man for giving her pleasure, only that she might be thought not to consent to't; and so to vindicate her honour forfeits her modesty.*

The fault lies, according to Wycherley, not with his plays, but with the lewdness of the women who read or see them. The woman furnishes the obscenity, not the inoffensive words—it is her indecent mind that gives the words meaning. "Nothing" is "secure" from the lascivious imagina-

---

5. For a more detailed discussion of attacks on *The Country Wife*, see David Roberts, *The Ladies: Female Patronage of Restoration Drama, 1660–1700* (1989). Roberts argues that the Maids of Honour were especially responsible for damning the play. See chap. 4, "Women at Court and Patronage of the Stage."

tions of such women because they see the entire world in carnal terms, only pretending to a kind of sexual modesty for the sake of superficial reputation. Extending the sexual content of his argument, Wycherley compares the attacks on his plays to false charges of rape in which the women in reality fault the poet for their own lecherous thoughts, just like the victims of rape who hang the man who "pleased" them only to maintain their "honour." Effectively paralleling spectatorship with sexuality, Wycherley suggests that for women the appropriate course for both is passive acceptance; resistance to either visual or actual violation could constitute a loss of modesty (an view reiterated in some contemporary conduct manuals).[6] Considering the multiplying rapes at the end of the play and the endorsement of passive femininity with which the play concludes, this image takes on particular force.

Having established that those women who claim that their modesty is offended by his plays are only proving their wanton nature, Wycherley attacks the more general claims of female modesty as a mere social mask that can be put on by even the basest bawd. *"For,"* he notes, *"by that Mask of modesty which Women wear promiscuously in publick, they are all alike, and you can no more know a kept Wench from a Woman of Honour by looks than by her Dress."* Modesty here becomes a "mask," much like the vizard masks worn by prostitutes and fashionable ladies alike. Moreover, Wycherley suggests that beneath this mask women are all alike, all capable of the adulterous imaginings he cited earlier; there is no essential difference between the lady and the whore. Unlike Collier's later postulation of a physical mechanism of modesty, Wycherley contends that female modesty is purely superficial, no more than a mask that can be donned by anyone who wishes to create an effect. Beneath this mask, the lady and the prostitute are interchangeable. It is for this reason, Wycherley contends, that the ladies do not like his plays, for through satirical "plain dealing" these dramas threaten to strip away the mask of modesty and expose the vileness beneath, the very point that Dennis, an admirer of Wycherley, was to make forty years later.[7] Yet for all his claims of innocence, Wycher-

---

6. A seventeenth-century version of this attitude can be found in *The Excellent Woman Described by her True Characters and Their Opposites* (1692), a conduct book by T.D., which faults Lucrece for her active response to rape: "If she had not been at all Criminal, she might without doubt have found more remedy for her trouble in her Conscience than in Death. They say she resisted more out of humour, or some secret considerations, than out of Vertue" (81). In other words, like the ladies in the theater, Lucrece tried too hard and overacted; she would not have had to go to such extremes had she been innocent.

7. "I have been sometimes apt to entertain a Suspicion, that 'tis not the luscious Matter which disturbs [women] in Comedy, but the secret implicite Satire upon the Sex. For a Woman in Comedy never grants the last Favour to one to whom she is not marry'd, but it

ley finds himself locked in sexually coded language, arguing that "'tis the plain dealing of the play, not the obscenity, 'tis taking off the ladies' masks, not offering at their petticoats, which most offends them."

Wycherley dramatizes his theories of gender and spectatorship in the course of the play, most notably in the character of Olivia who perfectly exemplifies the sexual hypocrisy he describes in the "Epistle Dedicatory." In the exchange between Olivia and her "plain dealing" cousin Eliza, Wycherley demonstrates the false modesty he complains of in his dedication. Referring wittily to his own play, he uses Olivia to represent the type of woman who complained loudest about the immodesty of *The Country Wife.* Spectatorship, according to Wycherley, is essentially neutral; it will not affect the truly modest woman who can indeed watch immodest productions without a blush. Eliza, Wycherley's mouthpiece in this scene, states, "I think a Woman betrays her want of modesty, by shewing it publickly in a Play-House . . . for the truly modest and stout say least, and are least exceptious, especially in publick" (2.1.403–6). Her argument leaves women at something of an impasse; if they complain or are even aware of indelicacies, then they are automatically defined as tainted. To prove her chasteness, a woman must remain silent and inactive so that the female audience becomes a largely passive body where the only women who blush are those who are corrupt enough to know what to blush at—like Olivia.

The true corruption of Olivia's mind is revealed when she attempts to justify her outrage to her cousin:

ELIZA. Why, what is there of ill in't [*The Country Wife*], say you?

OLIVIA. O fie, fie, fie, wou'd you put me to the blush anew? call all the blood into my face again? But, to satisfie you then, first, the clandestine obscenity in the very name of *Horner.*

ELIZA. Truly, 'tis so hidden, I cannot find it out, I confess.

OLIVIA. O horrid! does it not give you the rank conception, or image of a Goat, a Town-bull, or a Satyr? nay, what is yet a filthier image than all the rest, that of an Eunuch?

ELIZA. What then? I can think of a Goat, a Bull, or a Satyr, without any hurt.

OLIVIA. I, but, Cousin, one cannot stop there.

ELIZA. I can, cousin.

OLIVIA. O no; for when you have those filthy creatures in your head once,

proclaims the Man's Triumph and her Shame. It always shews her Weakness and often her Inconstancy, and sometimes her Fraud and Perfidiousness." "To Judas Iscariot, Esq; *On the present State of the Stage,*" published in *Original Letters* (1721). *Critical Works,* 2:166.

the next thing you think, is what they do; as their defiling of honest Mens Beds and Couches, Rapes upon sleeping and waking Countrey Virgins, under Hedges, and on Haycocks; nay, farther—

ELIZA. Nay, no farther, Cousin, we have enough of your Coment on the Play, which will make me more asham'd than the Play it self.

(2.1.409–27)

Eliza, Wycherley's example of a modest woman, has difficulty picking out the finer points of obscenity that Olivia dwells on in loving detail. Only immodest women have anything to fear from immodest "images"; where Eliza can imagine a bull or a goat without becoming aroused, Olivia's mind's eye is full of images far more wanton than any in Wycherley's play, and her blush is a guilty marker of knowledge not purity. As Eliza exclaims, Olivia's fantasies are more immodest than anything in the play. Olivia continues on (despite Eliza's remonstrances) to claim that she cannot even look at china without thinking about sex, thanks to *The Country Wife*'s notorious china scene, and has thus had to break "all my defil'd Vessels" (2.1.437). Wycherley's point, of course, is that it is Olivia who has defiled the china, not his play.

Olivia's mental state, her ability to invest even mundane objects with a sexual meaning, translates into her behavior, which provides a perverse vindication of the innocence of the stage. As Olivia makes very clear, she refuses to go to "nasty Plays" (2.1.402), therefore her lewd behavior is innate, not learned from the stage. (By contrast, Eliza, who expresses her willingness to see any of Wycherley's plays, is a model of propriety.) This distinction is significant, for the play pivots around Olivia's sexuality; it is the source of Manly's betrayal, her humiliation, and his revenge. Through her, Wycherley mocks female sexual desire as well as the desire for autonomy, inevitably conflating the desirous woman with the prostitute, to which Manly reduces Olivia by the end of the play. In *Technologies of Gender*, De Lauretis observes that sexuality "is construed not as gendered (as having a male form and a female form) but simply as male. Even when it is located, as it very often is, *in* the woman's body, sexuality is an attribute or property of the male."[8] Wycherley's entire play could be said to elaborate on this precept. At the core, Olivia's problem is that she refuses to accept the parameters for male control of female sexuality. Her active pursuit of her own desires sets up a gender imbalance that must be resolved before the play can conclude in an orderly manner. *The Plain Dealer* provides a means of separating ladies from whores by establishing

8. Teresa de Lauretis, *Technologies of Gender: Essays on Theory, Film, and Fiction* (1987), 37.

a principle of gender based on familiar binary oppositions (male/active/subject, female/passive/object); the play begins with these oppositions at risk and ends with them firmly established. The means to this end are extreme, as the society Wycherley depicts is reconfigured, almost magically, by acts of rape, real or attempted.

Olivia begins the play as something of a female rake, a woman who attempts to control her own sexuality, acting on her own desires to pick and choose among the men around her. In her first meeting with Manly, Olivia rejects him, announces that she has married without his knowledge, and casts an appraising eye over Manly's attractive companion, the cross-dressed Fidelia.[9] But events swiftly move out of her control, largely because of the corrupt moral/sexual sense that leads Olivia to mock Manly and to desire his effeminate comrade. As Manly later comments, she would be better fitted with a "Goat or Monky" than with a man (4.2.214). Despite the general similarity of plot, she differs radically from her namesake in *Twelfth Night*.[10] Although Shakespeare's Olivia preferred the effeminate page to his/her masculine master, she offered marriage, not adultery—and never chased him/her around her bedroom.

Fidelia's account of her second meeting with Olivia provides a vivid illustration of Olivia's dissoluteness, demonstrated through her innately libidinous conduct. On meeting Fidelia, Olivia displays a sexual hunger potent enough to corrupt even the most corrupt; as Fidelia reports, "she has impudence enough to put a Court out of countenance, and debauch a Stews" (4.1.77–78). When Manly questions this assessment, Fidelia describes the female gaze's capacity for communicating the unspeakable: "Her tongue, I confess, was silent; but her speaking Eyes gloted such things, more immodest, and lascivious, than Ravishers can act, or Women under a confinement think" (4.1.80–82). Here the female gaze is in itself obscene; Olivia's "speaking Eyes" convey a message she would never articulate, so that the gaze itself demonstrates promiscuity. Manly, even while trying to hold onto his ideal vision of Olivia, admits the potentially pornographic quality of the female gaze ("I know there are whose Eyes reflect more Obscenity than the Glasses in Alcoves," 4.1.83–84). Fidelia contests that she understands the import of such "eye-kindness," because

no Woman sticks there: Eye-promises of Love they only keep; nay, they are Contracts which make you sure of 'em. In short, Sir, she, seeing me,

9. In the Introduction to the New Mermaid edition of *The Plain Dealer*, James L. Smith describes Olivia as "an affected, prudish, greedy, vain, deceitful, money-grubbing nymphomaniac" (1979), xxii.

10. Celimene, Olivia's counterpart in Moliere's *The Misanthrope*, is guilty of little more than hypocrisy as she allows men to court her and then abuses them behind their backs.

with shame and amazement dumb, unactive, and resistless, threw her
twisting arms about my neck and smother'd me with a thousand tasteless
Kisses: believe me, Sir, they were so to me. (4.1.93–98)

Because "eye-promises of love" are the only "contracts" that women
keep, they represent the only reliable gauge of female passion with the result that the female gaze acts as a monitor of desire.

Crucially, the scene shows Olivia adopting an unsuitably masculine
position, appropriating the active male role and pursuing the passive Fidelia, who in contrast stresses her more traditional feminine position, being "dumb, unactive, and resistless" (strikingly similar to the familiar
admonition that a woman should be "chaste, silent, and obedient"). As
the play progresses, Olivia will be punished for her transgressions against
Manly and more generally against proscribed gender roles. Just as
Olivia's unchecked sexuality is the means by which Wycherley satirizes
her and the "overnice" women she represents, it is on her sexual body
that the playwright and his character inflict their punishment. In what
amounts to a rape, Manly takes Fidelia's place in Olivia's bed and exacts
his revenge by taking that from her which she would not give to him.[11]
Savoring the prospect of making her sexual satisfaction depend on one
she affects to despise, he declares, "Yes, so much she hates me, that it
would be a Revenge sufficient, to make her accessory to my pleasure, and
then let her know it" (4.2.259–60). By means of this theft of sexual favors,
Manly denies Olivia control over her sexuality, reestablishing the male
sexual and social dominance that will triumph by the end of the play.

As Olivia's pursuit of Fidelia becomes more grotesque and her conviction that a woman has satisfied her lusts more ridiculous, her attempt at
sexual autonomy vanishes, and she is reduced to the status of a common
whore, a "wench" at whom Manly flings money in payment for services
rendered (5.3.116).[12] The figure of Olivia as a prostitute is developed
throughout the play, from her first scene with Manly when he compares
her to "Suburb Mistresses" with their "mercenary love" (2.1.643, 650) to
the play's final scene. Bitter and undeceived, Manly descries her as a
"Mercenary Whore . . . Ay, a Mercenary Whore indeed; for she made me
pay her, before I lay with her" (5.2.120–23). She has betrayed Manly doubly, first by appropriating his money, and second by rejecting his sexual
advances. As Manly comments when overhearing Olivia boast that she

11. Percy G. Adams's useful essay, "What Happened in Olivia's Bedroom? or, Ambiguity in *The Plain Dealer*," explores differing interpretations of this scene in an especially cogent
manner, ultimately concluding that Wycherley has been deliberately ambiguous. *Essays in
Honor of Esmond Linworth Marilla* (1970), 174–87.
12. "Here, Madam, I never yet left my Wench unpaid" (5.3.114–15).

had deceived him in order to get his money, "Damn'd Money! it's Master's potent Rival still; and like a saucy Pimp, corrupts, it self, the Mistress it procures for us" (4.2.242–43). The play makes the connection between sexual and monetary dealings unavoidable, a connection crucial to the representation not only of Olivia but of the Widow and even of Fidelia.

The link between women, sex, and money is perhaps most clearly explicated in the figure of the Widow Blackacre. She is a rich widow whose money is inescapably tied to her person; who possesses one possesses the other. Thus, a widow's position is the inverse of that of the prostitute; the widow, like the prostitute's customer, must pay for sexual pleasure. As with most late-seventeenth-century plays, the spectacle of the older woman is the occasion for ridicule,[13] and as a result most references to the Widow's sexuality remain in the realm of the figurative rather than the real. Like Olivia, she places material desires over honor, and as with Olivia, this refusal to assume a traditional feminine role results in the Widow's downfall.[14] The steady erosion of her powers culminates finally in a "rape" of the Widow, absurdly paralleling the rape of Olivia and Vernish's near rape of Fidelia. Captured by Oldfox, she is tied to a chair and threatened with his "parts." Taking his words literally she shrieks, "Acquainted with your parts! A Rape, a Rape! What, will you ravish me?" (5.2.424–25). This threat turns out to be purely figurative, as Oldfox explains that he does indeed intend to ravish her, "but it shall be through the ear" (5.2.426–27). This threat of violation, figurative or otherwise, begins the final reinstatement of male control over the Widow. She is saved from Oldfox's "well-pen'd Acrostics" only to be threatened with a more serious assault, legal action by Jerry and his new guardian, Freeman. She is relegated control over her own body only because nobody else would want it—and even then the final decision is made not by the woman but by her former suitor. As with Olivia, the Widow's story ends with control of a woman's money and person returned to men at the end of the play as Freeman and Jerry reestablish the patriarchal order.[15]

The final piece of the female puzzle, Manly's erstwhile companion Fi-

---

13. For an even more extreme representation of the older woman as the object of sexual disgust see Duffett's *The Amorous Old Woman* (1674) in which, as in *The Plain Dealer,* a young man courts a much older rich widow. In the play's climatic scene, the title character insists that her suitor watch her prepare for bed. She then proceeds to strip off not only her clothing but her eyebrows, an eye, her hair, and ultimately a leg. This grotesque dismembering proves to be too much for her suitor, and he quickly decamps.

14. See Derek Hughes, "*The Plain Dealer:* A Reappraisal," for an assessment of the similarities between Olivia and the Widow.

15. For a fine discussion of the Widow's role within the fractured ideology of *The Plain Dealer* see Burke, "'Law-Suits,' 'Love-Suits.'"

delia, stands in contrast to both the widow with her comically debased sexuality and Olivia with her whorish tendencies; in *The Plain Dealer*'s schema of female sexuality, she represents a feminine ideal: passive, masochistic, and untainted by money's corrupting touch. Although Fidelia spends most of the play in men's clothes, Wycherley carefully designates her behavior and appearance as feminine. She is no hardened campaigner—Manly chides her repeatedly for her cowardice—and she bursts into unmasculine tears at several points during the play, including in the first scene where Manly threatens never to see her again. Unlike the more aggressive cross-dressed heroines in the plays of Behn, Shadwell, or Southerne,[16] Fidelia inhabits her male role awkwardly. She is apprehensive of almost everything, cannot fight, and is distinctly uncomfortable in her role as Olivia's admirer. Moreover, she has adopted her unfeminine garb for a laudably feminine (if seemingly paradoxical) reason, maiden modesty. She confesses to Manly that she donned male garb "partly out of shame to own my love to you, and fear of a greater shame, your refusal of it" (5.3.94–96). Even her love for Manly remains untainted by lust as she admits at the end of the play that her love has a moral rather than carnal basis; she followed him to the Indies after she long "observ'd [his] actions thoroughly, with admiration" (5.3.146).

At the same time that he effaces Fidelia's appetites, Wycherley clearly establishes her as a sexual object for the members of the theater audience. The role was first played by Elizabeth Boutell, one of the leading breeches-role actresses in the 1670s. Boutrell was known not for her realistic representation of male roles, but, on the contrary, for her long chestnut hair and attractive legs, markers of female sexuality on the Restoration stage. Physical emblems written into the text emphasize these feminine features, most notably Fidelia's "long Womans hair" (5.3.81), which falls down in times of crisis and instantly reveals her sex. When Fidelia is forced to reveal her sex to Vernish she is physically threatened as Vernish gropes her to determine the truth of her words, an act which immediately incites his lust:

> VERNISH. How! A very handsom Woman I'm sure then: Here are Witnesses of't too, I confess.
> (*Pulls off her peruke and feels her breasts*)
>
> (Well, I'm glad to find the Tables turn'd, my Wife in more danger of Cuckolding, than I was). [*Aside*].
>
> (4.2.371–74)

---

16. See, for example, Hellena in *The Rover* (1677), Mrs. Gripe in *The Woman Captain* (1679), and Sir Anthony in *Sir Anthony Love* (1690).

His actions direct the audience's eyes first to her hair and then to her breasts, establishing her as a sexual object in their eyes as well as his. Explicitly sexualized by a man's rather than a woman's act and word, Fidelia is validated as a legitimate object of desire.

The result of this demonstration of Fidelia's sexual identity is yet another scene of rape, albeit one that operates very differently from the rapes of Olivia and the Widow. Vernish expresses his intent to make her enact her womanhood, a threat that becomes savage as he pulls her toward Olivia's chamber, where a bed will provide "the proper Rack for Lovers" (4.2.380–81). At the same time that this attempted violation increases Fidelia's status as sexual spectacle, it proves her sexual virtue; in the logic of Restoration drama, only the chaste can be truly threatened by rape—the proof of female chastity lies in the very act that could destroy it.[17] Where the Widow's rape becomes a mockery of her sexuality and Olivia's a proof of her whorish nature, Fidelia's represents a sadistic demonstration of female virtue, focused on the body of the actress. Ultimately, money becomes the link between women and sex, a link which Vernish sums up at the end of act 4: "*I'll fetch the Gold, and that she can't resist; / For with a full hand 'tis we Ravish best*" (4.2.425–26). The play's repeated acts of rape suggest an almost desperate attempt to assert a broad-based patriarchal rule, for, as Carole Pateman argues, "women's bodies symbolize everything opposed to political order";[18] in a properly ordered society, men control both money and female sexuality, dispensing gold and ravishing as they wish. In the end, Vernish's attempt on Fidelia is unsuccessful in part because she does not participate in the same sex/money nexus as Olivia and even the Widow. By contrast, Fidelia not only rejects gold but at the end of the play gladly gives herself and her fortune to Manly; as Peter Holland notes, "The revelation of Fidelia's wealth, not her sex, is the true resolution of the enigma she posed."[19] She makes no attempt to retain control over her wealth, possessing it only to give it up once more. Fidelia thus cannot be linked to the prostitute and represents no threat to patriarchal power structures. Despite her "manly" garb, she makes less of an attempt to appropriate male behavior than any female character in the play.

In contrast, Olivia represents the prototypical castrating woman whose machinations leave Manly financially and sexually powerless. Manly's

17. See also Marsden, "Rape, Voyeurism, and the Restoration Stage," in *Broken Boundaries: Women and Feminism in Restoration Drama* (1998), 185–200.

18. Carole Pateman, *The Disorder of Women: Democracy, Feminism, and Political Theory* (1989), 4.

19. Peter Holland, *The Ornament of Action*, 201.

only recourse is to prove that he is indeed "Manly"; as her threat has been sexual, his punishment is inflicted on her sexual body. In order to shore up the masculinity of the play's title character, its heroine must embody an exaggerated vision of female virtue. She cannot appear as an active, witty counterpoint to the hero, but instead adopts a passive role of virtuous suffering. The result is a play in which the heroine has been forced to deny her personal desires to the extent of pimping for her beloved. Seemingly, Wycherley demands the complete abandonment of female desire and presents rape as the punishment women are to expect if they express desire and step outside of their sphere. As J. Douglas Canfield notes, the ending of the play is a "wish-fulfillment" not simply in Manley's dominance over the town fops and fools, "but especially in the rape of the uppity women," adding that despite Manley's "restoration" in the end, the play's ideology is "threadbare": "The lingering question of the play is how long can the Court party and its hired guns, among them the playwrights, hold the Restoration compromise together."[20]

Participating in the concern over women's sexuality and its link to spectatorship, *The Plain Dealer* presents a stark picture of gender definition. By beginning with an exhortation against prudish women, quickly converted in the "Epistle Dedicatory" and through the character of Olivia into a depiction of women as carnally suspect, the play leaves its female characters in a nearly untenable situation in which modesty is reinvented as depravity and agency as evil. The danger Olivia represents can also be tied to those women who protested Wycherley's drama; like her, they were guilty of too much carnal knowledge, not too much modesty. In the play's strict justice, the active female is made into a sexual object and vehicle for male pleasure against her will. In contrast, Fidelia exemplifies the feminine role as sexual spectacle, displaying a physical womanliness while remaining passive to the point of masochism. To do otherwise would be to link her, like Olivia, to the active sexuality of the whore. In order for Fidelia to get her happy ending, she must be exhibited as female and must demonstrate that she both is not and does not desire to be "manly." Wycherley's play suggests that women who violate this traditional role, in essence attempting to become the hero rather than the heroine, will be punished and ultimately left powerless.

Twenty years later, the representation of female spectatorship, while again linked clearly to female sexuality, would suggest very different issues. The Restoration was over, and, with the ascension of William of Orange, the government and ultimately the social order were reimagined,

20. Canfield, *Tricksters and Estates*, 137, 139.

as Locke had demonstrated in his *Two Treatises on Government* (1690). In the theater, the marriages that Restoration rakes ridiculed but with which comedies so often ended had become a central concern of serious drama as well. Social contracts, both domestic and political, are central concerns of the drama of the 1690s, as audiences are encouraged to consider the problems of marriage and the ways in which this intimate bond serves as an analogy of the state.[21] The certainties of Wycherley's dark comedy are out of date in a world where the tie between husband and wife, ruler and ruled has become a contract that can be questioned and possibly dissolved. In its reconsideration of the situation of woman as spectator, *The Provoked Wife* articulates more directly the problem of female sexuality in a world controlled, even if tenuously, by men.

Provoked Wives and Other Subjects

> When plays such as "The Provoked Wife" are exhibited—it is charity to revile theatres.
>
> —Elizabeth Inchbald, headnote to *The Provok'd Wife*,
> in *The British Theatre* (1824), 9:5

Despite its ultimate lack of action, Vanbrugh's *The Provok'd Wife* generated far more moral outrage than did Wycherley's "excessively obscene" *Plain Dealer*. By the mid eighteenth century, *The Provok'd Wife*, a play with little actual plot, in which fornication is contemplated but never consummated, had become one of the most controversial of English comedies. Although twentieth-century commentary has often focused on the revision of the scenes involving Sir John, during the eighteenth century, it was the morality of the play's female characters that attracted the most attention.[22] Despite the absence of sexual action, critics condemned the looseness of its principles and in some cases argued that the entire play should be suppressed for the public good. Even stripped of its "rankest offences," Inchbald writes, "the present comedy had yet, perhaps, better—never be either seen or read."[23]

21. For a discussion of the centrality of marriage as a political analogy in the late seventeenth century, see Mary Landon Shanley, "Marriage Contract and Social Contract in Seventeenth Century Political Thought," *Western Political Quarterly* 32, no. 1 (1979): 79–91.
22. Collier, of course, objected to the unadapted play's farcical use of clerical garb as blasphemy; nonetheless, even with Sir John's drunken brawling in the clerical garb, he found *The Relapse* more abusive of the clergy than *The Provok'd Wife*. See *A Short View*, 108–9.
23. Inchbald, headnote to *The Provok'd Wife*, in *The British Theatre*, 9:3.

First performed in April 1697, *The Provok'd Wife* proved immediately successful and quickly came under fire from Collier.[24] Such attacks initially spurred the play's popularity, although the figure of Lady Brute came under increasing criticism, and more and more alterations were necessary in order to keep the play on the stage, reaching their logical conclusion with Inchbald's admonition that the play should be avoided completely. These criticisms, like the play's plot, center around Lady Brute's sexual virtue: will she succumb to temptation and sleep with the seductive Constant? Saddled with a repulsive husband who persecutes her incessantly, she is a sympathetic figure with whom, Collier would argue, women in the audience might very well identify. Therein lies her danger, for unlike Wycherley, Vanbrugh does not present a series of clearly established moral lines. Lady Brute's dilemma, to sin or not to sin, to assert her own desires or to suffer passively, has no easy answer. *The Provok'd Wife* provides precisely the kind of dangerous example Collier feared—far more so than *The Plain Dealer* with its rigidly drawn gender lines and its satire on women who try to move into male territory.

In his assessment of *The Provok'd Wife*, Gildon praises the play but quickly acknowledges that it had generated controversy, admitting that some critics had designated it "a loose play, without Design, or if there be a Design, 'tis such a one as the just Rules of Comedy exclude, since it teaches the Wives how they ought to return the Brutality of their Husbands" (144). He deflects the fear of female sexual agency implicit in this reading, claiming instead that the play's lesson is directed to husbands, not wives:

> It rather teaches Husbands how they ought to expect their Wives shou'd make them a Return, if they use them as Sir *John Brute* did his; such Husbands may learn, that slighted and abused Virtue and Beauty, may be provoked to hearken to the prevailing Motives of Revenge. I can never think any reasonable Man shou'd suppose a Woman entirely divested of a sense of Humanity, or insensible either of the Power of an agreeable Temptation, or of the Pleasure it yields: . . . when the Husbands ill Usage of his Wife deprives himself of her Love, he dismisses the surest Guard of their common Honour; and the other, that is her Pride and Care of her Reputation will not be of force enough against Revenge; and the strong sollicitations [*sic*] of an agreeable Person, that demonstrates a value for what the Possessor slights: So that it cannot be deny'd, that this Moral is of admirable Use; and offers a Truth to our consideration, which wou'd often prevent

24. Collier objected strongly to the scenes in which Lady Brute contemplates adultery and argues that while it goes against "the strict Statute Law of Religion" she might win her case if there was a "Court of Chancery in Heav'n" (1.1.94–96). He saw this as the play's greatest example of blasphemy, although he also condemned Sir John's masquerade as a clergyman.

the Ruin of Families, which generally begins with the Husbands Faults. (144–45)

By shifting the weight of the play's instruction to husbands, Gildon shifts as well the blame for the situation the play depicts. His sympathies clearly lie with Lady Brute: she is an example of "slighted and abused Virtue and Beauty" while it is her husband's "ill Usage" that has created the potential for "ruin" within the family. The crux of the play, as well as its potential aftermath, the socially catastrophic "Ruin of Families," is not female frailty but male brutality. The vigor with which Gildon discusses this subject (as well as the time he spends on it—he dedicates less than half the time to *The Relapse*) suggests that at the time the play was first produced, these were the moral issues that generated the most intense debate.

Just as Wycherley began *The Plain Dealer* with a commentary on female spectatorship that he ultimately used to explore hypocrisy and deceit, so too does Vanbrugh use the topic to dissect the sexual and social relations that will dominate his drama. Lady Brute's and Bellinda's discussion of the theater in act 3, scene 3 reveals some of the essential differences between the two playwrights' views on female sexuality. The dialogue is worth quoting at length:

BELLINDA. But my Glass and I cou'd never yet agree what Face I shou'd make when they come blurt out with a nasty thing in a Play: For all the Men presently look upon the Women, that's certain; so laugh we must not, tho' our Stays burst for't; Because that's telling Truth, and owning we understand the Jest. And to look serious is so dull, when the whole House is a laughing.

LADY BRUTE. Besides, that looking serious do's really betray our Knowledge in the Matter, as much as laughing with the Company would do. For if we did not understand the thing, we shou'd naturally do like other People.

BELLINDA. For my part, I always take that Occasion to blow my Nose.

LADY BRUTE. You must blow your Nose half off then at some Plays.

BELLINDA. Why don't some Reformer or other beat the Poet for't?

LADY BRUTE. Because he is not so sure of our private Approbation as of our public Thanks. Well, sure there is not upon Earth, so impertinent a thing as Women's Modesty.

BELLINDA. Yes: Men's Fantasque, that obliges us to it. If we quit our Modesty, they say we lose our Charms, and yet they know that very Modesty is Affectation, and rail at our Hypocrisie. (3.3.76–96)

Like Wycherley, Vanbrugh explores the problem of woman's modesty and female spectatorship, but unlike Wycherley, he admits that "nasty things" create a dilemma for women. Looking serious, as Eliza had said, betrays as much knowledge as laughing, but there seems to be no easy solution to the problem, unless, like Bellinda, a woman "blows [her] Nose half off." Although Vanbrugh voices the familiar charges that female modesty is more affectation than real and that ladies, in private, approve of lewdness, he counters these charges with a suggestion of male complicity. Men's "Fantasque" rather than innate female perversion constrains women to affect modesty; it constitutes an important part of male-defined feminine "Charm." Thus, as Bellinda suggests, it is men who have trapped women within a system of conscious affectation: without modesty (or the pretense thereof), women cease to be desirable, yet with it they become the subject of abuse like Wycherley's. Elsewhere, Constant voices a similar assessment of the male emphasis on chastity: "We recommend it to our wives, Madam, because we wou'd keep 'em to our selves. And to our daughters, because we wou'd dispose of 'em to others" (3.1.360–62). In both cases, women are a commodity whose value is increased when they possess the feminine virtues of modesty and chastity.

The larger context for Lady Brute's conversation with Bellinda complicates the notion of spectatorship as a register of female modesty still further. Although the two women discuss their responses to drama, these responses are embedded within a larger discussion over the nature of the woman as object. Lady Brute and Bellinda are less concerned with their own response to the play than they are to how they will appear to the men around them. As Bellinda notes, all the men "look upon the women" to see how they react, thus she spends time in front of her mirror practicing the appropriate demeanor, in essence, constructing herself for the male gaze. The female spectator thus becomes object rather than possessor of the gaze, and her response to drama ultimately becomes irrelevant except within the context of this dynamic of gaze and desire. Just before their discussion of the theater, Bellinda and Lady Brute define the male gaze as necessary to a woman's experience, thus defining women as objects of male gaze and desire: if there were no men, women would not wear fine clothes, go to church, stay in London, for without the male gaze, their lives would have no purpose or form. Thus, at the theater Lady Brute describes how she displays herself as a erotic object:

LADY BRUTE. I confess, That I love to sit in the Fore-front of a Box. For if one sits behind, there's two Acts gone perhaps, before one's found out.

And when I am there, if I perceive the Men whispering and looking upon me, you must know I cannot for my Life forbear thinking, they talk to my Advantage. And that sets a Thousand little tickling Vanities on Foot—

BELLINDA. Just my Case for all the World; but go on.

LADY BRUTE. I watch with Impatience for the next Jest in the Play, that I may laugh and show my white Teeth. If the Poet has been dull, and the Jest be long a coming, I pretend to whisper one to my Friend, and from thence fall into a little short Discourse, in which I take Occasion to shew my Face in all Humours, Brisk, Pleas'd, Serious, Melancholy, Languishing;—Not that what we say to one another causes any of these Alterations.

Here the female spectator is reconfigured into the object of the male gaze; as Lady Brute stresses the ways in which she constructs herself as physically desirable with her white teeth and most attractive "humours," Vanbrugh presents a picture of women who are endlessly objectified, on the stage, and within the theater itself. Female spectatorship, in other words, is simply another occasion for the commodification of women, this time staged by the woman herself.

Although women present themselves and are presented as objects for men's delectation, in this play as in *The Plain Dealer,* women's eyes speak their true desires. For Vanbrugh, however, these desires are natural and understandable rather than disgusting. Despite her attempts to construct herself as the conventionally attractive object of the male gaze, Lady Brute's eyes express her personal wishes, which put the lie to her decorous exterior. When she claims that she has no secrets for "my heart cou'd never yet confine my Tongue" (1.1.109–10), Bellinda corrects her, explaining that it is Lady Brute's eyes which she cannot control, "for I am sure I have seen them gadding, when your Tongue has been lockt up safe enough" (1.1.111–12). What these "gadding eyes" reveal is Lady Brute's unspoken but very real desire for Constant; in Bellinda's candid assessment, "never was poor Creature so spurr'd on by desire, and so rein'd in with fear!" (1.1.124–25). Constant, much less adept than Bellinda in interpreting the language of the female gaze, only begins to recognize the disconnect between Lady Brute's words and her wishes later, commenting inarticulately, "She said that—says she—she said—Zoons I don't know what she said: But she look'd as if she said everything I'd have her" (3.1.462–63).

Where *The Provok'd Wife* differs the most conspicuously from *The Plain Dealer* is in its representation of female sexual agency. Olivia, the woman who attempts to act on her desires, becomes the butt of Wycherley's satire on hypocrisy, both sexual and otherwise. In *The Provok'd Wife*, both the context and the characters are more complex. Unlike Olivia, Lady Brute is a sympathetic character in an intolerable situation, whose plight as an abused wife makes the question of women choosing to act on their desires a serious one. Although Olivia is driven by unthinking lust, Lady Brute contemplates her marriage vow and weighs it against her resentment toward her husband and her yearning for Constant. As their candid conversations indicate, she and Bellinda are well aware of how society's system operates; discussions of what men expect of women quickly become frank appraisals of marriage and the pros and cons of committing adultery. It was dialogue such as that in act 3, scene 3 where Lady Brute laughingly suggests that Bellinda "commit Fornication . . . if 'twere only to keep me in Countenance whilst I commit—You know what" (3.3.128– 30) which most troubled later critics. Both characters freely acknowledge their own sexual agency and question the viability of conventional morality. Crucially, in these scenes as throughout the play, sexual agency is not presented as a male prerogative.

As the play makes clear, Lady Brute is indeed tempted by Constant, and he makes no secret of his desire for her. In the end, however, it is the fact or fiction of women's sexual behavior, rather than the reality of their desire, on which the play turns. Lady Brute both likes Constant and hates her husband. Will she act on her desires or not? The play gives no answers (we know only that she has not cuckolded her husband—yet). Like the other comedies of the 1690s that examine troubled marriages (such as Southerne's *The Wives' Excuse* and Vanbrugh's own *The Relapse*), *The Provok'd Wife* pulls back from actually representing female sexual agency in action, suggesting that the conscious decision to commit adultery made by a sympathetic female figure simply cannot be plotted even when rapes (i.e., *un*conscious sexual actions) of innocent women are commonplace. Thus, schemes to discredit not only Lady Brute but the more conventional Bellinda as well turn on a false representation of their sexual actions. First Mademoiselle gives an exaggerated account of Lady Brute's meeting with Constant in St. James Park in which the tryst ends with consummation[25] (in reality, Lady Fancifull breaks up the scene before anything untoward could occur). Lady Fancifull's libelous story about Bellinda is more extreme still as she sends Heartfree a letter in which a putative "friend" claims to have slept with Bellinda, fathered a child with her, and "the Foundation laid" for another (5.5.120–23). The women are not the only objects of false rumors, as Lady Fancifull is equally creative in her

25. "He tro her down. Il tombe dessus, Le Diable assiste, Il emporte tout" (5.3.103–4).

version of Heartfree's past, but with an important difference: the way to smirch a male reputation is to suggest that he is married, not that he is sexually active. What closure the play achieves comes from the exposure of Lady Fancifull's machinations and from the uniting of Heartfree and Bellinda as, with some misgivings on both sides, they agree to attempt the "Matrimonial Project," what Heartfree describes as "*Hob's* Voyage— a great Leap in the Dark" (5.5.15, 27).

Despite the broad comedy of Sir John in his clerical (and, in later versions, female) attire, *The Provok'd Wife* is a profoundly female-centered drama. The play focuses squarely on Lady Brute, her marital problems, and her deliberations regarding whether or not to act on her desires. This concern over female sexuality and its potential corruption links *The Provok'd Wife* not only with the marriage plays with which it is commonly associated but also with the she-tragedies that form the focus of the remainder of this book. Lady Brute appears in a comedy, but the issues she deals with are similar to those that trouble the equally sympathetic heroines in dozens of female-centered tragedies: sexual agency and sexual stain. But where the tragedies portray these events as resulting, inevitably, in female misery, in Vanbrugh's complex comedy, even though the sexual act is averted (in contrast to contemporary tragedies) the moral lines remain fuzzy. Thus, Lady Brute can link a wife's sexual insubordination to the social contract, arguing that since her husband has violated his matrimonial vow to be kind, she is free to violate hers: "the Argument's good between the King and the People, why not between the Husband and the Wife?" (1.1.70–71). Using the language of contract theory, the play suggests that if Sir John is the "brutal," cowardly domestic king, then Lady Brute, like the people of England in 1688, may have the right to remove him as her ruler.[26] In questioning her husband's status as domestic ruler, Lady Brute implicitly interrogates the political order, an analogy Mary Astell would use just three years later in *Serious Reflections on Marriage*.[27]

26. As John Bull notes, this play, like many of the marriage plays of later seventeenth century, is "concerned with much more than the dilemma of a particular couple," using the problem of marriage to represent larger social and political issues, such as the changing social order and the politics of postrevolution England. *Vanbrugh and Farquhar* (1998), 57.

27. "If Absolute Sovereignty be not necessary in a State, how comes it to be so in a Family? or if in a Family why not in a State; since no Reason can be alledg'd for the one that will not hold more strongly for the other? If the Authority of the Husband so far as it extends, is sacred and inalienable, why not of the Prince? The Domestic Sovereign is without Dispute Elected, and the Stipulations and Contract are mutual, is it not then partial in Men to the last degree, to contend for, and practise that Arbitrary Dominion in their Families, which they abhor and exclaim against in the State?" *Reflections Upon Marriage*, in *The First Feminist: Reflections upon Marriage and other Writings by Mary Astell*, ed. Bridget Hill (1986), 76.

In *The Plain Dealer*, Wycherley presents an example of the use of theater for ridicule, which some playwrights would later attempt to use as a counter to Collier's arguments. The play clearly delineates virtue and vice, and the threat of feminine insubordination is firmly quashed. Female sexual behavior is ridiculed and the only opportunity for the female spectator's identification is with Fidelia, a passive emblem of feminine virtue, both sexual and monetary.[28] *The Provok'd Wife*, on the contrary, presents exactly the possibility of identification that Collier and his followers feared: a woman with sexual agency who questions the double standard of her society. Although Lady Brute does *not* act, and at the play's end is left with the same questions with which she began the play, the very fact that she seriously contemplates adultery (and that Vanbrugh allows his audience to believe she would be justified in acting on her desires) made the play problematic in its own time and offensive to later writers. Both plays examine female sexuality within a larger system of male control, but *The Plain Dealer* renders this sexuality ultimately innocuous by caricaturing it when women slip outside of the larger homosocial network of desire. *The Provoked Wife* presents a more sympathetic vision of female desire, but ultimately depicts a world in which the female subject designs herself as object of the male gaze, re-creating her sexuality as a commodity for male consumption, a material entity much like the estate for which she exchanges the use of her body. Whereas in Wycherley's play masculine prerogative ultimately contains the threat of female sexuality, such a division of power is not possible for Vanbrugh's characters. In its sympathetic treatment of potential female sexual agency *The Provok'd Wife* represents the inverse of its tragic contemporaries, in which women suffer terribly for sins which they never intended to commit; nonetheless in its contemplation of the larger implications of this sexuality the play raises similar concerns. As the following chapters will demonstrate, the women in these plays, like Lady Brute and Bellinda, are conscious of being the object of the male gaze, although for them this objectification both defines their roles as tragic heroines and all too often results in their destruction.

28. Money is discussed relatively infrequently in *The Provok'd Wife*. Lady Brute married for money and status or "ambition," without ever loving her husband, as she admits in the opening scene. Her ambition is the source of her unhappy marriage, but the play touches lightly on this subject, dwelling instead on the behavior of husbands and wives after they marry, as Gildon's discussion of the play indicates.

CHAPTER 3

Falling Women: She-Tragedy
and Sexual Spectacle

The Distress of Morena never fail'd to bring Tears into the Eyes
of the Audience; which few Plays, if any since *Otway*'s have
done; and yet, which is the true End of Tragedy.

—CHARLES GILDON, *The Lives and Characters
of the English Dramatick Poets* (1699), 111

Isabella: Do! Nothing, for I am born to suffer.

—*The Fatal Marriage* (2.2.66)

In the last decades of the seventeenth century, serious drama
was reinvented with a female face. The sweeping oaths and pledges of
honor prominent in an earlier generation of heroic drama had lost their
validity, especially in the aftermath of the Exclusion Crisis, and playwrights sought a new means of enacting honor and integrity. With the
heroic mode outdated and no longer convincing, writers turned to the
private realm, using the spectacle of female travail as the means to excite
audience interest and in many cases to communicate a political agenda.
In these plays, later dubbed "she-tragedy," women are presented to the
audience's gaze, established as desirable, and then driven into prolonged
and often fatal suffering. It is the distinctly female nature of this suffering
that gives these plays their name and provides the common link among
the serious dramas of this often ignored period of English theater.

The goal of this chapter is to examine the semiotics of she-tragedy and
to consider its implications for the cultural inscription of female sexuality. The movement that culminated in she-tragedy began in the 1680s with
the emphasis on pathos, a property contemporary writers referred to as

"distress." From 1680 onward, pathos dominated the theaters, with plays deriving their power not from their potential to shock, but from their ability to thrill with scenes of suffering innocence. Unlike the horror plays of the previous decade, the spectacle in these cases arises not from grisly scenes of blood or torture, but from displays of emotional and sometimes physical suffering inflicted on blameless victims who are almost inevitably female. Such scenes of suffering incorporated the suggestiveness of sex comedies popular in previous decades but avoided the aggressive sexuality displayed by women in the earlier plays, thus bringing the stage characters closer to popular ideals of feminine behavior. The cult of suffering enabled playwrights to represent truth visually rather than verbally; the evident intensity of the heroine's pain demonstrated the validity of both her emotion and the drama's action. The source of her distress also provided a ready means of expounding a political argument, whether it was in a post-1688 Whig drama in which an innocent maiden is undone by a tyrant, thus confirming the legitimacy of removing bad monarchs, or less frequently, a Tory nuanced play in which the sacred ties of family and implicitly of state have come undone, leading to moral chaos visited, inevitably, on the body of another innocent maiden. No matter the message, such displays of pathos provided drama with a new form of authenticity, demonstrated through a heroine's ability to suffer.

The chapter explores the means by which she-tragedy functions, providing an introduction to those plays, written largely between 1690 and 1714, which exploit the combination of pathos and sexual titillation. I examine the characteristics of she-tragedy and consider the cultural factors that made these female-centered plays the dominant mode of serious drama for so many years. She-tragedy came to the fore in the period following the drought of new drama that characterized most of the 1680s. In late 1694, Thomas Betterton, Elizabeth Barry, and a group of veteran actors left Christopher Rich's management to establish their own company at Lincoln's Inn Fields, thus greatly increasing the demand for new plays.[1] The serious drama of this period is a source of confusion and general distaste to many modern scholars who prefer their drama hard-edged and cynical rather than affective and emotional. Allardyce Nicoll, writing his multivolume history of English drama, describes the drama of this period as lacking orientation: "It is to be regarded as a blundering attempt on the part of men who knew not what they desired to furnish actable plays for the theater. They could give nothing definite to the stage; their plays are amorphous, chaotic in plot and undistinguished in char-

---

1. The company received an official license in March 1695.

acter drawing."[2] Robert D. Hume is equally impatient with the "love-and-drivel mode" of what he terms the "directionless tragedies" of the 1690s and early 1700s.[3] This attitude is due in part to a general twentieth-century distaste for the sentimental as well as the overtly sensational, in many ways the legacy of modernism and New Criticism with their fore-grounding of verbal wit over emotional display. This does not, however, accurately reflect the taste of the eighteenth century, in which plays of wit were often ignored while the affective tragedies of the 1680s and 1690s were revived again and again. Perhaps the problem lies not with the plays themselves but with our attempts to force them into formal categories. Although the generic approach can expose the diversity of serious drama, it also imposes limitations of our own making onto an age that seemingly had no need to work within such narrow boundaries.[4]

Although the plays of this period are diverse in form, thus troubling in Nicoll's and Hume's attempts to categorize them by type, they are remarkably coherent in their obsession with portraying the woes of women, particularly those women who have, voluntarily or involuntarily, committed a sexual sin. In this way, they can be seen an outgrowth of the pathetic plays of the 1680s, particularly those of Otway and Banks. Of course, not all drama of this period fits into the category of she-tragedy (Southerne's *Oroonoko* and Addison's *Cato* are conspicuous examples), but the emphasis on pathos, sexuality, and specifically female suffering dominates. Even a partial listing of the new tragedies staged during this period indicates the popularity of this female focus: *The Fatal Marriage* (1694), *Agnes de Castro* (1695), *The Mourning Bride* (1697), *The Unnatural Mother* (1698), *Queen Catharine; or, The Ruins of Love* (1698), *The Princess of Parma* (1699), *Love's Victim; or, The Queen of Wales* (1701), *The Fair Penitent* (1703), *Zelmane; or, The Corinthian Queen* (1705), *Almyna; or, The Arabian Vow* (1707), *Elfrid; or, The Fair Inconstant* (1710), *The Distrest Mother* (1712), *Jane Shore* (1714). In addition, stories of Boadicea appeared on both stages between 1695 and 1697[5] while two different versions of *Iphigenia* competed in December 1699.[6] Where plays lack feminine titles or references

2. Allardyce Nicoll, *A History of English Drama, 1660–1900* (1952), 2:61, 96.

3. Robert D. Hume, *The Development of English Drama*, in *The Late Seventeenth Century* (1976), 422.

4. One reminder of this generic flexibility is the designation "tragedy" applied to any serious drama.

5. Rich's company staged the anonymous *Bonduca; or, The British Heroine*, an adaptation of Fletcher's *Bonduca*, in 1695, and Betterton's company answered with Charles Hopkins's *Boadicea, Queen of Britain* in 1697. Both John Downes in *Roscius Anglicanus* (1708; reprint 1969), and Gildon in *A Comparison of the Two Stages*, ed. Staring B. Wells (1942), cite Hopkins's play as a particular success.

6. Betterton's company produced John Dennis's *Iphigenia* (an adaptation of Euripides),

to the defeat of love, they often add a suggestive subtitle, such as a revival of Rochester's adaptation of Fletcher's *Valentinian* advertised as *Valentinian, With the Rape of Lucina*, a description which promised spectators a display of eroticized suffering.[7]

These plays coincide with the attacks on the theaters described in the first chapter, yet, despite the intensely sexual nature of the plays and their characters, they appear immune from the censure of Collier and his followers. Aside from an occasional reference to a perceived blasphemous phrase (as, for example, in act 3, scene 4 of Congreve's *The Mourning Bride*),[8] the antitheatrical writers are mute on the potential evils of contemporary tragedy. The reasons for this silence are twofold. First, at the time of the antitheatrical debate, comedies outnumbered tragedies by a margin of more than three to one. They were more visible and hence the most obvious target of attack. But on a deeper level than mere logistics, the she-tragedies of the late seventeenth and early eighteenth centuries provide little threat to the stability of English sexual and political culture. She-tragedy depends on the spectacle of female distress to satisfy its audience. In it, scopic pleasure is dependent on the representation of the passive woman's suffering, which is inevitably sexually tinged. In these plays playwrights manipulate the female image, carefully constructing a system of spectatorship *within* the play, in which the heroine is designated as the desirable object of a specifically male gaze. Significantly, women rarely possess the gaze in these plays and thus they do not run the risk of "being wounded in the eye" with desire, something Collier feared would happen to the female spectators of comedy. Just as the male characters within the plays gaze on a series of female victims, the audience is encouraged to focus on these desirable yet ultimately vulnerable women. In contrast to the comedies which Collier et al. denounced, in she-tragedies women are not encouraged to transgress; the message presented is instead one of horrible retribution for even the most innocent offenses.

She-tragedy reiterates gender as a stable series of binary oppositions: male/female, subject/object, and actor/acted upon, oppositions that supported rather than threatened existing social structures. With the excep-

---

while shortly after Rich's company staged Abel Boyer's *Achilles; or, Iphigenia in Aulis* (a translation of Racine's *Iphigenie*). *A Comparison between the Two Stages* mocks the rival plays and playwrights ("Then comes the second *Iphigenia* in all her Charms, and like a superiour Mistress was resolv'd to eclipse her Rival") but notes that neither play was an outstanding success and that "both sleep in everlasting Tranquility," 24, 25.

7. April 16, 1706, performance advertised in *The Daily Courant*.

8. Collier objects to the reference Osmyn makes to hell and damnation in the scene. Congreve responded with considerable annoyance in *Amendments of Mr. Collier's False and Imperfect Citations, &c.* (1698), complaining "if there be Immodesty in that Tragedy, I must confess my self incapable of ever writing any thing with Modesty or Decency" (23).

tion of atypical figures such as Delarivier Manley's Homais in *The Royal Mischief,* these women accept rather than challenge their subordinate position within a patriarchal society, choosing, as does Southerne's Isabella, to suffer rather than to act. (Manley's supporters were quick to note that Homais's transgressions were punished by the end of the play, thus observing the dramatic stricture of poetic justice as well as maintaining proper social decorum.)[9] However, the manner in which they reiterate these familiar contrasts allows playwrights to articulate political or social agendas; the nature of these agendas varies from playwright to playwright and even from year to year. One opposition that is repeatedly blurred and then exploited is that of the woman who is both virgin and whore, chaste and unchaste. It is this conflation of contraries that threatens the social order of the play and which must, in the end, be destroyed. She-tragedy derives its considerable emotional power from the display of the defiled women and the prolonged distress of these sullied maidens. Ironically, the heroines of she-tragedy are often established as icons of implicitly English feminine virtue, in contrast to a series of exotic and immoral women, of whom Congreve's Zara is perhaps the most compelling example. This English virtue is first confirmed and then ultimately reified through the suffering the heroine endures.

To begin, I examine what might be called the formal components of she-tragedy, those devices commonly employed by playwrights to stage the suffering of their female characters. These elements remain constant from the steamy world of the 1690s to the chaster dramas of Nicholas Rowe and his contemporaries. After a consideration of the origins of she-tragedy, the chapter closes with an exploration of the serious drama of the 1690s, especially the decade's most popular she-tragedies, Southerne's *The Fatal Marriage* and Congreve's *The Mourning Bride.* Although the explicitly sexual content of tragedy diminishes in the eighteenth century, the spectacle of female suffering does not. The importance of such suffering is perhaps best epitomized in the quotation with which I began this chapter, in which Charles Gildon praises a play specifically for its skillful rendition of female "distress." Crucially, Gildon observes that an effective play "bring[s] Tears into the Eyes of the Audience," which, he claims, "is the true End of Tragedy."[10] Tragedy is thus defined not in terms of formal

9. Gildon writes that in contrast to her source in Sir John Chardin's *Travels,* Manley's tragedy "has receiv'd this Advantage, that the Criminals are here punish'd for their Guilt, who in the Story escape; a Poetick Justice, which ought ever to be observed in all Plays; for a Just Audience could never have been pleas'd with the Prosperity of *Homais,* and *Leavan* [*sic*], after so criminal an Amour." *Lives and Characters,* 91.

10. Gildon, *Lives and Characters,* 111.

principles but in affective terms accomplished through the spectator's vicarious enjoyment of suffering womanhood.

WHAT then is she-tragedy? As generally described above, it is subgenre of plays written between the late 1680s and first decades of the eighteenth century that focuses on the suffering and often tragic end of a central, female figure. Its most famous practitioners were John Banks, William Congreve, Thomas Southerne, and Nicholas Rowe, although a case can also be made for including Thomas Otway on this list. More specifically, these are intensely erotic plays that revolve around the sexuality of a central female figure, usually a woman tainted by sexual transgression, either voluntary or involuntary: Southerne's Isabella commits adultery through a second, bigamous marriage; Congreve's Zara indulges in adulterous desire; Rowe's Calista is unchaste and his Jane Shore the mistress or "whore" of a king. The defining characteristic of the genre, this obsession with tainted female sexuality, constitutes a "technology of gender" in which female sexuality is both demonized and defined as a treasure for homosocial exchange. In these plays, the woman does not control her own sexuality; rather, possession of her body is fought over and displayed by the play's male characters. In the semiotics of she-tragedy, control of a woman's sexuality is marked by control of the gaze, and the she-tragedy heroine spends much of her time on stage subjected to a gaze explicitly defined as male.

In the theater, as opposed to the experience of the solitary reader, the spectator gazes on a living image. She-tragedy's success depends in particular on the skillful manipulation of the female image, and the manner in which this image is displayed exposes some of the form's most distinctive qualities. On a fundamental level, unlike tragedies centered on a male hero, the plays depend on the symbiotic relationship between looking and loving. The connection between sight and desire plays an important role in the action of she-tragedy, and even more important it determines the function of the heroine in the plays. A passive and objectified figure, the she-tragedy heroine is a fictional woman represented by a living woman, whose physical presence betrays her femininity. Her visibility as a sexual object, not subject, must be established early in each play as it is the catalyst for the play's action and the direct cause of the heroine's ultimate distress. By contrast, in the tragedy of the late seventeenth and early eighteenth centuries, male characters are rarely situated as sexual objects. Moreover, male characters do not suffer in the same manner as do women: their misery might be said to be active rather than

passive, and they do not demonstrate the pathos that their female counterparts do. In she-tragedy, sexual objectification and suffering necessarily go together; the one is almost inevitably the cause of the other. A useful
comparison here might be made to *King Lear*, a play that does focus on
the sufferings of its title character and which in mid-eighteenth-century
stagings would become notable for its rendition of male pathos. As staged
in the later seventeenth century, however, the effect of male distress was
greatly diminished. In Nahum Tate's adaptation, Lear shares the stage
with Edgar and Cordelia; both roles are augmented by Tate. Lear's sufferings are abbreviated and interspersed with a variety of new scenes, including Edmund's attempted rape of Cordelia.

Suffering as sexual spectacle is pivotal to the construction and ultimate
effectiveness of she-tragedy. Within these plays, the male gaze is explicitly directed toward the sexualized woman, but this emphasis on spectatorship extends beyond the confines of the stage and into the theater
audience. As discussed in my opening chapter, Restoration and eighteenth-century theories of audience response expect a male spectator to
respond differently to visual representation than a female spectator.
These differences are essential to the gender relations delineated within
the torrid world of she-tragedy. Because the viewers described by critics
and depicted by playwrights are theoretical rather than factual, and because these interpretations of audience response inform dramatic structure and meaning, I want to begin by looking not at the actual audiences
but at the literary construction of these gendered spectators before turning to the plays themselves.

Early modern explanations of scopophilia defined men as natural
voyeurs and attributed their voyeurism to no less an event than the fall
of man, claiming that by the "misfortune of Humanity," men need the
sight of beauty in order to appreciate virtue.[11] Thus even Milton's Satan
is struck "stupidly good" (9.465) by the sight of Eve's beauty, although
the effect is only fleeting.[12] I want to look particularly closely at one detailed description of male scopic pleasure that provides a paradigm for
the staging of the female image in she-tragedy. Writing in 1714 about the
figure of Lady Jane Grey (the subject of three she-tragedies), fledgling

11. "Dedication" to Edward Young, *The Force of RELIGION; or, Vanquish'd Love. (Illustrated in the Story of Lady Jane Gray)* (1715). The epitaph reads "Gratior and pulchro veniens in Corpore Virtus," Virgil. All further references will be made to this edition and cited parenthetically.

12. John Milton, *Paradise Lost*, in *John Milton, Complete Poems and Major Prose*, ed. Merritt Y. Hughes (1957).

clergyman Edward Young provides an example of what for him represents the ideal male fantasy:

> There is not in Nature a more glorious Scene, than He enjoys, who by Accident oversees a Great, and Young, and Beautiful Lady in her Closet of Devotion, instead of Gaiety, and Noise, and Throng, so natural to the Qualities just mention'd; all is solemn, and silent, and private. Pious Meditation has carry'd her away into a Forgetfulness of her lovely Person, which no one but herself can forget! All her exquisite Features are animated with Religion in such a Manner, as to make any licentious Thought in the Beholder impious and shocking! All her Motions and Posture, whose Gracefulness in others might be a Foundation for Pride, and be thought an Excuse for Omissions in Duty, are full of Humiliation, and pious Neglect! ("Dedication")

Young's ideal spectacle is a classic case of voyeurism consisting of a gaze that creates desire within the male subject and establishes the person gazed on as object. Despite Young's protestations that "licentious Thought[s]" in the beholder would be shocking, he dwells on physical details, repeatedly commenting upon the "lovely Person" and "exquisite Features" possessed by the object of his gaze. Accented by a series of impassioned exclamation marks, his comments become increasingly excited as he continues his description.

Significantly, this gaze is not mutual, and in Young's description, this lack of mutuality becomes one of the scene's delights. The power of his gaze gives the male spectator authority over his female object; he can watch her unobserved and take careful note of that "lovely Person," constructing her as object. This position of male dominance carries through into the staging of the imaginary tableau: the man stands watching as the woman kneels passively in a position, as he notes, of "Humiliation." Most important, it is the male observer who controls the gaze: "Those Eyes, which cannot be shew'd in Publick without interrupting the Business of the World, fixing Thousands in Attention, and suspending the Pursuits of Avarice and Ambition, are devoutly rais'd, and importunately fasten'd on an invisible Object" ("Dedication"). Young pointedly establishes that the woman's gaze has been deflected; she turns her eyes upward on the "invisible Object" to whom she prays. Young's ecstatic description validates the male gaze while vilifying the female gaze. The gaze is indeed powerful, but when possessed by a woman it creates chaos, "interrupting the Business of the World" and transfixing thousands. As Young suggests, the ideal woman is the object not the possessor of the gaze, kneeling in supplication, her eyes turned away from the male spectator. But where Young attempts (not very successfully) to sublimate his excitement into religious ecstasy, she-tragedy explicitly encourages "licentious thoughts" through the sexual spectacle of the falling woman.

As Young suggests, notions of spectatorship are strictly gendered, and we can see the construction of this sexual system both within the plays and within the theaters where they were performed. Contemporary sources often exclude women from the sensual pleasures of watching; men are established as the gazing subject while women are relegated to the role of passive object of this gaze. When writers such as Collier and his followers theorize the female gaze and apply this connection between sight and desire to women, it becomes a source of consternation, a harbinger of social disintegration. Playwrights present a different model. Where men are naturally expected to feel "passion" on watching a she-tragedy, women are asked to identify with the female victim, expressing their fellow suffering with ideologically correct tears—a safer form of identification than that feared by writers of antitheatrical pamphlets. Nicholas Rowe, for example, addresses prologues to the "fair Judges" (6) in his audience, begging them to weep for his heroines and suggesting that if they find them lifelike they should use their gaze to "copy out the Dame" (15).[13] In one prologue, written for Rowe's *The Tragedy of Lady Jane Gray* (1715), female spectators are instructed to "lament in silent Woe" (39), showing their appreciation for the play and for its heroine through their tears. But the author of the prologue quickly turns from directing the female spectator's response to considering how the sight of all these tears will affect the men in the theater audience:

> The lovely Form through falling Drops will seem
> Like flow'ry Shadows on the silver Stream.
> Thus Beauty, Heaven's sweet Ornament, shall prove
> Enrich'd by Virtue, as ador'd by Love.
>
> (41–44)

The spectator here becomes the spectacle, her eyes veiled by tears, which obscure her gaze and increase her beauty. While her gaze is concealed, the male spectator, like Young's observer, can enjoy the sight of the woman's "lovely form" so that for the female spectator, the act of watching only serves to emphasize her role as object. (One might think here again of the scene in *The Provok'd Wife* in which Lady Brute and Bellinda explain how at the theater they construct themselves as objects of the male gaze.) As

13. Prologue to *Jane Shore* (1714).

constructed by these authors, the gaze of the female spectator should be veiled by tears and her response to theater to imitate passive virtue and identify with the object of the male gaze. A mirror of the system of spectatorship within the plays, these constructions of the female spectator create two interlocking circles of spectatorship: one, the play onstage; and two, the theater auditorium, where men become desirous spectators and women are established as and aligned with the object of male desire.

Of course, this is the female spectator as a theoretical construction—a construct as troubling to late-seventeenth- and early-eighteenth-century writers as she would be to twentieth-century theorists and complicated today by the dearth of actual accounts of women's responses to she-tragedy. But what we do know is that the *real* women in the audiences liked she-tragedy; playwrights repeatedly seek the approval of "the fair" in their prologues, and revivals of the more popular she-tragedies were frequently staged "at the request of some ladies of quality." It is perhaps no surprise that female audiences liked these plays, given their emphasis on the heroine rather than the hero. As Austen's Catherine Morland would remark a century later, she preferred novels to history because history consisted of "the quarrels of popes and kings, with wars and pestilences, in every page; the men all so good for nothing, and hardly any women at all—it is very tiresome."[14] She-tragedy does indeed shift the focus of serious drama onto women and in that sense could be said to validate their personal experience in a way in which the more masculine serious drama of the Restoration did not. Nonetheless, if these female spectators are to "copy out the dame," this identification has its masochistic elements as the women they witness spend much of their time onstage in anguish. The centrality of the female protagonists certainly explains the popularity of these plays among women, yet the suffering that these characters endure makes the concept of identification in itself painful. As discussed in the introduction to this book, similar issues have troubled a more recent generation of theorists.[15] In the case of she-tragedy's early

14. Jane Austen, *Northanger Abbey*, ed. R. W. Chapman (1933), 108.

15. Mary Ann Doane struggles with this problem when examining the popularity of the woman-centered "weepies" of the 1940s and 1950s. In *The Desire to Desire: The Woman's Film of the 1940s* (1987), she outlines the difficulties in conceptualizing the female spectator (see especially chap. 1, "The Desire to Desire"), ultimately arguing that the women's films allow a space for the female spectator by deemphasizing female sexuality as spectacle. Subsequently, in "Film and Masquerade: Theorizing the Female Spectator," she suggests a form of masquerade in which the female spectator mimics a male spectator and thus participates in a sadistic rather than a masochistic impulse. Jackie Stacey deals directly with the issue of women identifying with the object of their gaze in *Star Gazing: Hollywood Cinema and Female Spectatorship*. However, the kind of identification she describes is very different from what a later-seventeenth-century theatergoer would have experienced as it comprises identifica-

audiences, it seems likely that the women in the theater audience shared with their male neighbors a vicarious pleasure in witnessing the suffering of the she-tragedy heroines while at the same time feeling a certain kinship with these distressed women because of their common gender.

Even within she-tragedy, spectatorship is an organizing principle. Filled with references to sight and spying, the plays invite the audience to survey the titillating spectacle of female sexuality, and like the pointing figures in landscape painting, the male characters function to direct our eyes toward the appropriate object. The female protagonists of she-tragedy, by contrast, like the pious figure in Young's vision, avert their eyes or lament the inefficacy of their gaze. This pattern of encouraging the spectator to focus on a female rather than a male object is reinforced by means of theatrical devices that deliberately present the heroine as a spectacle to be scrutinized by the audience. Each play establishes the sexualized heroine as the visual object early in the action and retains this focus through the psychosexual observations of the male characters. The paradigm of male spectator and female object is particularly noticeable in conventional scenes such as those in which the heroine is "discovered," recumbent, in a seemingly acquiescent position, by a male character whose subsequent comments effectively establish her as sexual object.[16] Such scenes share virtually identical components: the reclining woman, her eyes hidden, and the man whose gaze controls the scene.

A few examples serve to illustrate the workings of such scenes and their import within the plays. Not surprisingly, minor plays often serve as the best exemplars of this mechanism (the best plays in this genre use the technique less crudely), as the plays themselves, like the scenes cited here, are often formulaic. Charles Gildon, for example, in his first attempt at tragedy, *The Roman Bride's Revenge* (1697), seeks to titillate his audience with the suggestion of rape, presenting his heroine seemingly at the mercy of a political/sexual tyrant:

> Scene *opens, and discovers* Portia *lying in a Melancholy posture on a Couch.* Enter *the* Emperor.
>
> EMP. Such was *Europa,* such bright *Danae* was,
> And such was *Laeda,* thus transporting fair,
> When with dilusive Arts great *Jove* compress'd 'em!

tion with a specific actress, something which the physical design of the Restoration and early-eighteenth-century theater as well as the less elevated social status of the early actresses would have obviated.

16. The visual impact of these scenes was emphasized by the staging: the previous scene would draw to reveal the recumbent actress, focusing attention on her.

> Oh! that I cou'd, like him, but change my Form,
> T'assume that likeness, that would please you most.
> Gods might unenvy'd, keep their Joys above,
> I'd wish no other Heav'n but my Love.
>   (*She starts from her Couch, on discovering the Emperor*)
> POR. Ha! is he here? and at this dead of Night!
> Oh! guard my Virtue Heav'n from the Tyrant!
>
>   (15)

The emperor's comments establish Portia as the object of his desirous gaze but also direct the audience's gaze to her recumbent body. His references to Europa, Danae, and Leda, all famous victims of divine rape, make the sexual content of the scene explicit, as do Portia's own references to the late hour (the time of illicit sexual encounters) and her outspoken fear for her own "virtue." Although the suggested rape never actually occurs, the scene allows the audience to imagine such a rape and to enact it on Portia's recumbent body.

A similar scene appears in the anonymous *The Fatal Discovery; or, Love in Ruines* (1698). Here, Cornaro enters and discovers his beloved Eromena (unbeknownst to him, the incestuous product of a union with his mother fifteen years before):

> And see she's here, my fate has guided me
> To what I wish — She sleeps, her face is lovely
> And her Charming Eyes, tho' they are cover'd,
> Pierce me to the heart; her Rosie Lips tho' they speak not,
> Invite the lookers on to taste their sweetness—And, I must—
> What, to kiss is no Crime, It may be she'll not wake,
> But if she shou'd, I'm sure she cannot blame me:
> They that will leave Locks open to a Thief,
> Must needs expect a Robbery
>   (*kisses her*)
>
>   (21)

Cornaro's description of his mistress's beauties guides the audience's gaze while his overt desire designates her as sexual. Importantly, her eyes are closed and her gaze thus averted (though her eyes' "charm" still "pierce[s] [him] to the heart"); the scene depicts the male gaze as active and the female object as passive, with her very passivity inviting sexual violation. Cornaro's final lines rationalize "stealing" a kiss first by claiming that a kiss taken without the other party's volition is no crime, then, in a rapid turn around, by describing the kiss as a justifiable crime—a theft of property carelessly exposed to view. Defining Eromena as a treasure for male appropriation rather than as a sexual subject, he objectifies female sexuality and thus controls it.

The lurid possibilities of such scenes of mediated voyeurism appear even more graphically in another anonymous play, *The Unnatural Mother* (1698), by "a Young Lady," which combines the tableau of the passive woman with miscegenation. The unnatural mother of the title tries to destroy her daughter by drugging her and arranging a sensational tableau for her daughter's lover and, of course, the audience to consume. The "*Scene draws, discovers* Bebbemeah *asleep on a Couch, with a black Slave in her Arms*" (27). Here the sexual potential of the scene is made explicit—the heroine is discovered in a pose which, although false, is carnally suggestive. The scene is staged with the male voyeur present, but the audience does not need the mediation of his gaze in order to interpret the sexual import of the tableau. Rather, his words intensify the audience's understanding of the heroine's now tainted sexuality:

> MUZ. Is it possible that heavenly Form, surprising Fair, should hide so black a Soul? had the great Rulers of the enamel'd Sky descended and told me this, I would not have believe'd 'em; but with my own Eyes wide open, to thy shame, to view thy lustful Sin, there is not one bare Hope left me, that I might be deceiv'd . . . Did I not see your fair white Arms lay twin'd about that sooty fellow's Neck, and all that melting lovely Body in his black lustful Arms? is this to be forgiven by a young Lover, who almost died each day for the enjoyment of that Treasure a poor despis'd Slave has rob'd thee of? (28)

The playwright's heavy-handed references to blackness of soul and fairness of body reiterate the confusion of black and white displayed physically only moments before. More strikingly, Muzuffer's repeated emphasis on the impact of seeing Bebbemeah's defilement establishes the significance of female sexuality as spectacle: with his "own Eyes wide open" he "views" her "lustful Sin"; he has "seen" her "heavenly Form," "that melting lovely Body" in "black lustful Arms." The blackness of the slave here represents a physical indicator of the enormity of her crime. Muzuffer's reference to the "Treasure" the slave has "rob'd" her of evokes the conventional trope of female virginity as a prize for male possession. Ironically, the sense of male control of female sexuality is illusory; Bebbemeah's mother here controls both her daughter and Muzuffer, at least temporarily. Although the two are united at the end of the play, the innocent heroine has been established in the eyes of both her lover and the audience as not only sexual but corrupt.

Scenes such as these, with their male commentaries on the tableaux presented to the audience and their passive heroines in what Young termed a posture of humiliation, do more than simply establish the heroine as the object of male desire, although that is an important component of both the scenes and of the plays as a whole. Essentially, such conventions define the female figure as passive and sexual because of that passivity, the object rather than the possessor of the gaze. In contrast, the male figure controls the scene. He is the active subject who mediates the audience's response—he becomes, in this sense, the prototype of the spectator. These are the fundamentals on which she-tragedy rests: display of the woman, emphasis on the vision of female sexuality, frequently, as in the scene from *The Unnatural Mother,* a corrupt sexuality exposed to audience view, and the ultimate suffering of the woman whose sexuality has become the object of the audience's gaze. Although the she-tragedy heroine may *do* nothing, (as Southerne's Isabella explains, she can do nothing, "for I am born to suffer"), her physical presence is at the center of the play, and she-tragedy's pleasure as well its moral and political message depends on the graphic representation of the heroine's suffering, passivity, and desirability.

As demonstrated in *The Unnatural Mother,* designating female sexuality as tainted is another significant component of she-tragedy. The she-tragedy heroine is traditionally virtuous, yet her chastity is threatened or even destroyed by a sexual crime in which she participates unwittingly or even unwillingly. Most often, these crimes involve violations of socio-sexual codes perpetrated on women. Although miscegenation and same-sex desire are relatively uncommon,[17] the she-tragedies of the 1690s and early eighteenth century are littered with examples of incest and rape. These formulaic plot lines serve to implicate the plays' female characters without forcing them outside of their passive role as object rather than subject of desire. In this way, such transgressions provide a means of making the she-tragedy heroine simultaneously innocent and corrupt.

As a dramatic convention, incest operates on a symbolic rather than visual level. By violating ancient sexual taboos, incest suggests the disintegration of larger social structures. Its complete perversion of family ties becomes a stand in for upheavals in the political realm, such as attempts to change the laws of succession or to depose a king, and during the late seventeenth and early eighteenth centuries the trope was more often used by Tory sympathizers. Ultimately, these structures must be restored (e.g., through the revelation of mistaken identity), or sacrifice of the perpetra-

17. Occasionally these plays toy with other forms of sexual taboo such as lesbian desire (as in Charles Hopkins's *Friendship Improved; or, The Female Warrior* [1700]).

tors, however blameless, becomes necessary to reestablish order. In she-tragedy, the innocent woman's incestuous behavior ultimately becomes the focal point of the drama, and her suffering provides a visual demonstration of the horrors inherent in a world so disordered. Although the most famous example of incest appears in *The Orphan*, where Monimia's unwitting coupling with her brother-in-law epitomizes the domestic and political crisis of the Exclusion Crisis, examples of father/daughter, mother/son, brother/sister, even aunt/nephew incest appear repeatedly.[18] The sexual situations suggested by such plot lines are inherently titillating and the distress they produce in the plays' female victims is invariably extreme. The popularity of incest was seemingly so great that John Dennis even insinuates brother/sister desire into his version of *Iphigenia* (1700). In this unconvincing version of the story, Orestes and Iphigenia meet and fall in love; when they discover that they are brother and sister they are delighted so that incest functions to titillate and yet can be resolved cozily. (Other dramatic versions of the Iphigenia plot avoided such patently implausible ploys.)

The exceptionally lurid *Fatal Discovery; or, Love in Ruines* (1697–perf., 1698–pub.) with its convoluted tale of multiple incest uses female sexual appetite as a catalyst for complete social and moral disorder. By using two heroines, the author splits his representation of female sexuality into two discreet forms, one the dangerous sexual passion of Bergingaria and the other the passive, suffering femininity of her daughter Eromena. The source of the play's moral chaos lies in excessive female desire: in the play's opening scene, Bergingaria confesses that fifteen years before, her "wanton Love" for her husband resulted in disaster. When her husband tired of her bed, she sought to lure him back and, overhearing him plan a tryst with a maid, she tried to take the maid's place, only to mistake the room and sleep instead with her son. A daughter is born of this incestuous union, and, inevitably, the son falls in love with his sister/daughter. Before his mother can prevent the union, he weds and beds Eromena. In such a world, where even the most basic social relations are awry, humans cannot trust to instinct, as Cornaro laments after his ill-fated wedding night, "My Daughter, Sister and my Wife, and all / My marry'd bedded Wife . . . Where was the Sacred power of Instinct now?" (42–43). Yet the ultimate source of this calamity is not instinct but female desire. Male sexuality appears as both natural and stable, while, unless regulated, female

18. For example, *The Fatal Discovery; or, Love in Ruines* (perf. 1697, pub. 1698) features both mother/son and father/daughter incest (both consummated), the "Young Lady's" *The Unnatural Mother* includes brother/sister desire, and Delariviere Manley's *The Royal Mischief* uses aunt/nephew incest to blacken the character of its villainous heroine.

sexuality can be unnatural, dangerous, and potentially out of control. Thus, Bergingaria bemoans her earlier rebellion against sexual control:

> Why hinder'd I the Pleasures of my Husband,
> When 'twas not in my power to give him any?
> He us'd me like a dear and only Friend,
> I wanted nothing but a wanton Love;
> I ought t'have been like him, so much himself,
> That my Desires shou'd then have ceased with his.
>
> (1–2)

As the play documents, a woman's "wanton Love," even for a husband, results in social and domestic chaos, and in her lament Bergingaria presents the only possible solution to such disruption: she should have subdued her desires until they became invisible, becoming so much a part of her husband that her desires would have been indistinguishable from his. In this way, it becomes possible to erase female desire and to control it. Otherwise, inexorably, unregulated female sexuality becomes incest. Although rarely depicted in such uncompromising terms, she-tragedy almost inevitably uses incest to link female sexuality with moral disintegration.

With their emphasis on the physical degradation of the victim, representations of rape can literally be said to be more of a spectator sport than incest, where the titillation depends on the audience's comprehension of the sin rather than on its actual representation. Scenes of attempted rape, relatively rare in Elizabethan and Jacobean drama,[19] were common on the English stage once actresses provided the means to illustrate the potentially titillating effects of ravished womanhood. They become especially common after 1680, during the years when pathetic plays and she-tragedies achieved their greatest popularity. Although in earlier Tory plays, such as Tate's *King Lear* (1681) or Otway's *Venice Preserv'd* (1682), attempted rapes often demonstrate the moral degeneracy of those who seek to usurp power, in the largely Whig she-tragedies of the 1690s, rape becomes the justification for displacing improper rule. Even more so than the trope of incest, depictions of rape employ the spectacle of the violated

---

19. Karen Bamford takes issue with a similar statement I made in an earlier article ("Rape, Voyeurism, and the Restoration Stage"). She claims that rape was indeed common on the Renaissance stage. As her discussion of Jacobean rape scenes makes clear, however, her definition of rape is much broader than mine and included Iachimo's survey of Imogen's bedchamber in *Cymbeline* as well as the proposed (but never attempted) rape in Webster's *Appius and Virginia*. As she admits, many of these scenes, such as that in *Titus Andronicus* or Heywood's *Rape of Lucrece*, are "innocent of eroticism." *Sexual Violence on the Jacobean Stage* (2000).

woman for ideological effect. In these plays, rapists are typically tyrants who use their position of power as a sanction for rape. Thus their sexual assaults on their female victims visually represent the more generalized assault on their subjects' liberties. Coupled with representations of degenerate Oriental courts and harems, a popular combination, rape became an especially potent argument against absolutist French/Catholic rule and for the strongly Protestant policies of William III.

In Restoration and early-eighteenth-century drama, rape presents an explicitly sexual situation that foregrounds the sexuality of the actress. Although rapes do not actual occur onstage, the audience is frequently presented with a preliminary scene in which the virtuous heroine is threatened by the villain, and in some plays in which the rape is successful, subsequent scenes in which the ravished woman is presented to eyes of other characters and the audience. Dwelling on the sexual component inherent in violation, these scenes provide an effective stage dynamic focused on the body of the actress. As the joint appearance of actresses and scenes of rape indicates, rape becomes possible as theatrical spectacle only when visible signs of the female are present: breasts, bare shoulders, and loosened or "ravished" hair. Such coded signs identify the actress as the focus of desire so that the rape becomes the physical manifestation of the desire perpetrated by the rapist but implicit in the audience's gaze. Thus the audience, like the rapist, "enjoys" the actress, deriving its pleasure from the physical presence of the female body. The scopic appeal of these scenes lies in their volatile blend of sexuality and suffering.[20] This violent sense of pathos appears most conspicuously in the scenes of attempted rape, where violence represents an essential part of pathos, and where the ravished woman becomes the source of visual pleasure. The effect of such scenes depends on the objectification of the heroine, on her representation as both object of pity and object of desire. The attempted rapes yoke these seemingly disparate emotions together through violence. Both emotions are made available to the audience through the heroine's desirability and through her suffering.

The means by which rape operates in drama can be seen in plays such as Nicholas Brady's aptly named tragicomedy *The Rape; or, The Innocent Imposters* (1692). Brady's play is a stolidly Whig drama that announces its political affiliation in the play's dedication to Charles, earl of Dorset, praising Dorset for his *"true Affection to the* Protestant Religion *and* English

20. Jean Hagstrum discusses the roots of the term *pathetic,* finding in these roots "ancient associations with passivity in pain and love" and linking the use of pathos near the beginning of the eighteenth century with violence. *Sex and Sensibility: Ideal and Erotic Love from Milton to Mozart* (1980), 6.

Frontispiece to Dryden's *Amboyna* showing the aftermath of a rape.

Liberties."[21] In his play, Brady negotiates the problem of rightful rule by setting his play in ancient Germany and contrasting the Goths, who demonstrate a proper English concern for liberty, with the Vandals, whose tyranny is ultimately distilled in the rape around which the play's action revolves.[22] Brady's play displays, at length, the conventions common to dramatic representations of rape in the later seventeenth century. Its central incident involves the rape of the virtuous Eurione by the evil Genselarick, and the play is remarkable for the extent to which it dwells on the vision, real or imagined, of ravished womanhood. This focus begins early in the second act as the villain expatiates on his desire for Eurione, visualizing the upcoming scene with relish:

> Methinks I see already
> Her dying Looks, her seeming faint Resistance,
> And feel the mighty Transports of hot Love!
>
> (21)

The audience is given ample opportunity to savor the rape themselves; although the rape necessarily occurs offstage, the progress of Genselarick's evil designs is relayed to the audience by a vivid description of Eurione's shrieks. Immediately after the rape, the scene draws to display the erotic spectacle of the ravished woman: "*the Scene draws, and discovers Eurione in an Arbour, gagg'd and bound to a Tree, her hair dishevel'd as newly Ravish'd, a Dagger lying by her*" (25). The elaborately coded tableau carefully presents Eurione to the audience's gaze: Eurione's "Ravish'd" hair becomes the signifier of her violation, the ropes and gag certify to her helpless state, while a dagger, the symbolic representation of her violation, lies by her side. This exhibition of erotic symbols establishes the crisis of ravished womanhood around which the play centers. The visual import of the tableau is echoed two scenes later when the violated Eurione is again displayed, this time as the object of the collective gaze of the Goth aristocracy, while her mother Rhadegondra exclaims, "Behold my Lords, the Ruines of your Princess!" (29).

The graphic spectacle of female distress evoked by Rhadegondra provides the play's political mandate, justifying the Goths' rebellion against the tyranny that the rape represents. The provocative combination of sex

---

21. Nicholas Brady, dedication to *The Rape; or, The Innocent Imposters* (1692).

22. The play even portrays a false heir to the throne, a woman who has been raised as a man because her Vandal father threatened to kill a female child. Her mother has a male child smuggled into her bed at the birth, à la the warming pan scandal. The true ruler, of course, is a Goth—a man who has been raised as a woman.

and sight that makes rape such an effective political tool ultimately constitutes the defining quality of she-tragedy. Saturated as they are with erotic scenes, these plays dwell on the spectacle of female sexuality made monstrous (characters such as Eurione even define themselves as "monsters" or "pollutions"). Unlike the male heroes of most Restoration and early-eighteenth-century tragedies, the existence of she-tragedy heroines is defined by suffering not by agency, and it was the intensity and physical nature of this suffering that titillated theatergoers and constituted the plays' greatest appeal. The essential power dynamic of these plays is established by exposing the heroines as the helpless objects of a gaze designated as specifically male. The plays' pleasure as well as their moral and political messages depend on the intensely visual nature of these heroine's suffering, passivity, and desirability.

Early Forms of She-tragedy

Although she-tragedies reached their peak in the 1690s and the first decade of the eighteenth century, their origins lay in the pathetic plays of the 1680s, most notably in the women-centered tragedies of Thomas Otway and John Banks. These works, in particular Otway's *The Orphan* (1680) and to a lesser extent Banks's *Vertue Betray'd; or, Anna Bullen* (1682), established a pattern of mingled titillation and suffering, dependent on displaying the afflictions and ultimate death of a central female figure. These plays became part of the popular repertoire, providing a point of reference for the works that were to follow. In the eyes of the critics and playwrights of the late seventeenth and early eighteenth centuries, the great legacy of Otway and Banks to the stage was the exquisite distress of their heroines, and it was this trademark quality by which subsequent writers were judged and which they sought to follow.

Of the two playwrights, it was Otway who was the most influential, deemed by his contemporaries the finest tragedian since Shakespeare, even excelling Shakespeare in the important category of distress. The finely wrought distress of the women in Otway's two most popular plays made him a benchmark for tragic writing. Not surprisingly, both *Venice Preserv'd* and *The Orphan* were popular throughout the 1690s and the early eighteenth century. Written specifically for Elizabeth Barry, the greatest tragic actress of the age, the roles of Belvidera and Monimia provide a finely tuned rendition of female woe. But it was *The Orphan* that became the prototype for she-tragedy as well as the play by which the pathos or "distress" of other plays was calibrated. Throughout this period, performances of *The Orphan* outnumbered those of *Venice Preserv'd*.[23] Even more telling, when referring specifically to one of Otway's plays as evidence of his genius, commentators inevitably turn to *The Orphan*, and particularly to Monimia's plight, her distress, and her ultimate tragic end. (One indication of how deeply embedded the play became in English culture is Charlotte Smith's use of the name Monimia for her heroine in *The Old Manor House* (1793), relying on the name's connotations of innocence and suffering to create sympathy for her character.) Where Belvidera balances Pierre as tempter to Jaffeir in *Venice Preserv'd*, Monimia is the central focus of *The Orphan*, the blameless catalyst for the play's tragic action and the locus of desire.

Readings of *The Orphan* have often tended to concentrate on the play's political import and its relation to the politics of Otway's age.[24] Although the play's political subtext cannot be denied, its topical connections to the Exclusion Crisis were not the key to its continuing success on the stage. In the years after 1690, it was Otway's delineation of female characters, especially the depiction of their tragic passions, which had the power to move an audience to tears—and which kept these plays on the stage year after year. Ironically, by concentrating on the political undercurrents of the play, recent scholarship has focused upon the homosocial exchanges that surround the play's title character rather than on Monimia herself. For Restoration and eighteenth-century audiences, however, as with the male characters within the play, it was Monimia on whom the action centered. She is not only the focus of all eyes, but of all desires—the central object around which the play revolves. The archetypal she-tragedy heroine, sexually tainted and yet morally pure, she and her sufferings become the focus of the audience's gaze and the source of its viewing pleasure.

Otway's play, with its vision of rape and incest visited on the body of an innocent woman, provided a pattern that a generation of tragedies would follow, with varying degrees of luridness. First, the she-tragedy heroine must be designated as desirable. It is no exaggeration to state that Monimia's body is the object of the male gaze throughout the play, and each male character in turn displays an obsession with her sexuality, an obsession that ultimately begets catastrophe. Before we even see Monimia, she is established as an object of desire as the brothers Castalio and

23. The two plays seem to balance each other sometime after 1705, and by the end of the century there is no significant difference in the number of performances.

24. For a good discussion of the political implications of *The Orphan*, see Jessica Munns, *Restoration Politics and Drama: The Plays of Thomas Otway, 1675–1683* (1995), chap. 4, "The Beast of Reason."

Polydore debate their attraction to her. When Monimia enters, she is accompanied by a page[25] who tells her, and indirectly the audience,

> Madam, indeed I'd serve you with my soul;
> But in the morning when you call me to you,
> As by your bed I stand and tell you stories,
> I am asham'd to see your swelling Breasts,
> It makes me blush, they are so very white.
>   (1.221–25)

The page's words direct the audience's eyes to the breasts of the actress playing Monimia, effectively sexualizing both the character and the woman who represents that character on the stage. Monimia's brother arrives, driven by an erotically charged dream within which he sees her,

> Thy garments flowing loose, and in each hand
> A wanton Lover, which by turns caress'd thee
> With all the freedom of unbounded pleasure.
>   (2.224–31)

Even the aged Acasto comments on Monimia's sexual allure after she has lost her virginity to Polydore.[26] These men gaze on Monimia, and through their actions and words invite the audience to follow the direction of their gaze. The effect is to make graphic Monimia's essential role as object of desire rather than sexual subject. With the site of the tragedy delineated as Monimia's bed and within it the body that has been displayed for the audience's scopic pleasure, the sexual thrill necessary for the emotional effect of she-tragedy is in place. Although, as Jessica Munns observes, Monimia is more than a passive victim, she nonetheless is acted on rather than actor.[27]

Crucially, Otway contaminates the woman whom he has so carefully established as object of the gaze, rendering her sexuality corrupt. As Polydore takes Castalio's place within Monimia's bed, he commits both rape and incest,[28] and in doing so defiles irrevocably the object of his desire.

---

25. Played traditionally by a young girl.
26. ACASTO: Though I'm deceiv'd, or you are more fair to Day;
   For Beauty's heighten'd in your Cheeks, and all
   Your Charmes seem up, and ready in your Eyes. (4.1.37–39)

27. Munns, *Restoration Politics and Drama*, sees Monimia as a representation of Julia Kristeva's "abject," "the emblem of sexuality as pollution and danger that has been inscribed throughout the text" (161). Her agency arises from her ability to articulate this pollution rather than conceal it.
28. Incest by sleeping with the wife of his brother and rape by deceiving the otherwise

Monimia's horror on discovering the dual sin is extreme (she faints and for the rest of the play refers to herself as a "pollution" devoid of humanity), but rather than responding with anger, she blames herself. Unable to endure the shame of her sexual stain, she drinks poison in the final act. In a death scene notable for its quiet pathos and absence of rant, she tells Castalio "none can ever love thee like *Monimia*" and begs him to "Speak well of me . . . 'Twill be a noble Justice to the memory / Of a poor wretch, once honour'd with thy Love."[29] Her final words poignantly sketch the poison's effect: "How my head swims! Tis very dark: Good night [*Dyes*]" (5.470). Although both Polydore and Castalio die before the end of the play, it is Monimia's demise, with her mournful and self-deprecating pledge of love, that playgoers found most memorable. This spectacle of corrupted sexuality, suffering, and ultimate death was to become a defining element in the wave of she-tragedies that emulated Otway. Each betrays a preoccupation with the sexuality of the central female character, projecting this obsession not simply verbally but visually, combining sexual spectacle with often exaggerated displays of female suffering.

John Banks, whose historical tragedies centered on doomed figures from England's past, provided another model for she-tragedy. In Banks's plays the tragedy not only focuses on a central female character but makes her distress the play's emotional core. Even *The Unhappy Favourite; or, The Earl of Essex* (1682), one of Banks's earliest and politically safest plays, includes a preponderance of female distress, despite the play's male title character. The plot revolves around three central women, the villainous countess of Nottingham; the virtuous Queen Elizabeth, duped into believing Essex a traitor; and Essex's wife, the countess of Rutland. Essex remains a static hero, undone by the scheming countess of Nottingham. Despite its title, this play, the most frequently revived of Banks's works, was often described by his contemporaries in terms of its ability to wring tears from its female audience.[30] The vividness of scenes such as the countess's mournful parting from her husband provide a prelude to the wholesale focus on suffering femininity that dominates the plays which followed.

Banks's other plays also deal with historical figures, but in each of his

---

unwilling Monimia. Polydore's angry soliloquy at the end of act 1 where he plans to "rush upon her in a storm of Love, / Bear down her guard of Honour all before me, / Surfeit on Joys till even desire grows sick" (1.373–375), echoes the claims of dozens of stage rapists.

29. Thomas Otway, *The Orphan*, in *The Works of Thomas Otway*, ed. J. C. Ghosh (1932). All further references to Otway's works will be taken from this edition and cited parenthetically.

30. See for example Gildon, *Lives and Characters*, 7: "This has always been Acted with Success, and never fail'd to draw Tears from the Eyes of the fair Sex."

subsequent tragedies these figures are young women, innocent victims of political schemes who desire only love and whose executions provide the plays with the requisite duress. Each play stresses the physical beauty of the doomed heroine, her sexual desirability, the pathos of her innocent suffering, and her ultimate execution. Such emphasis on historical precedents, however, no matter how depoliticized, could be dangerous, as Banks was to discover. Of the three she-tragedies that followed *The Unhappy Favourite,* only *Vertue Betray'd; or, Anna Bullen* (1682) made it past the censor. Although written in 1683 and published 1694, *The Innocent Usurper* was not staged, while *The Island Queens; or, The Death of Mary, Queen of Scots,* with its sympathetic treatment of a Catholic threat (Mary Queen of Scots) to the Protestant throne of England, appeared in printed form in 1704 only after it had been rewritten and retitled *The Albion Queens.*[31] Banks's version of the Lady Jane Grey story was to enjoy a brief vogue, at least in print, at the time of the Hanoverian succession, when anti-Catholic sentiments ran high and Protestant martyrs, particularly young and beautiful ones, were fashionable.

Banks's second historical drama, *Vertue Betray'd; or, Anna Bullen* (1682) was the first of his she-tragedies to become a popular success. In this version of the life of Henry VIII's second wife Anne Boleyn, Anna is the blameless victim of a series of court intrigues. Although she remains faithful to the king, her enemies accuse her of adultery, and the play ends with her execution. The final scene, like that in *The Orphan,* focuses on Anna's "miseries" and on her innocence. In it, she pays a brave but tearful farewell to her daughter, Princess Elizabeth, and then, robed in chaste white, goes quietly to her execution. As she is called to the block she remarks plaintively, "My Lord, I've but a little Neck; / Therefore I hope he'l [the Heads-man] not repeat his Blow."[32] The "little Neck" she will bare for the executioner epitomizes her defenselessness and the meekness with which she submits to her fate. The play concludes with a gruesome account of Anna's death, more tears from the characters who have surrounded her throughout the play, and a final vindication of her virtue. In making wronged innocence their central focus, plays such as *Vertue Betray'd* provide a new and more sustained examination of feminine distress. If Banks's focus on female sexuality was somewhat less intense than Otway's, his heroines are no less sexually defined and no less the object of the masculine gaze.

31. See Jayne Elizabeth Lewis, introduction to *The Island Queens; or, The Death of Mary Queen of Scotland* (1995). As Hume notes, "the execution of monarchs, especially female 'usurpers,' became an increasingly touchy subject." *The Development of English Drama,* 217.
32. John Banks, *Vertue Betray'd; or, Anna Bullen* (1682; reprinted 1981), 74.

Other forerunners of she-tragedy can be found in two plays frequently revived in the late seventeenth and early eighteenth centuries: Lee's *The Rival Queens* and Shakespeare's *Othello*. Each appeared regularly on the stage in the 1690s and early eighteenth century, and each was identified in terms of its female characters by contemporary viewers.[33] Although Shakespeare may not have demonstrated sufficient focus on female distress for a late-seventeenth-century audience, *Othello* nonetheless contains the by-now familiar components of male obsession with the heroine's sexuality and a tainting of that sexuality that concludes with the death of the innocent yet corrupt woman. In 1699, Gildon commented that *Othello* "is still often acted, and esteemed one of the best of our Author's Plays."[34] It may indeed be that this popularity led to Thomas Rymer's attack on *Othello* in *A Short View of Tragedy* (1698). Lee's *The Rival Queens*, like the plays of Otway and Banks, revolves around the adversity and death of its central female characters. Neither Roxana nor Statira is pathetic, however, and the play itself stresses their role as queens rather than their distress. But contemporary accounts suggest that the two actresses most celebrated for their roles in she-tragedy may have worked to mitigate the lack of feminine pathos. Discussing the continuing popularity of *The Rival Queens*, Betterton comments, "The Players, when this Tragedy first appeared, made it a Favourite one to the World, but for want of a *Barry* and a *Bracegirdle,* the Characters of *Roxana* and *Statira* are a perfect burlesque on the Dignity of Majesty and good Manners."[35]

Betterton's stress on the distinction between old and new methods of female representation expresses a need to refine and thus re-create not only *The Rival Queens* but all female tragedy within the fashionable mode. As his comment indicates, the actresses who redefined the roles of Roxana and Statira were central to the play's continued popularity. He goes on to describe Mrs. Barry's Roxana in terms that emphasize her rendering not simply of "Majesty and good Manners," but more to the point, of female distress:

> Tho' before our Eyes we had just seen Roxana with such Malice murder
> an innocent Person, because better beloved than herself; yet, after Statira

33. See for example Samuel Cobb, who uses Desdemona's death to illustrate Shakespeare's skill in moving the passions: "I feel a Pity working in my Eyes / When Desdemona by her Husband dies." "Of Poetry," in *Poems on Several Occasions* (1707), 192.

34. Gildon, *Lives and Characters,* 128.

35. Thomas Betterton, *The History of the English Stage, from the Restauration to the Present Time Including the Lives, Characters and Amours, of the most Eminent Actors and Actresses. With Instructions for Public Speaking; Wherein the action and Utterance of the Bar, Stage, and Pulpit are Distinctly considered* (1741), 19.

[played by Bracegirdle] is dead, and Roxana is following Alexander on her knees, Mrs. Barry made this Complaint in so Pathetic a Manner, as drew Tears from the greatest Part of the Audience.[36]

By injecting the role of the passionate and headstrong Roxana with pathos, Barry was able to draw tears from her audience, stressing the pathetic in her character (note the description of Barry's Roxana "following Alexander on her knees"). Although known for her representation of passionate characters such as Roxana, Barry was equally renowned for her ability to wring tears from her audience, as in the scene described above, and perhaps even more famously in her portrayal of Monimia. Her comment that she could not speak the line "Ah poor Castalio" (5.304) without weeping was cited as evidence of her ability to make the simplest words moving.[37]

Where Barry's characters were typically impassioned, Anne Bracegirdle, who frequently shared the stage with Barry, was known for her depiction of helpless maidens; as Elizabeth Howe notes, even the roles in the comedies written for her were notably passive.[38] In tragedy, she routinely embodied suffering innocence, epitomized by plaintive tears, so much so that the anonymous burlesque *The Female Wits* used the motif of a weeping Bracegirdle in its caricature of the Lincoln's Inn Fields actors.[39] Her representation of virtue under siege, in roles such as the victimized Eurione in *The Rape*, provided a complement to those written for Barry, and the two actresses frequently appeared in the same play. Having two talented actresses so capable of embodying distress provided theater managers with the means to present the scenes of woe the public craved. The result was nearly two decades of she-tragedy.

Southerne, Congreve, and the She-Tragedies of the 1690s

By the mid 1690s, as playwrights adopted the style and subject matter of Otway and Banks, she-tragedy began to appear routinely on the

---

36. Edmund Curll, from his biography of Barry, cited by Elizabeth Howe in *The First English Actresses: Women and Drama, 1660–1700* (1992), 157.

37. Gildon claims that Barry told him this. He recounts the anecdote in *The Complete Art of Poetry* (1718), 1:290.

38. "The typical Bracegirdle heroine is passive; her task is to protect her reputation and discern if her lover is worthy of her, not to initiate action." Howe, *The First English Actresses*, 88.

39. The Bracegirdle figure is depicted "whining": "My Innocence is white as Alpine Snow, / By these Tears, which never cease to flow." *The Female Wits; or, The Triumvirate of Poets at Rehearsal* (perf. 1697, pub. 1704; reprint 1967), 50.

stage. The growing popularity of women-centered dramas was spurred by the tremendous success of the two greatest tragedies of the decade, Thomas Southerne's *The Fatal Marriage; or, The Innocent Adultery* (1694) and William Congreve's *The Mourning Bride* (1697), both works which dwelt on the spectacle of suffering and sexuality. Obsessively focused on a single tragic heroine, *The Fatal Marriage* enjoyed greater popularity than either of Banks's staged plays, while *The Mourning Bride* was one of the first popular tragedies to capitalize on the paired talents of Barry and Bracegirdle, a combination that was to define she-tragedy for more than a decade.[40] In the last years of the century, many playwrights would attempt the genre that Southerne and Congreve had made popular, although few achieved the success of *The Fatal Marriage* or *The Mourning Bride*.

Where *The Mourning Bride* became the pattern for many subsequent dramas, *The Fatal Marriage* had few direct imitations, at least in form.[41] Unlike most serious dramas of the time, *The Fatal Marriage* is a tragicomedy, with a comic subplot in which a mercenary old father is tricked into believing he is dead interspersed with tableaux of Isabella's decline into sorrow and madness. Seen as an intrusion by many critics even at the time, the comic scenes were ultimately omitted from the play, leaving it unrelentingly tragic. In its serious scenes, Southerne's play demonstrates a distinct kinship with *The Orphan,* and it is a measure of the success of the play that in it Southerne was seen by his contemporaries as a successor to the great Otway (both Downes and Dryden linked Southerne's play to Otway's two greatest tragedies).[42] Like *The Orphan, The Fatal Marriage* concentrates on the sexual contamination of a virtuous heroine and her subsequent suffering and death. But Southerne goes beyond Otway, expanding the role of his heroine and exhibiting her sufferings at greater length. In this he diverges radically from his source, Aphra Behn's novella, *The History of the Nun; or, The Fair Vow-Breaker* (1689). Where Behn portrays a heroine who not only commits an "innocent adultery" but

40. Barry and Bracegirdle both appeared in *The Fatal Marriage* as well, however Bracegirdle played the role of Victoria in the comic subplot. Isabella and Victoria appear in but a single scene together and never exchange dialogue.

41. One of the few tragicomedies other than Southerne's is the anonymous *The Fatal Discovery; or, Love in Ruines* (perf. 1697), in which the double incest plot (mother-son, son/father-daughter) alternates with comic scenes of a young wife persuading her old husband that he is not a cuckold.

42. Downes, *Roscius Anglicanus*, 38; Dryden in a letter, *To My Dear Friend Mr. Congreve* (1694). In her comments on the play, Elizabeth Inchbald cites Dryden's comment, adding "every reader will own the comparison just, for they have both unbounded force in the description of poignant grief" (headnote to *Isabella,* in *The British Theatre*, 7:3).

murders both husbands and betrays remarkably little remorse for her crimes, Southerne excises the murders and focuses obsessively on the adultery and its aftermath. His Isabella is a victim of circumstance, a mournful figure who nonetheless accepts the blame for all she endures. Southerne develops the image of the innocent heroine, a victim of desire in a homosocial economy over which she has no control. In contrast to Behn's heroine, Southerne's Isabella accepts her fate passively, refusing in one instance to act because "I was born to suffer" (2.2.66). Eroticizing the heroine and her plight, Southerne's play presents a world in which all eyes converge on the heroine's bedchamber, on the bed in which the "fatal marriage" is consummated and the "innocent adultery" committed. Isabella's horror-struck repetition of the word "bed" after her husband's return fixes the audience's attention even more firmly on that "warm witness of [her] broken vows" (4.3.40) and its symbolic representation of her sexual stain.

The main plot focuses unashamedly on the sexual degradation of the central female figure; as Elizabeth Inchbald was to note more than a hundred years later, "the characters which surround Isabella are merely placed there by the author, to give effect to all she says and does."[43] Isabella, believing her husband Biron is dead, marries her former suitor Villeroy in gratitude for his financial assistance. Biron lives, however, and his existence has been concealed by his younger brother; the day after the marriage, he returns. Unlike so many overtly Whig dramas, *The Fatal Marriage* does not represent the suffering of its victimized heroine as the result of tyranny; rather, Southerne links Isabella's misery to the distinctly mercenary aspirations of the play's male characters. After Biron's death, Carlos admits that he concealed Biron's whereabouts and allowed Isabella to wed Villeroy because "I could not bear a younger Brothers lot / To live depending, upon curtesie" (5.4.220–21). Southerne's Tory sympathies appear perhaps most clearly in the play's explicitly political articulation of family ties as a repentant Count Baldwin argues that Carlos's actions represent a disruption of natural order, for "Parricide is highest treason sure / To sacred Natures laws" (5.4.243–44), a statement with almost Jacobite overtones in its equation of sacred bonds and proper rule. The commercialism that induces this domestic and political disintegration is introduced early in the play as both Carlos and his father conflate Isabella's misery, her "mis-fortune," with her lack of fortune and her financial ruin with her personal ruin. Carlos reiterates the relentlessly mercantile language by emphasizing how Isabella's poverty, the result of

43. Inchbald, headnote to *Isabella*, in *The British Theatre*, 7:4.

unnatural family relations, benefits Villeroy's "interest." Although Villeroy seeks to disconnect the word from its commercial implications, claiming "Her Happiness must be my Interest" (2.1.8), such mercenary associations have left the world of *The Fatal Marriage* hopelessly corrupt,[44] a theme that Southerne would later exploit to great success in *Oroonoko*.

With Isabella the object exposed for sale, the play emphasizes spectatorship within a homosocial domain and concludes with a sadistic vision of the sins of the father being visited upon the (innocent) female body, a body eroticized and displayed to spectators on and offstage. Love and desire are described in terms of sight, yet the gaze that arouses these sensations is not available to the play's female characters, isolating them as objects and presenting, at least in the case of the play's central figure, sexual subjectivity as ultimately masochistic. Thus, Isabella explicitly characterizes herself as object rather than subject. Beset by creditors, she laments her role as "common spectacle" (2.3.23), a role which she plays not only to the "lewd Rabble" (2.3.25) but to male characters and theater spectators as well. Southerne designs his heroine as the object of all eyes and carefully marks her as sexual spectacle. Isabella articulates her role within the play, and the role of countless other heroines, as a form of spectacle:

> Am I then the sport,
> The Fame of Fortune, and her laughing Fools?
> The common spectacle, to be expos'd
> From day to day, and baited for the mirth
> Of the lewd Rabble? must I be reserv'd
> For fresh Afflictions?
>
> (2.3.21–26)

She links her afflictions to her position as spectacle, and while Southerne would not wish to compare patrons of the theater to the "lewd Rabble," Isabella functions in much the same way for both audiences.

The link between sight and desire is most clearly expounded by Villeroy, who evaluates his love in terms of the pleasures of gazing on the object of his desire, and who invites others to follow suit. This evocation of scopic pleasure intensifies in act 3, scene 2, one of the play's central scenes. Set the morning after the bigamous marriage, the scene puts the private world of Isabella's bedroom on public display as Villeroy rejoices

---

44. Hughes astutely describes Southerne's vision as of "a universal Babel in which language has no power to signify or prescribe the nature of justice, and in which the only regulating principle is the sale of human flesh," *English Drama*, 376.

openly at having finally "possessed" Isabella, thus broadcasting her guilt (3.2.71–72). The couple is greeted with a song for the new bride, which encourages the spectators (both onstage and off) to study the bride for indications of sexual experience:

> *By her Eyes we discover the Bride has been pleas'd;*
> *Her blushes become her, her passion is eas'd;*
> *She dissembles her joy, and affects to look down;*
> *If she Sighes, 'tis for sorrow 'tis ended so soon.*
>
> (3.2.50–53)

Her eyes cast down, the bride is the center of a largely male group who study her for markers of sexual experience, such as her blushes. The incident described in the song is almost immediately reenacted as Villeroy displays the wedded and bedded Isabella to a group of friends. In this context, the blush that stains Isabella's cheeks as the scene ends becomes sexually suggestive, a marker of her transgression. ("A rising smile / Stole from her thoughts, just redning on her Cheek," 3.2.216–17.)[45] Southerne returns repeatedly not simply to the fact of Isabella's "innocent adultery," but to the spectacle of her tainted sexuality, a spectacle designed for and appreciated by a male audience.

When the duplicitous Carlos tells Villeroy, "I long to wish you Joy," Villeroy responds "You'l be a Witness of my Happiness" (2.3.134–35), thus establishing a homosocial economy based specifically on vision. These words sketch a world in which male bonds are built by *watching* the exchange of women and the public display of these pieces of sexual property. Isabella's long-lost husband Biron reiterates this principle, denouncing his male relatives:

> They stood,
> With malicious silent joy, stood by
> And saw her give up all my happiness,
> The treasure of her beauty to another;
> Stood by, and saw her married to another.
>
> (5.1.24–27)

45. A similar interpretation of blushes as sexual pleasure can be found in Charles Hopkins's *Boadicea* (1697), in which a rapist argues:

> And yet your lovely Cheeks begin to glow,
> And strugling [sic] warmth strikes out — why, let it now?
> Your yielding Heart, would to my Wish incline,
> Methinks I feel it beat, and leap at mine.
> Your panting Breast sends up your sighs apace,
> And soft Consent sits blushing on your Face. (22)

Although the act Biron refers to is that of allowing Isabella to wed another man, he couches his description in terms of almost voyeuristic pleasure, repeatedly stressing that his father and brother "stood by and saw"—and enjoyed—the spectacle of Isabella's debased sexuality. His words fetishize Isabella's sexuality, constructing her body as sexual "treasure." The homosocial exchange of this "treasure" becomes the play's essential action and watching this exchange its peculiar pleasure.

The female gaze cannot operate in such a world, as the fate of Isabella demonstrates. When she does possess the gaze, as when she looks on her son or on the sleeping Biron, the effect is markedly masochistic. In the first instance, the face of her son reminds her of her husband, causing pain. Later in the play, Isabella looks upon Biron, in a seeming reversal of the scenes of male voyeurism so prevalent in she-tragedy. The scene draws, showing Biron asleep on a couch. Isabella enters and beholds him, "Pleasure grows again / With looking on him . . . Sure I may take a Kiss—" (5.2.11–12, 14). But the effect of the female gaze is radically different from that of a man in a similar situation. Rather than becoming inflamed by desire and inviting the audience to participate in her excitement, Isabella suffers; she becomes the victim of her own vision, throwing *"her self on the Floor"* and noting that the act of watching has "unhing'd / the great Machine . . . The reas'ning faculties are all depos'd" (5.2.25–26, 28). The female gaze thus leads not to desire but to madness. Raving by the end of the scene, she has become spectacle rather than spectator, and has so far lost control of the gaze that she does not even recognize her husband.

Isabella's madness represents the final stage in *The Fatal Marriage*'s dramatization of female misery. In what would become a familiar pattern, a woman is pushed beyond sense by the extremity of her suffering and by the recognition of her own contamination. Although female madness appears in drama before the end of the seventeenth century, portrayed in popular plays such as *Hamlet* and *Macbeth*, for late-seventeenth- and early-eighteenth-century dramatists the most influential representation of female madness appeared in Otway, this time in *Venice Preserv'd* (1682), where Belvidera's anguish over her parting from Jaffeir drives her mad and ultimately results in her pathetic death. Although recognizable through its language, female madness in the she-tragedies of the 1690s and early eighteenth century is more than a matter of semantics. It is represented in terms of a series of conventional physical signs, much in the manner of Malvolio's yellow stockings and exaggerated smile: loosened hair and clothing as well as exaggerated displays of passion.

Not accidentally, these signs of madness are also sexually suggestive. Duncan Salkeld notes that at the end of the seventeenth century the topic of madness in Shakespeare's plays became "controversial," citing an exchange between Jeremy Collier and James Drake and concluding that the dispute illustrates "the attitudes of men of letters to female sexuality [and] says much about the patriarchal history of Shakespeare criticism."[46] But such assumptions go far beyond Shakespeare as many seventeenth-century playwrights equated female insanity with sexual experience; most often, it is precisely the carnality of this experience that results in madness. As with Isabella, for many of Belvidera's followers vision becomes a special burden, revealing as it does the extent of their self-proclaimed pollution. In Charles Hopkins's *Boadicea* (1697), for example, one ravished heroine (played by Bracegirdle) laments after her rape,

> O! wou'd I cou'd run mad—my Brain turns fast —
> I feel it whirle—and shall run mad at last.
> Break my poor Heart, turn my distemper'd Brain,
> Start Eye-Balls from your Spheres —
> And never let me see the Light again.
>
> (37)

Transgressive sexuality, here rape, occasions this desperation just as Isabella's "innocent adultery" resulted in hers. Madness inevitably results in death, as the crazed heroine often takes her own life, translating the blows of fate into violence on her own body.

Because they deprive the heroine of personal agency, representations of madness present a potent source of pathos. A victim of chance and the vagaries of her own mind, the heroine cannot act and becomes no more than a titillating spectacle. In *The Fatal Marriage*, the trope of madness is only one of the ways in which the play uses the specularization of female sexuality to affirm socially determined gender roles. With the heroine established as the passive object of a specifically male gaze as in the final mad scene, the play's obsession with the visual delineates appropriate gender relations. The audience is encouraged to share in the experience, to be, like Carlos, "a witness" to Villeroy's joy and Isabella's degradation. Through its display of female sexuality, and the subsequent contamination and destruction of this sexuality, the play identifies, punishes, and

46. Duncan Salkeld, *Madness and Drama in the Age of Shakespeare* (1993), 12. Collier objected to the "Freedoms" of Ophelia's language during her mad scene, declaring famously: "Since [Shakespeare] was resolved to drown the lady like a kitten he should have set her swimming a little sooner. To keep her alive only to sully her Reputation, and discover the Rankness of her Breath, was very cruel" (10). Drake defends Ophelia's honor, citing blasted romantic hopes as the source of her madness (*The Antient and Modern Stages Survey'd*, 293–96).

controls the potential threat of female desire. By exaggerating traditional sexual roles so that male desire is stated and demonstrated in contrast to female suffering, the play becomes intensely erotic yet ultimately safe. Ladies can weep for Isabella (thus creating that veil of tears) without wishing to imitate her fate.

The potency of vision becomes a central motif in the most successful tragedy of the 1696–97 season, Congreve's *The Mourning Bride*. Sir Richard Blackmore hailed Congreve's play as "the most perfect *Tragedy* that has been wrote in this Age," praising its diction and characterization, especially that of the passionate Zara, and its decency, as well as its lack of a comic subplot.[47] Gildon, with a penchant for "distress," was more stinting in his praise, finding the play derivative of the heroic tragedies of an earlier age, a view shared by several twentieth-century scholars.[48] Certainly these similarities exist, yet *The Mourning Bride* is more than a throwback to an earlier generation of tragic drama. More recently the play has been discussed as an embodiment of Congreve's Whig sympathies and as expression of anti-imperialist sentiments in the final years of the Nine Years War.[49] But Congreve's tragedy differs most notably from its heroic predecessors in its incorporation of pathos as well as passion, a quality that was a necessary part of serious drama by the end of the seventeenth century. In his play, the qualities of pathos and passion are embodied, literally, in the figures of its two heroines who become the exemplars of proper feminine virtue and of an exotic and dangerous zeal. It was this incorporation of dual heroines, one passionate and the other passive, that characterized much she-tragedy of the late 1690s, and Con-

47. Sir Richard Blackmore, preface to *King Arthur. An Heroick Poem. In Twelve Books* (1697), vii. Blackmore also praises Congreve's decision not to include a comic subplot, a device which he felt marred plays such as Southerne's *The Fatal Marriage*: "This *Tragedy*, as I said before, has mightily obtain'd; and that without the unnatural and foolish mixture of *Farce* and *Buffoonry*, without so much as a Song, or Dance to make it more agreeable. By this it appears, that as a sufficient *Genius* can recommend it self, and furnish out abundant matter of Pleasure and Admiration without the paultry helps above nam'd, so likewise that the Tast of the Nation is not so far deprav'd, but that a Regular and Chast Play will not only be foregiven, but highly Applauded" (vii–viii, reverse italics).

48. Gildon begins his commentary on Congreve in *Lives and Characters* with the somewhat ambiguous "if what Dr. *Blackmore* says of it be true" (23) and then quotes much of Blackmore's praise of the play, largely as an antidote to his own, more temperate recommendation. He finds *The Mourning Bride* inferior to the tragedies of Otway and Lee in terms of "Conduct of the Plot" and especially in the "Delineation of the Characters for the true End of Tragedy, *Pitty* and *Terror*; or, The *true* and *natural Movement* of the Passions" (23–24).

49. See Richard Braverman on *The Mourning Bride*'s specifically Whig implications (*Plots and Counterplots: Sexual Politics and the Body Politic in English Literature, 1660–1730* [1993], 201–7) and Bridget Orr (*Empire on the English Stage, 1660–1714* [2001]) on the play's use of a Spanish setting to voice concerns regarding the quest for empire (174–77).

greve's success in *The Mourning Bride* is the result of his ability to exploit the complementary talents of Barry and Bracegirdle. Although *The Mourning Bride* is not the first in this mold, it is probably the best—and certainly it was the most popular with eighteenth-century audiences.

Congreve's play rests on the opposition between and even confusion of its two heroines: Zara, the captive queen of the Moors; and Almeria, the play's mourning bride. A specularized object of desire throughout much of the play, Almeria's role is established in the play's opening scene as *"the Curtain ris[es] slowly to soft Musick, discovers Almeria in Mourning."*[50] She seems defined by suffering and appears attired in mourning, drooping with grief. While the music plays, the audience watches this passive figure of pathos, physically embodied by the attractive Anne Bracegirdle. Almeria spends much of the play demonstrating her grief, weeping, swooning, even "crawling on the Earth" (4.1.327) in a posture of humiliation before her father. Her speeches overflow with tears and masochistic images of pain, as when she suggests to Osmyn that they mutely accept their fate:

> O, let us not support,
> But sink each other, lower yet, down, down,
> But prone, and dumb, rot the firm Face of Earth
> With Rivers of incessant scalding Rain.
> (3.1.370–74)

Helpless in her grief, she is presented throughout the play as the incarnation of a specifically Christian beauty and virtue.

If Almeria represents a feminine ideal, Zara stands in direct contrast. As Osmyn comments to Almeria, "She's the Reverse of thee" (2.2.200). A woman with "a Soul, / Of God-like Mould" (3.1.222–23), she is tainted by "Passions which out-strip the Wind, / And tear her Virtues up" (3.1.228–29). Specifically, in acting on her desires, appropriating the gaze and with it the male role of sexual subject, she negates her more feminine "virtues" of "soul" and beauty. As Gildon notes, Zara descends from a long line of heroic tragedy heroines, with her passionate desire and evidence of queenly power. Zara is moreover specifically exotic, a Moorish queen whose origins make the contrast with the European, Christian Almeria more pointed. Yet, it is her presence in the play that sets it apart from those she-tragedies that would seek to imitate it and, as Bridget Orr notes, that defies easy allegorization.[51] Although Congreve wrote the role

---

50. William Congreve, *The Mourning Bride*, in *The Complete Plays of Congreve*, ed. Herbert Davis (1967). All further references will be taken from this edition.

51. *Empire on the English Stage*, 174.

of Almeria to showcase Bracegirdle, Almeria's proper feminine sufferings interested theatergoers less than the ardor of Barry's Zara. As Anthony Aston recounts, "Mrs. Barry out-shin'd Mrs. Bracegirdle in the Character of Zara in *The Mourning Bride*, altho' Mr. Congreve design'd Almeria for that Favour."[52] Although this was likely due in part, as Elizabeth Howe attests, to Barry's superior talent in tragic roles,[53] it owed much to Congreve's vivid characterization of Zara. Vital and dynamic, Zara controls the action for much the play. Aligned thematically and structurally with the imperialist king of Granada, who, like Zara, falls in love with an unwilling character and later masquerades in order to gain access to his beloved, she represents active desire rather than feminine distress.

Widely praised for its language (Blackmore described the diction as "Proper, Clear, Beautiful, Noble, and diversify'd agreeably to the variety of the Subject"),[54] *The Mourning Bride* is a play of words rather than action. Aside from the play's final act, with its macabre ending as first Zara and then Almeria mistake the headless corpse of the king for Osmyn, the plot remains relatively static, consisting largely of Almeria's woe, Osmyn's frustrated anger, and Zara's attempts to fix Osmyn's affections on herself. Its visual power lies in the horrors of its setting amidst tombs and dungeon cells and to a greater degree in the verbal imagings of its characters. Where *The Fatal Marriage* focuses literally on Isabella's bed, *The Mourning Bride* creates a similar effect of intensity from its elaborate verbal picturings of rage and desire. Thus the king details the tortures he plans to inflict on Osmyn (4.1), while Zara not only re-creates the sexually charged scene in which she first met Osmyn (2.2)[55] but imagines their deaths as the consummation of her desire (5.2). Only Almeria seems immune to this compulsion. In her role as passive sufferer, she describes her

52. Anthony Aston, *Brief Supplement*, quoted by Howe, *First English Actresses*, 158.

53. See Howe, *First English Actresses*, on the Barry-Bracegirdle pairing in tragedy, 156–62.

54. Blackmore, preface to *King Arthur*, vii. Collier seems to have been the only dissenting voice, objecting to what he saw as blasphemy (see note 9 above). Gildon quotes extensively from Blackmore, yet differs from him in the warmth of his praise, commenting that he finds the style of *All for Love*, the plays of Otway, and Lee's Lucius *Junius Brutus* more sublime than that of Congreve. *Lives and Characters*, 24.

55.
> Kneeling on Earth, I loos'd my hair,
> And with it dry'd thy wat'ry Cheeks; then chaf'd
> Thy Temples, 'till reviving Blood arose,
> And like the Morn vermillion'd o'er thy Face.
> O Heav'n! how did my Heart rejoice and ake,
> When I beheld the Day-break of thy Eyes,
> And felt the Balm of thy respiring Lips! (2.9.47–53)

Visual details such as Zara's loosened hair as well as the rush of blood to Osmyn's cheeks make this imagined scene erotically suggestive.

pain rather than her desires, the sole exceptions being those moments when she imagines her own death in graphic detail (2.2.) or when she recounts the torments she would go through for Osmyn (4.1).

In contrast to *The Fatal Marriage*, even the emphasis on debased sexuality is muted in this play, consisting largely of Zara's unnatural attempt to establish herself as sexual subject but most vividly demonstrated in the picture Osmyn sketches of Almeria's potential sexual union with Garcia:

> Then *Garcia* shall lie panting on thy Bosom,
> Luxurious, revelling amidst thy Charms;
> And thou perforce must yield, and aid his Transport.
> (3.1.358–60)

Although this event never occurs, Osmyn's vision is almost pornographically explicit, picturing as it does not only Almeria's exposed sexual "Charms" but the moment of climax itself. (It is typical of Congreve's emphasis on the verbal that he uses Osmyn's words to urge the spectator to re-create this imagined scene in his mind's eye rather than attempt to represent any such scene.) The responses of Osmyn and Almeria to this imagined scene reflect conventional gender oppositions: the male subject actively expresses his emotional right ("Hell, Hell! have I not Cause to rage and rave?" 3.1.361) while Almeria articulates her role as victim and succumbs to another cycle of misery, detailing not only her sufferings but her role as passive object ("O, I am struck; thy words are Bolts of Ice, / Which shot into my Breast, now melt and chill me. / I chatter, shake, and faint with thrilling Fears": 3.1.367–69).

The contrast between Osmyn's obsessive imagining and Almeria's self-destructive objectification presents a clear delineation of the erotic force of spectatorship and its relation to gender. Sight is the predominant motif in the play; characters not only watch each other; they watch each other's eyes. But control of the gaze is strictly gendered; for women, sight and desire are an unstable combination, leading to potential incest and actual carnage. For men, however, sight both initiates and perpetuates desire. The king becomes infatuated with Zara simply by looking on her, and Osmyn continually re-creates the vision of Almeria in order to feed his desire. Complaining that sight itself is "impotent" when its object is absent, he conjures up a vision of Almeria to gaze on, turning to "the Mind, whose undetermin'd View / Revolves, and to the present adds the past . . . I have *Almeria* here. / At once, as I have seen her often" (2.3.224–29). Such mental imaging is presumably more potent, as Osmyn has complete control over this image of Almeria. His internalized voyeuristic gaze is ultimately masturbatory, suggesting that the image is more satisfactory than the sexual being that this image represents.

But Congreve's most explicit exploration of sight, gender, and desire occurs in the third act. Zara, wearing a black veil, presents herself to Osmyn, hoping that this disguise will trick him into passion. As long as her face remains veiled, his response is one of pleasure ("Is it my love?" he asks eagerly, expecting Almeria), but lifting the veil extinguishes his ardor. Zara laments:

> ZARA. What, does my Face displease thee?
> That having seen it, thou do'st turn thy Eyes
> Away, as from Deformity and Horrour.
> If so, this Sable Curtain shall again
> Be drawn, and I will stand before thee seeing,
> And unseen. Is it my Love? ask again
> That Question, speak again in that soft Voice,
> And look again, with Wishes in thy Eyes.
>   (3.1.148–55)

The scene presents a quickly subdued challenge to the gendered gaze on which she-tragedy depends, as Zara strives to satisfy her desires by designating Osmyn as sexual object. In contrast to Almeria, whose image Osmyn can control through his own internal eye, Zara appropriates the gaze, acting herself as the voyeur, as she says, "seeing and unseen."

Unlike the women in the theater audience whose veils of tears serve to objectify them, and unlike the heroines in she-tragedy circumscribed by the male gaze, Zara's "sable curtain" allows her to control the gaze and thus, in effect, to control male sexuality, if only for a moment. Yet, despite her efforts, Zara is ultimately powerless, her usurpation of the gaze doomed to failure; ironically, her real goal is not to control the gaze, but, like Almeria, to be the object of the desirous gaze. In the end, the female gaze proves unreliable, as both Zara and Almeria mistake the king's headless corpse for that of Osmyn. Zara's impetuous nature leads to her death (she stabs her eunuch Selim, who enters to correct her error, and then drinks poison) while the more yielding Almeria shrinks back from the mangled body and swoons into the real Osmyn's arms. But where Osmyn can take onanistic pleasure from his inner gaze, Almeria, unlike Zara, refuses to take on such an unfeminine role:

> Can I believe
> My Sight, against my Sight? and shall I trust
> That Sense, which in one Instant shews him dead
> And Living?
>   (5.2.292–95)

Although she ultimately concludes "Yes, I will; I've been abus'd / With Apparitions" (5.2.295–96), she proves her femininity by swooning and by concluding the play once again veiled in tears.

In the end, the play enacts a lesson in gender propriety as Almeria prospers, albeit tearfully, while Zara's desire and unfeminine sexual aggression lead to her death. Although Blackmore lauds the conclusion for its representation of poetic justice, where "Vice, as it ought to be, is punish'd, and Opprest Innocence at last Rewarded,"[56] the punishment or reward of female characters in *The Mourning Bride* and in the Barry/Bracegirdle era in general depends almost entirely on the deployment, willing or unwilling, of female sexuality. Women die or retire triumphant based on two qualities largely unrelated to their actual vice or innocence: one, the extent to which their sexual virtue has been compromised; and two, their degree of "passion" and their willingness to pursue the object of their desire (almost always with disastrous results). Thus, amorous women and villainesses meet the same fate as the innocent victims of rape, incest, or adultery.

These two plays represent distinctive and deeply influential qualities of she-tragedy at the end of the seventeenth century, before Jeremy Collier's attack on the theaters and before the advent of the more straitlaced drama of the early eighteenth century. *The Fatal Marriage,* with its literal focus on debased sexuality and on the suffering woman as a sexual object, provides a compelling example of distress as visual spectacle. The play's power lies in the opportunity it provides for the audience to participate in watching first the humiliation Isabella suffers in poverty, then her unwitting sin, and finally her horrified recognition, madness, and death. Despite the addition of the comic subplot, the power of the play lies in its unremitting examination of Isabella and her miseries; not surprisingly, it was one of Elizabeth Barry's most famous roles and it remained for decades a tour de force for leading actresses such as Susannah Cibber and Sarah Siddons.

If *The Fatal Marriage* represents she-tragedy at its most visually intense, *The Mourning Bride* represents female sexuality through discourse rather than action. Although spectators are invited to witness Almeria's distress, the play discusses images rather than providing these images for the audience's delectation. Its impact on subsequent drama, however, derived not from the beauties of its diction but from Congreve's skillful deployment of the very different talents of the play's two female leads. In a centuries-old pattern in which one success spawns a rash of imitations, nearly a dozen plays appeared in the next five years that combined the talents of actresses such as Barry and Bracegirdle and the sexual specta-

---

56. Blackmore, preface to *King Arthur,* vii.

cle of *The Fatal Marriage*.[57] During their careers on the stage, Barry and Bracegirdle played together in at least thirty new tragedies, the bulk of these appearing after *The Mourning Bride*. Certainly the use of dual heroines in tragedy was not unique to the Barry/Bracegirdle era,[58] but it received added stature with the success of the Barry/Bracegirdle pairing in *The Mourning Bride* and prompted numerous other playwrights to follow suit. In the final years of the seventeenth century, the formula of the two female leads, one often characterized by passion and the other by helpless virtue, dominated tragedy. Such roles were not restricted to Barry and Bracegirdle, however; the managers of Drury Lane tried to duplicate the popularity of the formula by staging its own double-plotted tragedies.

Despite the number of these plays produced at the two rival theaters, few survived beyond a few nights, and even fewer were revived in subsequent years. Bemoaning the lack of good drama, Gildon, the author of *A Comparison between the Two Stages* (1702) observes, "You can't name me five Plays that have indur'd six Days acting, for fifty that were damn'd in three."[59] Among the "five Plays" were Mary Pix's *Ibrahim*, which was revived several times between 1696 and 1705, and possibly Charles Hopkins's *Boadicea Queen of Britain* (1697).[60] (Not coincidentally, both plays were Barry and Bracegirdle productions, and both featured scenes of rape and its aftermath.) Writers attempted to duplicate the winning formula of successful plays such as *The Fatal Marriage* and *The Mourning Bride*, so

---

57. The development of the formula was furthered by the evident friendship and lack of professional competition between the two women. As Colley Cibber in *An Apology for the Life of Colley Cibber*, ed. B. R. S. Fone (1968), notes, in the complex theater politics preceding the breakup of the United Company, the Patentees attempted to give some of Barry's chief roles to Bracegirdle:

> Mrs. Bracegirdle had a different way of thinking, and desir'd to be excus'd, from those [roles] of Mrs. Barry; her good Sense was not to be misled by the insidious Favour of the Patentees; she knew the Stage was wide enough for her Success, without entring into any such rash, and invidious Competition, with Mrs. *Barry*, and therefore wholly refus'd acting any Part that properly belong'd to her.

Cibber, *An Apology*, 106.

58. For a discussion of actress pairings, see Howe, *The First English Actresses*, chap. 7. Howe's account of plays written for Rebecca Marshall and Elizabeth Boutell in the 1660s and 1670s (152–56) is especially useful, as she argues that the partnership of Barry and Bracegirdle may have been intended to emulate the popularity of this earlier pairing.

59. Blackmore, preface to *King Arthur*, 2.

60. *A Comparison between the Two Stages* describes Hopkins's *Boadicea* as having done "very well" (20). For a discussion of Pix's *Ibrahim*, see chap. 4. Hopkins's *Friendship Improv'd; or, The Female Warrior* (1699) also seems to have had some success. The play was republished in 1702, which may suggest a revival at that time. Genest argues for a revival; however, *The London Stage* is more cautious and notes only the publication. John Genest, *Some account of the English Stage: From the Restoration to the Present*, 10 vols. (1832); *The London Stage, 1660–1800: A Calendar of Plays, Entertainments, and Afterpieces*, 5 parts, ed. Emmett L. Avery et al. (1962–1968).

that in the final years of the seventeenth century playgoers saw a stream of she-tragedies, each with its suffering heroine and sexual subtext. Some copied the formula of previous plays so closely that their plays read like replicas, such as Henry Smith's *The Princess of Parma* (1699). Smith's play features a romantic triangle (and happy ending) much like *The Mourning Bride,* and in it the tearful "Almira," played by Bracegirdle, and Barry's passionate and ruthless villainess both love the same man.

Although plays such as *The Princess of Parma* may not have been great theater, the very formulaic nature of these plays illuminates popular gender ideology in a way that a more complex or original play would not. The elements that reappear again and again, women in distress, often sexually compromised and helpless to control their lives and bodies, are precisely those qualities that playwrights and theater managers believed would attract audiences into the theaters. On a less strictly commercial level, through the image of the suffering woman, she-tragedy provides a comforting ideal of gender relations that offsets the threatening aspects of uncontrolled female sexuality and its related power. Such corrupted and dangerous energy is destroyed by the end of the tragedy, but not before the audience is given a chance to savor the titillation it occasions; it is, in a sense, a way for spectators to have their cake and eat it too.

The shift from the masculine drama of the Restoration proper, when Charles was king and rakes ruled the comedies, to woman-centered tragedy is one of the most remarkable in English theater and one of the most unremarked. Making women rather than men the protagonists of serious drama required a new kind of plot in which the heroine is the spectacle and her sexual presence the basis of the plot. This vision of the heroine as victim provided playwrights with a new source of social and political argument; it is not what she does but what is done to her—and by whom—that is essential. The obsessive focus on the suffering woman and her sexual virtue that is the hallmark of she-tragedy becomes the means to articulate a social agenda based on gender propriety as well as specific political ideologies, both Whig and Tory. Perhaps most noteworthy, she-tragedy was not merely a passing fad. Although she-tragedies ceased to be written after the early decades of the eighteenth century, plays such as *The Fatal Marriage* and *The Mourning Bride* remained on the stage throughout the eighteenth century. These plays presented generations of theatergoers with an eroticized image of the suffering woman, an image, as John Dennis would later claim, necessary for the sexual morality of the British nation. The domestic sphere inhabited by she-tragedy heroines becomes the means by which playwrights conceptualize the national virtues of internal stability and potent global power as dependent on female sexual virtue.

CHAPTER 4

Women Writing Women:
Female Authors of She-Tragedy

Not all women involved in theater in the later seventeenth century were on the stage or in the audience. Although the majority of playwrights in the later seventeenth century were male, in the last decade of
the century, a new generation of female playwrights emerged. The three
most prominent of these were Mary Pix, Catharine Trotter, and Delarivier
Manley, all active professional writers and all authors of woman-centered
tragedies that premiered during the 1695–96 theater season.[1] They were
joined in the next three years by two more women playwrights, an anonymous "Young Lady" and Jane Wiseman, each the author of a tragedy.
These tragedies pose a series of important questions regarding the connection between a writer's sex, her literary context, and the works she
produces: in a literary climate where pathos and sexual spectacle had become the norm, how did women writers respond to these inherently
misogynist conventions? Can the generation of female playwrights who
succeeded Aphra Behn be said to constitute a specifically feminine line of
drama, one distinct from that of their male contemporaries? In short,
what happens when women write she-tragedy?

In exploring this question, my emphasis falls on Pix, Trotter, and Manley, the most accomplished and prolific of the new women playwrights,
and the ones not coincidentally who were memorialized in the anonymous burlesque *The Female Wits; or, The Triumvirate of Poets at Rehearsal*
(perf. 1696, pub. 1704). All three began their careers as playwrights dur-

---

1. Manley also had a comedy, *The Lying Lover; or, The Jealous Husband,* staged during this
time, although it was less successful than *The Royal Mischief.*

ing the 1695–96 theater season, and the three women were certainly ac-
quaintances, if not necessarily fast friends. As Paula Backscheider has
noted,[2] the three represented a community of women writers, supporting each other (at least at first)[3] and conspicuously writing verses in each
other's praise. In these commendatory verses, published with the early
plays of each author, the three women present themselves as part of a
specifically female tradition, following the earlier precedent set by
Katherine Philips and Aphra Behn. Although the male authors of similar
verses also published with the plays tend to link the women's writing
with their sexual identity, stressing the women's desirability and comparing the literary debut to a loss of virginity,[4] the women describe each
other in more warlike terms. Pix begins her poem in praise of Manley's
Royal Mischief by comparing her to "some mighty Hero" who "snatch
Lawrels with undisputed right, / And Conquer when you but begin to
fight." Likewise, in her homage to Trotter, Manley laments the passing of
Orinda and Astrea, but claims that Trotter "with stronger Arms, [men's]
Empire have disjoin'd." Although in their own prologues the women often fall back on the familiar trope of the timid woman looking for help
from the men of honor, when they describe each other their terms are notably more vigorous.

Although the three women looked back to Behn and Philips as literary
foremothers and sought, in the words of Manley, to "loose the Reins" and
give men's "Glory Chase,"[5] unlike Behn and even Philips,[6] they were not
part of the male literary establishment, although they sought to position
themselves within it. Of the three, Pix was the most dedicated playwright,

2. See *Spectacular Politics: Theatrical Power and Mass Culture in Early Modern England*
(1993), chap. 3, "Representation and Power."

3. Manley would later turn against both Pix and Trotter, satirizing them sharply in *The
New Atalantis.*

4. See for example the epilogue attached to Manley's failed comedy, *The Lost Lover*
(1696), which compares the playwright to a woman giving up her virginity, or Wycherley's
prologue for *Agnes de Castro* in which the author compares Trotter's bringing forth of a play
to childbirth ("And like the Pregnant of Sex, to gain, But for your pleasure, more Disgrace
and Pain") and concludes:

Then be not, as Poor Women often find,
Less kind to her, but as she'd more inclin'd,
At venture of her Fame, to please Mankind.

Such sexually suggestive comments were not applied to Pix, who was older than Trotter and
Manley and known for her girth.

5. "To the Author of Agnes de Castro," published with the play, 1696.

6. For the extent to which Philips participated in the largely male patronage system, see
Maureen E. Mulvihill, "A Feminist Link in the Old Boys' Network: The Cosseting of Katherine Philips," in *Curtain Calls: British and American Women and the Theater, 1660–1820*, 71–104
(1991).

writing twelve plays during the course of her career along with a novel. Manley, by contrast, wrote in a wide variety of forms, from roman à clefs such as her notorious *New Atalantis*, to autobiography and political journalism. Trotter included among her writings a novel, five plays, and a variety of philosophical and religious treatises.

Today, *The Female Wits* is better known than the women it ridicules. Largely an ad feminam attack on Manley, the short burlesque is modeled directly on Buckingham's *The Rehearsal* as its preface and not-so-subtle subtitle suggests. Despite its title, the play is largely dedicated to mocking Manley's *The Royal Mischief* and represents the author as Marsilia, a vain, oversexed, and attention-starved fool. Pix and Trotter make briefer appearances, Pix as the cheerful "Mrs. Wellfed," and Trotter as Calista, a self-consciously learned lady. Although each is briefly held up to ridicule, neither is subjected to the venom directed at Manley. The burlesque was staged originally in October 1696, after Manley had removed *The Royal Mischief* from Drury Lane and taken it to the rival theater at Lincoln's Inn Fields where it was subsequently staged with moderate success. Using Drury Lane actors and actresses playing themselves, the play ridicules Lincoln's Inns Fields' star performers, most notably Elizabeth Barry and Anne Bracegirdle, as well as Manley.[7]

The burlesque chooses as its targets the three women writers who had aligned themselves together as the followers of Behn and were seemingly resolved on entering the largely masculine world of play writing. Given the boldness of their stated enterprise, it is almost surprising that Pix and Trotter do not receive a more vigorous pummeling. The attack on Manley, by contrast, involves personal as well as partisan spite. Perhaps following the burlesque's assertively inclusive title ("The" female wits rather than "A" female wit), scholars in recent decades have tended to read the play as evidence that the three women playwrights were seen as a distinct threat to their male contemporaries, although the nature of this threat varies from scholar to scholar. Lucyle Hook, for example, claims that the women playwrights were subjected to an attack that Derek Hughes has described as "brutal" because they were the "chief purveyors" of a sentimentalized drama.[8] As the previous chapter has indicated,

---

7. Marsilia instructs Mrs. Knight to imitate Barry's distinctive style of rant ("in this Speech, stamp as Queen *Statira* does, that always gets a Clap," 32), and later coaches Miss Cross in Bracegirdle's trademark pathos: "Give me leave to instruct you in a moving Cry. Oh! there's a great deal of Art in crying: Hold your Handkerchief thus; let it meet your Eyes, thus; your Head declin'd, thus; now, in a perfect whine, crying out these words, By these Tears, which never cease to Flow." *The Female Wits; or, The Triumvirate of Poets at Rehearsal* (perf. 1697, pub. 1704; reprinted 1967), 50.

8. "By the 1690s, another type of heroic drama, equally unrealistic but tinged with sen-

they were neither the originators of she-tragedy with its heavy use of pathos nor even the "chief" writers in this genre. Nor, as this chapter will demonstrate, did all three women incorporate pathos into their drama. More recently, feminist scholars have interpreted the burlesque as evidence of a theatrical battle of the sexes in which Pix, Trotter, and Manley represent "a specifically gendered threat to the masculine province of dramatic poetry."[9]

I prefer to read *The Female Wits* as slightly less freighted with sinister overtones. Certainly the play is misogynist and uses the fact of the female wits' sex as the occasion for ridicule. But seeing the three as a threat to the male literary world seems a bit extreme; unlike their predecessor Behn, these women were not members of the theatrical establishment. They were all new playwrights with little or no clout in the theaters, and their willingness to align themselves together as women made them an obvious and easy target. It might be appropriate here to remember Samuel Johnson's oft-quoted quip regarding female preachers as being like dogs walking on their hind legs ("it is not that it is done well but that it is done at all"). The so-called "female wits" were the later seventeenth century's "walking dogs," less threats, perhaps, than anomalies. The burlesque bears this out, focusing more attention on Marsilia's absurdities (and on the absurdity of her play) than on the so-called "triumvirate." The author does, however, seem intent on undermining the assumption of community asserted by the female wits in their commendatory verses; the play shows Marsilia denigrating both Mrs. Wellfed and Calista, Calista sneering at Mrs. Wellfed's lack of learning, and the two secondary women competing for the attentions of Powell, each promising him a better part in her next drama. Nonetheless, the two neglected women end the play amicably, leaving the rehearsal for a communal dinner at the beginning of the third act.

Any attack on a female community of writers, however, is secondary to the play's burlesque of Manley and *The Royal Mischief.* Specific refer-

---

timentality, was enjoying a certain success. The chief purveyors of this new drama which pleased the Ladies were a group of women who seemed impervious to masculine criticism. . . . Although *The Royal Mischief* was the immediate pretext for *The Female Wits,* the true cause of the attack was the surprising success of the women playwrights with the Ladies in the boxes who were beginning to enjoy the 'Solace of Tears' and to dominate theatrical taste in the middle 1690s." Introduction to *The Female Wits,* ii, iii. Pix, Trotter, and Manley were certainly not the main writers of pathos in 1696 (indeed only Pix could be said to include pathos in her tragedy), nor particularly powerful in the theater at this early stage of their careers.

9. Laura Rosenthal, *Playwrights and Plagiarists in Early Modern England: Gender, Authorship, Literary Property* (1996), 175.

ences to Manley's tragedy appear repeatedly, testifying to the play's relative success on the stage as well as to its memorable excesses. Although the bulk of the play focuses on the rehearsal of Marsilia's ridiculous tragedy, it does portray her as encroaching on male territory when she proclaims her intention of altering Ben Jonson's *Catiline* and thus becoming one of the previously all male "sons of Ben." Here the sense of threat is more palpable; it is this transgression rather than her personal vanity or pursuit of other men that moves Aw'dwell to exclaim, "Surely this Scene will chace her from my Soul" (10). Although this reference is a relatively small part of the burlesque, it is notable that what is represented as the height of Manley's literary ego is not only an intrusion into a masculine realm but worse yet a desecration of one of England's literary heroes ("Your Ladyship has laid his Honour in the Dust," exclaims Praiseall, 10).[10]

Nearly three hundred years after the publication of *The Female Wits*, women playwrights of the Restoration and early eighteenth century have been linked by a gendered and, in its own way, equally invidious trope. Drawing on Behn's veiled comparison of herself to a masked woman, a potential courtesan, in the prologue to *The Forc'd Marriage* (1670), some recent critics have been quick to align writing for the stage with sexual impurity and to imply that the women writers saw themselves and were seen as somehow tainted.[11] (Jacqueline Pearson even uses the analogy as the title of her book about female playwrights in the Restoration and eighteenth century, *The Prostitute Muse*). More recently, this analogy between female playwright and prostitute has come under attack from feminist scholars who rightly observe that to romanticize such a connection is not only anachronistic but ultimately denigrates the female playwright.[12] Certainly, the three women discussed in this chapter construct themselves and each other in a very different manner, one that emphasizes their role as writers, albeit writers who were new to the world of theater. Although the three writers who are the focus of this chapter did indeed underscore their sex in the prologues and prefaces to their plays, the tropes they use to construct themselves vary from the woman warrior entering the literary lists to the helpless damsel, calling on the protection of

10. See Rosenthal for a nuanced and insightful examination of *The Female Wits'* attack on Manley's proposed adaptation of Jonson.

11. The association between playwright and prostitute is most famously expressed by Catherine Gallagher in "Who Was that Masked Woman? The Prostitute and the Playwright in the Comedies of Aphra Behn," *Women's Studies* 15 (1988): 23–42.

12. See for example Rosenthal's response to Gallagher, 114–16. Marta Straznicky provides a cogent discussion of the problems of publicity in "Restoration Women Playwrights and the Limits of Professionalism," *ELH* 64 (1997): 703–26.

sympathetic men in her audience. They never even hint that play writing compromises their virtue, whether it be in writing for money or making themselves public.

As debates such as how women playwrights perceived themselves and were perceived suggest, our understanding of the women writers who followed Behn remains murky. In particular, the problem of she-tragedy and the woman writer raises important issues concerning our assumptions regarding the woman writer and her age. Historically grounded scholarship examines the ways in which women's writing is shaped by social constructions of gender. But what of the professional woman writer, especially the playwright whose immediate financial success depended on pleasing a specific audience? In what ways does her cultural and biological experience shape her response to the literary marketplace? These questions have been rarely considered with regard to the woman playwright. We perpetuate this silence by tacitly isolating women such as Pix, Trotter, and Manley from their literary context. Our own pressures of publication often encourage us to examine the woman writer as unique or resistant; we thus create a gendered literary history that may not actually exist.[13] Although dedicating a chapter solely to the works of women writers can be seen as participating in this isolationist pattern, considering these writers within and against their contemporaries is necessary in order to recontextualize their works. In this way, the examination of three playwrights who wrote women-centered tragedy can provide a case study testing the extent to which a distinctly "female" voice can be distinguished in women's writing.

Mary Pix and the Practice of She-tragedy

The most prolific of the "Female Wits" was Mary Pix, who wrote thirteen plays over the course of ten years. Best known today for her comedies, she nonetheless wrote six tragedies, of which one, *Ibrahim, the Thirteenth Emperour of the Turks*, achieved some lasting success on the stage.[14] It was this play on which Gildon lavished such praise, describing the "distress" of its ravished heroine as exciting tears, an effect he celebrates as the proper end of tragedy. His comment that the distress of Morena "never fail'd to bring Tears into the Eyes of the Audience" emphasizes that the play was revived more than once, each time evoking

---

13. Margaret Ezell makes this point eloquently in *Writing Women's Literary History* (1993).
14. First staged in 1696, it was revived on at least three separate occasions: 1702, 1704, 1715. This is all the more impressive as the vast majority of she-tragedies never returned to the stage after their original appearance.

the same powerful effect, an unusual commendation for the often un-successful serious drama of the late 1690s. Moreover, while admitting that versification was not Pix's strength, he nonetheless linked Pix to the playwright most Restoration writers believed stood heir to Shake-speare's genius and whose ability to sway the emotions of his audience was legend. Claiming that in its depiction of "the Passions" *Ibrahim* evokes emotions "which few Plays, if any since *Otway*'s have done; and yet, which is the true End of Tragedy" (111), Gildon's comment stands as rare praise to any playwright, let alone a woman, in marked contrast to more recent assessments of Pix's tragedies. Often considered by fem-inist critics to be conservative, Pix is described by Jacqueline Pearson, for example, as "attempt[ing] to write in a gender-neutral way, but in fact this means assuming male viewpoints and stereotypes" (201), while Derek Hughes claims Pix "distinguished herself as a slavish upholder of male authority."[15]

Although her plots may reiterate patriarchal authority in their use of she-tragedy conventions, Pix deliberately addresses her plays to the women in her audiences. Each tragedy includes a plea to the ladies for their support, as in the prologue to *The Double Distress:*

> Our modest Muse no Fop nor Ruffian brings;
> But treats of Heroiens and of sacred things:
> Be kind, ye Fair, since of the Fair she sings.[16]

Here Pix not only reiterates her own proper feminine nature (she is, as she claims, a "modest Muse"), but stresses the importance of women within her play. Rejecting the male "Fop" and "Ruffian," she links "Her-oiens" and "sacred things," concluding that her play is distinctly female. This appeal to a feminine audience is heightened in the prologue and epilogue to *Ibrahim* where Pix first endows her play with traditional womanly qualities (it is a "harmless, modest play" in need of "protec-tion") and then concludes her epilogue by conferring the same passive qualities on herself:

---

15. Jacqueline Pearson, *The Prostituted Muse: Images of Women and Women Dramatists, 1642–1737* (1988), 201; Derek Hughes, *English Drama, 1660–1700* (1996), 419. Robert D. Hume, writing twenty years before Hughes, is less concerned with issues of gender, and while his comments on Pix's plays are brief, he bestows some kind words on her tragedies (he describes *Ibrahim* as a "vigorous melodrama," *Development of English Drama,* 423). For a lengthier assessment of critical responses to Pix, see Marsden, "Mary Pix: The Women Writer as Commercial Playwright," *Studies in the Literary Imagination* 32, no. 2 (fall 1999): 33–44.

16. Pix, prologue to *The Double Distress* (1701).

By the great Rules of Honour all Men Know
They must not Arm on a Defenceless Foe.
The Author on her weakness, not her strength relies,
And from your Justice to your Mercy flies.[17]

By making her sex the occasion for pathos (the author stands in the same predicament as her distressed character, threatened and in need of protection), Pix links herself with the heroines of her drama, arguing not for the strengths of her play, but claiming her weakness as a woman and her need for chivalrous protection. Pix's careful self-construction defuses the potential threat of female authorship, stressing instead the conventional power dynamic of helpless woman and protecting male that her tragedies reproduce.

Although Pix's plays clearly delineate a sympathetic representation of women, they do so within the conventions of a literary tradition that upheld patriarchal power structures. Thus it is perhaps not surprising that the tragedy in which Pix achieved her greatest success was the one in which she participated most fully in what were to become the recognizable conventions of she-tragedy. Rape, pathos, and the subsequent display of the tainted woman all have their part in *Ibrahim*, combined in a direct and effective single plot. The key to *Ibrahim*'s dramatic power is its emphasis on the erotic, comprised especially of the repeated display of female sexuality. Despite the title of *Ibrahim*, the play focuses intensely on the figure of Morena, the young, beautiful, and helpless daughter of the Mufti who is desired by both the Sultan Ibrahim and Amurat, general of the sultan's forces. Morena's "distress" arises when the sultan rapes her, an act engineered by Sheker Para, Ibrahim's favorite mistress, who herself loves Amurat. Although many of the events in *Ibrahim* are drawn from Sir Paul Rycaut's *History of the Turkish Empire*, Pix's interpretation of Turkish history is all her own.[18] Although her memory for factual details

17. Pix, epilogue to *Ibrahim, the Thirteenth Emperour of the Turks* (1696).

18. In her preface, Pix acknowledges Rycaut's continuation of Richard Knolles's *Turkish History* as the source of her play. As the play demonstrates, she ignores much of the military and political history of Ibrahim's reign in order to focus on the Sultan's sexual habits. It seems likely that she originally read an edition of Rycaut similar to the 1687 folio in the British Library, which contains both Knolles's history and Rycaut's continuation: *The Turkish History from the Original of that Nation to the Growth of the Ottoman Empire with the Lives and Conquests of their Princes and Emperors. By Richard Knolles . . . with a Continuation to this Present Year MDCLXXXVII, whereunto is added, the Present State of the Ottoman Empire by Sir Paul Rycaut. The Sixth Edition, with the Effigies of all the Kings and Emperors, newly engraven at large on copper*, 3 vols. (London, 1687). Pix may or may not have seen this edition, but it is almost certain that her source, like the British Library copy, included both Rycaut's continuation and 1687 folio edition of his earlier *Present State of the Ottoman Empire*. In one volume she

may not have been exact (she admits that she misremembered Ibrahim's place in Turkish history—he was the twelfth rather than the thirteenth emperor), she shares the common association of Turkey with the exotic and sensual.

Set within the Turkish sultan's court, a site of imagined sexual excess governed by a tyrant with insatiable appetites, the play displays a prurient interest in the sexual proclivities of this deviant landscape with its harem, courtesans, and eunuchs. The titillation of the exotic is represented most concretely near the beginning of the play when Ibrahim chooses a new virgin for his harem. Sheker Para has selected twenty virgins "and set [them] in order for your view" (4). These "fresh Viands" are presented for Ibrahim's and the audience's inspection as "*The Scene draws and discovers the Ladies set in Order for the Sultans Choice, who takes out his Handkerchief, and walks round them*" (4). Here the male gaze within the play serves to direct the spectator's gaze, this time on a variety of female objects. The sexual import of the scene is explicit; once the sultan drops his handkerchief, the favored virgin will be led to his bed, and "*the Scene shuts upon the rest.*" The spectator thus participates vicariously in the sultan's sexual speculations, as do Sheker Para and her eunuch Achmet, who comment on the scene. In addition to discussing the sultan's choice, they compare the gender politics of the harem to those of Europe:

> SHEKER. How different, *Achmet* is this from the *European* stories;
>   I have read there, twenty Heroes for the Ladies
>   Burn and die, here twenty Ladies for the Hero.
>   *Ach.* It shows that Mankind maintains his Charter
>   Better here, yet loses sure the sweetness.
>   Of submissive love.
>
>   (4)

Specific sexual behavior thus becomes the means of articulating a nationalist politics in which the oriental "Charter" represented by the sultan and Sheker Para is contrasted first verbally and later visually with the European and implicitly English virtues of Morena and her sweet submissiveness. Similarly, the play's rape reiterates the familiar plot of much Whig she-tragedy in which sexual brutality demonstrates political tyranny.

---

could thus have read about the rape of Morena (unnamed and unmutilated in Rycaut's account) and the ceremony of the handkerchief which Rycaut describes in *The Present State* and which Pix dramatizes in the first act of the play.

Such tantalizing exhibitions are only the backdrop for the play's chief spectacle, the figure of the virtuous Morena and her prolonged and oft-displayed suffering. Pix juxtaposes Morena's innocent virtue with the lustful scheming of Sheker Para; while Sheker openly pursues Amurat, planning with almost masculine relish "to quench these raging fires, / In full possession of my fierce desires" (6), Morena exhibits the sweet "submissive love" that Achmet had found so foreign to Eastern passion. The collision of these very different female principles generates much of the play's plot. Although the faithful Achmet offers to tear out Morena's eyes to revenge his mistress, Sheker vows to "spoil the Worship Shrine" (14) in a more potent manner, by destroying not her beauty but her sexual purity. The rape that follows becomes the play's principal action and precipitates the inevitable tragic outcome.

The rape occurs at the end of act 3 after the unwilling Morena is dragged into Ibrahim's presence. The sight of her beauty inflames him, and in typical tyrannical fashion, he orders her carried to his bed. Although Morena begs for death, dismemberment, or torture, he muses that "there may be a new unknown delight / To conquer all these struglings" (24). The scene becomes an extended display not only of Morena's sexual desirability and distress, two deeply interlocked qualities, as the sultan's comment suggests, but of graphic violence. When a watching eunuch protests, Ibrahim stabs him, an act that leads to still more bloodshed as Morena "*catches hold of the* Sultans *naked Scimiter*" and "*Draws it thro' her hands*" (24) in a masochistic attempt to deter the sultan. Like her earlier pleadings for death or torture, this attempt fails, only spurring Ibrahim to great heights of desire ("By Heaven rage is mixt with love," he cries, "And I am all on fire!" [24]). The bloody hands, along with the conventional disheveled or ravished hair and disordered clothing, vividly manifest Morena's violation. Her mutilation becomes a visual substitution for the unrepresentable act of rape; the blood on her hands symbolizes the blood of her broken hymen, a clever theatrical device that allows Pix to present a symbolic rape on the stage.

Pix emphasizes the importance of this titillating scene of sexual defilement by replaying it twice in the following acts. The fourth act begins immediately after the actual rape, and focuses, both literally and figuratively, on the body of the ravished woman. Morena is led in, "*her hair down, and much disorder'd in her dress*" (25), sexually coded markers of her violation and of her chaste resistance to the rape. Next, the rape itself is replayed when a friend informs Amurat of the defilement of his beloved, narrating the event in graphic detail, and inviting him—and again the audience—to

—suppose
Her prayers, her tears, her cryes,
Her wounding supplications all in vain.
Her dear hands in the Conflict cut and mangled,
Dying her white Arms in Crimson Gore,
The savage Ravisher twisting his [fingers]
In the lovely Tresses of her hair,
Tearing by the smarting Root,
Fixing her by that upon the ground:
Then—(horrour on horrour!)
On her breathless body perpetrate the fact.

(28)

Narrative goes where representation cannot—into the act itself, the "fact" perpetrated on Morena's helpless body. Description quickly becomes reality as the scene draws and reveals the prostrate Morena, distraught and disheveled. Even though Amurat insists that her "Virgin Mind" remains pure (40), it is the "polluted" and sexualized female body that becomes the literal focus of the drama.

Although *Ibrahim* contains an attack on absolutism, Pix's straightforward political message is enabled by a sophisticated manipulation of erotic spectacle. Pix illustrates the inherent corruption of absolute power (as opposed, we are to assume, to the liberties of England under William III) and demonstrates these excesses through the spectacle of female suffering. Despotism is represented and undone because of its assault on helpless femininity. Yet, while Ibrahim's tyranny causes the tragedy, the real impact of the play's last three acts arises from the spectacle of Morena's prolonged suffering and eventual death. The play ends almost immediately after her death, emphasizing her role as visual and emotional center of the tragedy. (Ibrahim, by contrast, is dispatched at the beginning of the act.) The play's power, as in the she-tragedies of Pix's male contemporaries, lies in its obsessive focus on the body of Morena, first virginal, and then, most crucially, publicly violated and held up for display.

Although Pix went on to write five more tragedies over the course of the following decade, none achieved the popular success of *Ibrahim*. Her next tragedy, *Queen Catharine; or, The Ruines of Love* (1698), explicitly courts the favor of the women in the audience and touts the travails of its two heroines.

To please your martial men she [the author] *must despair;*
And therefore Courts the favour of the fair:

From huffing Hero's she hopes no relief,
But trusts in Catharine's *Love, and* Isabella's *grief.*[19]

Despite Catharine's tender love scenes with Owen Tudor and her ward Isabella's protracted sorrow, the play seems to have been unsuccessful and was never revived.[20] Talky and overlong, it lacks both the sensationalism and the pathos that had invigorated *Ibrahim.* Two other plays (*The False Friend; or, The Fate of Disobedience* [1699] and *The Double Distress* [1701]) were also unsuccessful. Despite Pix's experimentation with prose in *The Czar of Muscovy* (1701), the play did not find favor with contemporary audiences.

In her final tragedy, *The Conquest of Spain* (1705), Pix recycles the plot of *Ibrahim,* but at greater length and with less extensive use of exotic spectacle and female distress. Like *Ibrahim, The Conquest of Spain* centers around the rape of a virtuous maiden and the resulting anguish and turmoil. Perhaps the play's most interesting element is Pix's emphatic reiteration of the essential purity of her ravished maiden. As in *Ibrahim,* where Amurat defends Morena's "Virgin Mind," exclaiming "Shall I forsake the Christal Fountain, / Because a Rough-hewn Satyr there / Has quencht his Thirst?" (40), Pix's hero insists he will still marry Jacincta, explaining "[Thy beauties] and thy noble Mind are still the same, / Sublime and Chast, unsullied by the Tyrant."[21] Such sentiments are markedly different from those expressed in Nicholas Brady's *The Rape* (1692), for example, where the inherent corruption of the raped woman is the basis for much of the play's action. This sense of contagion is even used as a stratagem for capturing the rapist, for, explains one character, a prince's "Royal Blood will prompt him to endure / Ten thousand deaths, rather than marry one / That's Ravish'd by another."[22]

As these passages indicate, even in those works that most strongly adhere to the patriarchal structures of she-tragedy, Mary Pix does more than "slavishly uphold" the masculinist point of view. Unlike their contemporaries, her heroes can see beyond the merely physical event of rape. Such expressions are rare in late-seventeenth-century drama; most male characters, when confronted with the violation of their beloved, bewail fate and vow revenge but make no claims for the woman's unchanged

19. Prologue to *Queen Catharine; or, The Ruines of Love* (1698).
20. *The London Stage* provides no information regarding the number of nights *Queen Catharine* ran; however, its absence in the list of plays Gildon attributes to Pix suggests that it was not a success. See *Lives and Characters,* 111–12.
21. *Conquest of Spain* (1705), 39.
22. Nicholas Brady, *The Rape; or, The Innocent Imposters* (1692), 34.

purity. Although sexuality may still be destiny in her plays as she follows the conventions of the genre and dispatches her ravished maidens, in the process she argues for a more exalted vision of female virtue.

Rather than holding Pix up to a standard of twenty-first-century feminism, it might be more accurate to describe her as a writer eager to satisfy the taste of the theatrical marketplace; alone among the female wits, her plays were revived in later years and even her critics admitted "she has done some things well enough."[23] Her single successful tragedy incorporates both strong sympathy for its distressed heroine and skillful appropriation of the more sensational elements of she-tragedy in its most misogynist form. In doing so, it became a commercially viable play, and her willingness to follow dramatic trends may well have been one reason for the praise she earned even from more hostile critics. Cognizant of contemporary tastes and willing to promote them within her drama, Pix wrote an effective tragedy and several successful comedies. Reading her within a framework we have constructed and which her contemporaries seem not to have shared overlooks and even denigrates the woman writer who sought to be financially successful in a male-dominated field.

Catharine Trotter and the Tragedy of Virtue

Catharine Trotter, the rather priggish Calista in *The Female Wits*, was, unlike Pix, known primarily for her tragedies.[24] In contrast to both Pix and Manley, Trotter cultivated a demeanor of modesty and virtue, and moral debates dominate her plays. (Manley would later satirize Trotter's modesty as carefully cultivated artifice in *The New Atalantis* [1710].)[25] Her plays stand apart from the general trends of later-seventeenth-century tragedy, neither evoking an earlier heroic age nor following the sexually tantalizing conventions of the 1690s. Even the prologues to her plays stress the higher goals of this female playwright, although the prologue to *Agnes de Castro* (1695), her first play, uses some of the conventional tropes of the helpless woman seeking the protection of men of "Wit" and "Honour" ("Conscious of her Faults she flies to you, / To save her from

23. *The Female Wits*, 11.

24. Trotter wrote four tragedies, *Agnes de Castro* (1696), *The Fatal Friendship* (1698), *The Unhappy Penitant* (1701), and *The Revolution in Sweden* (1706). Her lone comedy, *Love at a Loss; or, Most Votes Carry It* (1700), failed after one night. No reason was given for the failure; the comedy is original and witty and was recently successfully revived in London.

25. "She has an air of youth and innocence which has been of excellent use to her in those occasion[s] she has since had to impose upon the world as to matters of conduct." Delarivier Manley, *The New Atalantis*, ed. Ros Ballaster (1992), 158.

the Thoughtless Damning Crew").[26] Trotter soon abandons this stance, and in subsequent works such as the "Dedication" to *The Unhappy Penitent* (1701) and the prologue to *The Revolution of Sweden* (1705) presents the female playwright as patriot and moral conscience.

On the surface, *Agnes de Castro*, Trotter's earliest and perhaps most successful tragedy, would seem to fit the mold of she-tragedy. Based on the Behn novel of the same title,[27] its cast is dominated by women, and both of its virtuous heroines die unjustly before the end of the play, while a third woman, the villainous Elvira, runs mad in the final act. But a closer examination of the play reveals that *Agnes de Castro* is in actuality very different from its near contemporaries such as *Ibrahim* or *The Fatal Marriage* and from the host of she-tragedies soon to follow. The play is remarkable for its lack of pathos and for the total absence of sexual spectacle. The sin central to the play's action is not sexual but violent—the murder of the princess Constantia—and the play consecrates feminine merit and the joys of female friendship rather than enticing its audience with overwrought scenes of suffering. Almost austere in its avoidance of exoticism and in its emphasis on virtue, *Agnes de Castro* shows women whose passions are under their own control and who choose the joys of friendship over those of heterosexual love.[28]

The central character, Agnes herself, is a chaste, even severe figure. Although beloved by the prince and lusted after by Alvaro (Elvira's corrupt brother), she remains not only cold to love but almost asexual. Instead of scenes that objectify Agnes and stress her sexual desirability, Trotter represents her heroine involved in a series of debates over the joys of pure virtue. In an animated discussion with the king, who strives to persuade Agnes to agree to a marriage with Alvaro, Agnes argues for a single life in political, not romantic, terms:

> Who wou'd resign a Quiet, though Poor, freedom,
> To be with glitt'ring, gaudy trappings deck'd;
> Which but inform the World, whose Slaves they are.
> No, Sir, I value Liberty far more,

26. "Prologue spoken by Mr. Powell," *Agnes de Castro* (1696).

27. *Agnes de Castro; or, The Force of Generous Love* (1688), itself a translation of a work by S. B. de Brillac. Trotter follows Behn's plot closely, inflecting the general story with her own concerns through her emphasis on the two central female characters rather than the Prince (Don Pedro in Behn's novel) and on the larger role Elvira plays in her tragedy. Unlike the novel, in which Constantia dies of grief, Trotter has her villainess kill the princess by accident, mistaking her for Agnes.

28. While Robert D. Hume links Trotter's tragedies to earlier heroic drama (see *Development of English Drama*, 423, 448), his description of the plays as distinctly stoic is perhaps more appropriate.

> Than to forsake it, though for Golden Chains,
> A shining Prison, is a Prison still.
>
> (12–13)

When the king rebukes her, she responds that if Heaven had designed her for love, it "had surely given me a Heart more tender . . . I feel no melting, no soft Passion there; / None but for Charming Liberty" (13). Agnes's reasoning (which sounds strikingly similar to that which Mary Astell would use five years later in her *Reflections on Marriage*) is not simply that she dislikes Alvaro but that she rejects marriage as a concept altogether, as a state whose inherent lack of freedom renders it inferior to the joys of independence. In Agnes, Trotter presents her audience with a heroine who is able to control her own sexuality and who finds heterosexual passion unappealing. Instead, Agnes's affections are focused on the princess, whom she describes as "the sole Disposer of my Actions" (14) and "Object of my Hopes . . . My Light, my Guard, my All" (25). When, in the final scene of the play, Agnes thaws slightly toward the prince, she does so in honor of the princess, who, as her dying wish, had charged Agnes to love the prince. Any traditional heterosexual emotion Agnes expresses, then, comes via the ardent friendship she experiences with the princess. She even defines the king in terms of Constantia; when he challenges her "sure you know me not," she responds, "I know you, Sir, to be *Constantia's* Father" (13).

Likewise, the princess describes Agnes as "my Souls best comfort" (3) and says that she is as "equal dear to me" as her husband (5). Even the revelation that her beloved husband loves her friend does not erode her fondness. "Fear not for *Agnes*," she assures her husband, "I love her, and her being dear to you, / More strongly recommends her to my care" (9). As Emma Donaghue notes, the prince and Agnes share rather than divide Constantia's heart, and this dual loyalty ultimately gives her emotional stability.[29] Elvira had thought to divide the two women by betraying the prince's wayward affections, but her machinations cannot alter their love for one another. Instead of creating competition, the mutable emotions of a man intensify the connection between the two women, a benevolent revision of the homosocial bond described by Eve Sedgwick.[30] As Elvira's serving woman observes, the two women "mingl[e] Kisses with the

---

29. Emma Donoghue, *Passions between Women: British Lesbian Culture, 1669–1801* (1995), 131–32.

30. See *Between Men: English Literature and Male Homosocial Desire* (1985), esp. chaps. 1 ("Gender Assymmetry and Erotic Triangles") and 2 ("*The Country Wife*: Anatomies of Male Homosocial Desire").

tend'rest Words, / As if their Rivalship had made 'em dear" (20). Notably, the intense bond described in *Agnes de Castro* is repeatedly characterized as pure; in the terms set up by the play, this purity does not necessarily mean that the women's love is not erotic but rather uncorrupted, even by the specter of jealousy. Before Trotter's play, expressions of female friend-ship, so-called "passionate" or "romantic" friendships, had been largely confined to poetry, in works such as those by the much admired Kather-ine Philips as well as Anne Killigrew, Elizabeth Singer Rowe, and others. In *Agnes de Castro*, such sentiments are enacted on the stage, not simply described, creating a very different representation of female desire. Trot-ter's heroines demonstrate the mutual depth of their feelings, yet at all times their behavior is controlled, unlike that of the heroines of most con-temporary drama. Although their love for each other is the play's domi-nant feature, trying to determine whether this affection can be labeled distinctly lesbian avoids the broader implications of Trotter's characteri-zations of women who insist on personal agency and possess the means to control their own sexuality, lesbian or otherwise.[31]

By contrast, the men in *Agnes de Castro* are notably weak and ineffec-tual. They not only do not dominate the action, but Trotter portrays them as relatively powerless whether acting for good or evil. The prince, the play's quasi-romantic lead, is the victim of his helpless love for Agnes, unable to fight his passion at the same time he abhors his emotional infi-delity to the princess. Like many a she-tragedy heroine, he defines him-self in terms of his suffering. "Is there another wretch on Earth like me?" he asks, finding little more to do than pour out his "Woes in soft Com-plaints," asking himself

> What can be thy relief?
> No, think of none, none, but in suffering more;
> T'attone thy Crime, be exquisitely wretched.
>
> (10)

In his acceptance of suffering and final desire to be "exquisitely wretched," the prince speaks the language of pathos, a language that in late-seven-teenth-century drama had been almost exclusively female. Even his final

---

31. Kathryn Kendall has discussed the possibly lesbian nature of Agnes's and the princess's love in several articles. See "From Lesbian Heroine to Devoted Wife; or, What the Stage Would Allow," *Journal of Homosexuality* 12 (May 1986): 9–21; "Finding the Good Parts: Sexuality in Women's Tragedies in the Time of Queen Anne," in *Curtain Calls: British and American Women and the Theater, 1660–1820*, 165–76 (1991); "Catharine Trotter Cockburn and Me: A Duography," in *The Intimate Critique: Autobiographical Literary Criticism*, ed. Greedman, Frey, and Zauhar, 273–82 (1993).

suicide attempt is thwarted by his father, who accuses him of being a coward. Similar male weakness appears in the figure of Alvaro, the play's male villain and a pale shadow of his sister Elvira. A passive rather than an active agent of evil, he must be prompted by the king to consider raping Agnes and guided by his sister in her machinations. Even the king himself finds Agnes's moral authority a threat. Determined to punish her "insolence" in opposing the marriage to Alvaro, he encourages Alvaro to rape her and through the act establish his authority ("'Tis in your choice, t'obey or be obey'd," [16]). The rape never occurs, and Alvaro's—and the king's—authority is never confirmed.

The king remains an oddly ambivalent figure in Trotter's play. He voices the prerogative of a corrupt patriarchal authority in emphasizing man's need for female submission, yet in the play's final act, he becomes a monarch with a moral conscience. Horrified that he misjudged Agnes and thus nearly committed "that detested Crime, abominable Murther" (42), he quickly releases her and forgives his son. As the king's words and the trial of Agnes indicate, the central crime in this female-centered play is murder rather than rape. This shift in emphasis results in a play where the focus falls on female friendship rather than on female sexuality, on a bond that even the uncontrolled excesses of male passion cannot destroy. These friends, unlike the Isabellas, Monimias, and Euriones of orthodox she-tragedies, are firm in their personal certainty of virtue. Agnes and the princess are equally notable for their almost stoic acceptance of grief, and the play openly rejects the copious expressions of misery that were the hallmark of pathos. Only the prince indulges in such emotions, and when, at the play's end, he endeavors to fall on his sword claiming nothing "shou'd make me live, / Thou do'st but lengthen out my Woes a moment . . . Why wou'd you have your Son be miserable?" (47), his behavior presents a startling contrast to Agnes's composed dignity. The king recapitulates the play's stoic philosophy as he chides his son,

> Hop'd you to live in Luxury and Ease,
> Courted by Joys, and Pleasures without end?
> Did you ne'r hear of Pains, and Cares, in Life?
>
> (47)

By implication aligning himself with Agnes, the king ultimately upholds her moral authority, and as the play ends with the prince determined to die of grief, the male characters represent a fallen world, one which cannot compare with the integrity of that inhabited by the princess and Agnes.

Trotter's emphasis on the abstract joys of conscious virtue results in a play that depends little on the visual embellishments common in later-seventeenth-century tragedy. Within the theatrical context of the 1690s especially, *Agnes de Castro* is remarkable for its absence of spectacle, sexual or otherwise. The rape that the king helps Alvaro plan never occurs; in fact, the abduction of Agnes, which Alvaro masterminds, becomes a simple exit. The dramatic events in which the prince rescues Agnes and returns her to court are described, not acted, and the play is almost devoid of pathos. What little of the pathetic it contains can be found in the prince's lamentations and in the death of the princess, although the death scene itself becomes more a paean to sorority than a display of suffering as each woman protests her love for the other.

Whatever sensationalism the play supplies is furnished by Trotter's villainess, the evil Elvira, whose insanity offsets the calm virtue of Agnes. Where Elvira lapses into madness after seeing the ghost of the princess, Agnes remains calm despite charges of murder, commenting "how strange a charm is Vertue in a Soul!" (32). She never weeps or wavers from her convictions, giving in to weakness only once when she swoons after the death of the princess. By contrast, Elvira spends the final act irrevocably mad, and it is with her madness that Trotter finally employs stage spectacle, using devices such as a discovery scene and displays of female frenzy. With the final act constructed as a test of Agnes's innocence, Elvira represents the key evidence for the defense (in her visitation, the ghost had promised Elvira that "thou thyself art Witness, / And unsuspected shall accuse thyself" [34]). The act begins with the discovery of "Elvira *asleep on a Couch*" (37). The scene closes immediately after, but it will open again to reveal Elvira in a frenzy, and she confirms her guilt by stabbing her woman Bianca before being carrying off the scene (40–41). In the end, like many of her contemporaries, Trotter concludes her play with its entire female cast either dead or raving. Nonetheless, *Agnes de Castro* differs from the vast majority of plays of the time in that its noble heroines do not participate in the familiar representation of femininity, which emphasizes helpless distress and elevates womanly passivity. Although Trotter eschews the sexual spectacle and pathos that such a dynamic encourages, her play is also unlike the heroic plays of an earlier generation. Rather than locating authority in the oaths and honor of those earlier plays, or in the female distress of her contemporaries, she establishes moral authority in purely female virtue—embodied specifically in friendship of Agnes and the princess—which overcomes the perversions of heterosexual love. Ultimately, nothing in the play can equal the purity of Agnes's and the princess's love. It alone remains uncorrupted and incorruptible.

Trotter's emphasis on the bond between Agnes and Constantia significantly alters the complexion of her drama. By using the tropes of romantic love to express the intensity of the friendship, Trotter replaces the male-female sexual bond that lies at the heart of she-tragedy with an exploration of a strictly female relationship. While, as George Haggerty has observed, "the erotics of male friendship are rarely more vividly represented than in the heroic tragedies of Restoration and early eighteenth century,"[32] similarly intense depictions of female friendship had been largely absent in drama, although not in poetry. In the tragedy of the later seventeenth century, male-female ties typically determine women's role in tragedy. They become the means for eroticizing female characters as well as defining the relations that establish political power, as *Ibrahim* demonstrates. By downplaying such conventions, Trotter presents a radically different psychosexual dynamic in her tragedy. With the friendship of Agnes and Constantia as the play's emotional center, *Agnes de Castro* circumvents the customary delineation of the objectified woman as victim along with the processes of spectatorship that depend on this fundamental spectacle. Virtue rather than distress becomes the play's central "spectacle." Lacking the voyeuristic imperative of its contemporaries, the play patently does not fit the familiar parameters of she-tragedy, despite its plot of female death and madness.

Although none of Trotter's subsequent tragedies are so clearly centered on women as *Agnes de Castro,* the plays contain a similar emphasis on virtue, especially feminine virtue, while at the same time avoiding the sexual sensationalism so characteristic of almost all drama of the 1690s. Thus, although *The Fatal Friendship* (1698) does contain a case of bigamy (not consummated), it is a man who commits the sin in order to preserve the life of his friend and who suffers in the end. The female characters remain blameless. In *The Unhappy Penitent* (1701), the sexual sin is marriage itself, as the play becomes a moral debate over absolute honor versus love. Margarite, the play's principal female character, agrees to marry her beloved Lorrain before she is absolutely certain an old, political betrothal has been dissolved. This precipitous marriage constitutes the sin for which she will be punished, not by death or by protracted displays of suffering, but by voluntary exile to a convent. Her friend Ann lectures her on the importance of self control over one's passions, no matter how lawful those passions may be:

---

32. George E. Haggerty, *Men in Love: Masculinity and Sexuality in the Eighteenth Century* (1999), 23. Haggerty cites examples of such male friendships in *All for Love, The Rival Queens, Valentinian,* and *The London Merchant.*

But when indulgent to our vicious Passions,
In defiance of Heav'n, it self, we will be happy,
Break through all restraints to our desires;
Some sudden Disappointment dashes th'enjoyment.

(36)

The "vicious Passions" to which Ann refers are those which led Margarite to marriage, not vice; her sin, if indeed it can be called such, lies in virtuous heterosexual love. But Ann's lecture reiterates the message of stoic denial of passion that permeates *Agnes de Castro*, a message counter to the emphasis on sexual passion and its deleterious effect on women that dominates the serious drama of Trotter's contemporaries.

The Revolution of Sweden (1706), Trotter's final tragedy and her most political play, contains little that even approaches visual titillation other than the appearance of two cross-dressed female characters, one fleeing from an abusive husband. The play's larger goal is heroic, as Trotter's prologue explains. Although her audience may expect "a soft Effeminate Feast," Trotter has loftier goals:

To publick Virtues she'd your Souls incite,
A Woman thus may give you safe Delight;
Her warmest Scenes will raise no dangerous Flame

. . . .

Nor will she less we hope engage the Fair,
Since Publick Good is now that sexes Care;
They must a Noble Heroine approve,
Parting with Life, nay what we prize above,
To save the Nation, vanquishing her Love.
This Pattern may prevail to disingage
All the Fair Politicians of the Age,
From every Byass that our Feuds increase,
Renouncing Private Ends, for Publick Peace.
Nor can the vainest haughtiest Man, disdain
A Woman's Precepts in Great ANNA's Reign.[33]

Carefully distancing herself from the assumption that a woman playwright would write only "warm scenes" of love, Trotter stresses that in her play as in her age, "Publick Good" is in the hands of women, using, of course, Queen Anne as her unassailable example. Her play elaborates on this theme not simply by glorifying Gustavus Adolphus of Sweden, but by stressing the loyal women who supported his rebellion against

33. Prologue to *The Revolution of Sweden* (1706).

tyranny. Rather than focusing on Gustavus's exploits, the play centers on the conflict between a noble husband and wife, where the husband's uxorious love puts his concern for his wife above his concern for his country. When she is captured, he gives himself up in an attempt to rescue her, a move which she deplores ("Oh insupportable!" she exclaims, "I've only now in Death to think my self / The wretched cause of *Arwide* and my poor / Deserted Countries Ruin" [35–36].) By contrast, when she (falsely) believes him a traitor to his country, she painfully but patriotically reveals his treachery.

"Renouncing Private Ends" might well stand as the motto not only for *The Revolution of Sweden* but for most of Trotter's dramas. Instead, Trotter uses her drama to instruct on "publick" themes, most commonly evoking the precepts of stoicism but on occasion returning to the heroic, as in *The Revolution of Sweden*, to accomplish her didactic aim. Consciously avoiding the style of female-centered drama favored by her male contemporaries and by female playwrights such as Mary Pix and the anonymous "Young Lady," she represents an ideal of female virtue that goes beyond the sexual. By replacing the male-female sexual bond that lies at the heart of she-tragedy with an exploration of female friendship, Trotter dismantles the binary opposition of male/subject and female/object that constitutes a central component of voyeurism in she-tragedy. In her plays, women can control their sexuality while it is men who seem to lose control (even in *The Unhappy Penitent* Margarite marries on the urging of Lorrain). Without feminine pathos as a central spectacle, her dramas avoid the conventions of she-tragedy, replacing dramatic voyeurism with displays of active, women-centered virtue.

Delarivier Manley—Drama and the Sensational

Unlike Pix or Trotter, Delarivier (or Mary de la Riviere) Manley was not primarily a dramatist; she wrote only four plays over the course of her career, dedicating most of her energies to writing Tory propaganda and later the novels and novellas for which she is now more commonly known. Contemporary accounts, including her own, describe her as a flamboyant figure, which made her an easy target in *The Female Wits*.[34] Manley was the author of three tragedies, *The Royal Mischief* (1696), *Almyna; or, The Arabian Vow* (perf. 1706, pub. 1707), written a decade later,

---

34. See for example Jonathan Swift's *Journal to Stella* and Manley's semiautobiographical *Adventures of Rivella* (1714; reprint 1999).

and *Lucius, First Christian King of Britain* (1717) a decade later still.[35] With the exception of *The Royal Mischief* and its connections to *The Female Wits*, these dramas have been largely overlooked. The two tragedies that parallel in time those of Pix and Trotter are, like her fiction, expressly woman-centered, with a strong female character as the central protagonist. Both were Barry-Bracegirdle productions, with Barry playing the strong central character, while in each case Bracegirdle was typecast as the gentle, affecting woman in a supporting role. Yet *The Royal Mischief* and *Almyna* can be called she-tragedy only in their focus on female characters. Pathos and passive suffering have little place in these plays. Instead, as a penciled-in reference to Lee's Roxana in the British Library copy of *The Royal Mischief* suggests, Manley's plays evoke the heroic mode of Restoration tragedy rather than conforming to existing dramatic trends or constituting a new literary departure. Where her contemporary and sometimes friend Mary Pix adopted new trends in drama, Manley looked back to the larger-scale heroics of an earlier generation of drama seen in plays such as Nathaniel Lee's *The Rival Queens*.

The Royal Mischief was Manley's most popular play, achieving a respectable run of six nights with Thomas Betterton's new company and drawing enough attention to be parodied by *The Female Wits*. Although Manley had complained that her first play, a comedy, had failed because audiences were prejudiced against a female writer, her preface to *The Royal Mischief* suggests that the contemporary audience objected more to the "warmth" of the play and its main character and less to the gender of the author.[36] Without question *The Royal Mischief* is deeply sexual, and the main action of the play involves the voracious sexual appetites of the central female character.[37] Manley claims that all drama describes some kind of passion and that she chose to write about "gentle love," as that "which is easiest to our Sex." She continues, somewhat disingenuously that "I did not believe it possible to pursue [love] too far, or that my Lawrel shou'd seem less graceful for having made an entire conquest." Like Wycherley a generation earlier, her comments are directed to the "Ladies," whom she

35. In her will, Manley mentions the manuscript of an additional tragedy, *The Duke of Somerset*, as well as a comedy. Neither play was staged.

36. "The principal Objection made against this Tragedy is the warmth of it, as they are pleas'd to call it" ("To the Reader"). In Lucyle Hook's words, a "miasma of hot surging sex [. . .] hovers over the entire production." Introduction to *The Female Wits*, viii.

37. *The Female Wits* makes a brief reference to the objections to Manley's play in act 1 when Marsilia quotes a passage from her play and Mrs. Wellfed comments, "Won't the Ladies think some of those Expressions indecent?" Marsilia responds, "Sure, Madam, I understand the Ladies better than you. To my knowledge they love words that have warmth, and fire, &c. in them" (4).

faults not for damning her play but for listening to "aspersions of my En-emies." Ironically, it is Wycherley's *Plain Dealer* that she uses as her ex-ample of truly obscene drama:

> I am amaz'd to know the Boxes can be crowded, and the Ladies sit atten-tively, and unconcern'd, at the Widow *Lackitt*, and her Son *Daniel*'s Di-alect, yet pretend to be shock'd at the meaning of blank Verse, for the words can give no offence; the shutting of the Scene I judge Modester (as being done by Creature of the Princess,) than in any terms to have had both the Lovers agree before the Audience, and then retire, as resolving to perform Articles. ("To the Reader")

Manley's claim that her language is clean blank verse that ought not to give offense, especially as nothing sexual is discussed or displayed on-stage is studiously naive. Although it is true, for example, that Homais and her lover do not discuss their tryst, the probable course of events is made clear when Levan carries Homais into her bedchamber and the eu-nuch Acmat shuts the scene on love's "Sacred Mysteries" (22). Manley concludes her defense by observing that in *The Royal Mischief* Homais is punished for her sins, a point Charles Gildon would echo in his defense of *The Royal Mischief* in *The Lives and Characters of the English Dramatick Po-ets*. (After an encomium of Manley's learning and talent, he praises the play for its "Poetick Justice, which ought ever to be observed in all plays.")[38] Manley's final comments not only stress that her audience is fe-male but suggest that it was women who objected to the "warmth" of her play. At the same time, she seeks to establish a sense of community with her female audience by charging her (presumably male) detractors with sexism. When the ladies read her play, she claims, "they'll find the preju-dice against our Sex, and not refuse me the satisfaction of entertaining them, nor themselves the pleasure of Mrs. Barry."

"Pleasure" is certainly an important component of Manley's grandiose drama. In contrast to the traditional portrayal of women as passive ob-jects of the male gaze, Manley creates a play that delineates a woman's active pursuit of her desires. *The Royal Mischief* is a lavish creation, full of extravagant settings and even more extravagant desires, especially those of its lusty heroine, the wicked Homais. Everything in the play centers around Homais and all action is driven by her desires. She has amorous connections with every man in the play, except Acmat, her eunuch and

38. Gildon contrasts Manley's version of Homais's story with its source in Sir John Chardin's travels, observing that in her rendition the story "receiv'd this Advantage, that the Criminals are here punish'd for their Guilt, who in the Story escape." *The Lives and Char-acters*, 91.

confidant. She is married to the old Prince of Libardian; lusts after his nephew Levan, Prince of Colchis; was once beloved by Osman, the chief vizier; and lost her virginity to his cousin Ismael. The other two female characters, Selima, the wife of Osman, and Bassima are conventionally virtuous, but lack Homais's energy. While Bassima, played by Bracegirdle, represents the antithesis of Homais's wanton passion (although trapped in marriage to a man she does not love she remains coldly virtuous), her scenes of chaste dialogue cannot balance the racy progress of Homais's lust.

In a departure from the conventions of she-tragedy, the play begins not with a discussion of Homais (a structure that immediately objectifies the female character), but with Homais and Acmat discussing Homais's life and loves, especially her current desire for the seemingly unattainable Levan. The effect is to establish Homais as a sexual subject, rather than the object of male desire. In the play's opening scene, Acmat recounts Homais's many conquests, reminding her, for example, that "*Ismael* you have enjoy'd / (And sure such Fires did never wait possession)" (2), a rare instance of a female character using the traditionally male terminology of sexual enjoyment, a sexual grammar that demands a subject and an object. Here the object "enjoy'd" and possessed is male, a pattern Homais will continue throughout the play. But Manley's innovation only goes so far. In the moral universe of the play, Homais can be represented as sexual subject because she is wicked. Indeed, her passions, epitomized by her incestuous desire for her husband's nephew, define her character as depraved and socially unacceptable; thus she must be destroyed by the end of the play, a point which both Manley and admirer Charles Gildon emphasize. Nonetheless, our pleasure, as well as that of the play's original audience, lies not in watching a display of female suffering, only faintly realized in the figure of Bassima, but in the vivid enactment of female desire. As Manley comments in her preface, Elizabeth Barry "excell'd and made the part of an ill Woman, not only entertaining, but admirable."

In more abstract terms, the play's actions can be seen as a conflict between male political power and female sexual agency.[39] Homais's husband, the Prince of Libardian, has confined her in his castle, yet she evades Libardian's control and arranges liaisons with Levan, as well as the death of her enemy and former suitor Osman and other egregious acts

---

39. For a brief account of the play's specific political implications, see Ros Ballaster, "The First Female Dramatists," *Women and Literature in Britain, 1500–1700*, ed. Helen Wilcox, 267–90 (1996), 284.

of defiance. Her prime weapons in her attempt to satisfy her desires are her eyes, and *The Royal Mischief* repeatedly asserts the power of the female gaze. As depicted by Manley, the female gaze is distinctly non-Lacanian in affect; rather than the familiar dynamic described by Lacan—and enacted in the drama of the later seventeenth century—in which the gaze establishes an object of desire and in doing so creates desire within the possessor of the gaze, Homais's manipulation of her gaze excites desire within the male object, which ultimately allows the female subject to control the man. Thus the female gaze is potentially dangerous because it can, in the words of Edward Young, "interrupt the Business of the World"[40] and thus disrupt masculine authority. Unlike conventional she-tragedy, in which women are presented as objects of a male gaze, Manley's play reverses the objectification of women through the emphasis on Homais's eyes and their ability to subdue men to her wishes. As the loyal Acmat reminds her:

> ACM. [Y]ou know not half your Power,
>   Those Eyes did never vainly shoot a Dart,
>   Such are their Fires, so sparkling, so attractive,
>   So passionately, soft and tender,
>   So full of that desire they give, as though
>   The Glorious Heaven stood ready for Possession:
>   You never look but to command our love,
>   And give your Lover hope—
>   Then how shou'd you despair.
>
>   (2)

A skillful player of sexual politics, Homais shoots "darts" with her eyes, which both excite male desire and vanquish male power. As even the eunuch Acmat observes, she has but to look "to command our love." The ease with which she manipulates the men in the play, always through her gaze, demonstrates this female power. Levan quickly falls prey to her seductive ways, and even her husband, the old Prince of Libardian, who knows the sins she has committed, succumbs to the power of Homais's eyes. ("Did I once listen to what Passion speaks, / Those lovely Eyes wou'd soon perswade my Heart, / With all your Guilt, to doat upon their Shrine" [38]). For Manley, the female gaze equals power; Homais controls men because they desire her while her passions only makes her stronger.

What we do not see in the play is a connection between Homais's gaze and her own desires, and the implied link between the two is only de-

---

40. Edward Young, dedication to *The Force of* RELIGION.

scribed, not depicted. In a pivotal seduction scene, Acmat presents Levan with a portrait of Homais and follows it with a description of Homais's erotic response to a likeness of Levan. Acmat's description becomes itself a titillating spectacle for Levan's consumption:

> ACM. Sure there's a Sympathy between you, for
>   Thus she bears her, when she sees your Picture,
>   Which drawn at length, almost as Graceful as
>   The Original, is the chief Ornament
>   Of her Apartment, answering
>   Exactly to her waking Curtains.
>   How often have I seen this Lovely *Venus*,
>   Naked, extended, in the gaudy Bed,
>   Her snowy Breasts all panting with desire,
>   With gazing, melting Eyes, survey your Form,
>   And wish in vain, 't had Life to fill her Arms.
>   (17–18)

Although Acmat recounts a rare example in serious drama in which the gaze of a woman does indeed lead to desire, the real outcome of his words is to re-create a male gaze and allow Levan to imagine Homais in her bedchamber. Relayed through the eyes of Acmat, this multilayered fantasy encourages Levan to visualize the naked Homais, with her "snowy Breasts all panting with desire," and through such vicarious pleasures, to effect Homais's seduction of Levan. The image of Homais and the portrait was obviously a compelling one as *The Female Wits* resurrects it,[41] yet it represents Homais's careful manipulation of male appetite rather than an expression of her own desire. Because Homais's passions drive the play, male characters become sexual objects (such as Levan) or figures of impotence (such as her aged husband and eunuchs such as Acmat). Throughout the play, Homais controls and contains the male gaze, allowing herself to become the object of the gaze as a means to an end—the enjoyment of her own desires. The sexual dynamic is under female control, epitomized by the power of Homais's gaze.

At the same time that she reiterates the power of the female gaze, Manley avoids staging the female distress that had become such a crucial component of serious drama in the 1690s. Even though we are told that

41. Betty Useful takes the position of Acmat, this time detailing her mistress's fascination for her stepson's portrait: "her Curtains by me drawn wide, discover your goodly Figure; each Morn the Idol's brought, eagerly she prints the dead Colours, throws her tawny Arms abroad, and vainly hopes kisses so Divine, wou'd inspire the painted Nothing, and mould into Man" (*Female Wits*, 36).

Selima, a secondary female character, has gone mad after her husband was shot out of a cannon (an episode which brought ridicule on the play) and roams the plain, "gathering the smoking Relicks of her Lord" (46), we do not see any instance of this distress. Instead, the audience sees Homais die unrepentant, lamenting the weakness of the men around her,

> O thou too fainly Lover! Cast thou hear him?
> That Coward *Ismael* too, who reapt my formost Joys;
> . . . .
> What an effeminate Troop have I to deal with?
> I'le meet and sink him in the hottest Lake;
> Nay, plunge to keep him down—O! I shall Reign
> A welcome Ghost; the Fiends will hugg my *Royal Mischief.*
> (46)

Even in death she takes on a male role, "reigning" in hell rather than being subject to "effeminate" men such as the "coward" Ismael or her "fainly" lover, Levan. Manley avoids the moral complications that accompany this dissolution of gender lines by making Homais an unrepentantly sinful character. Nonetheless, the dearth of female suffering and the resultant lack of pathos prevents the objectification of women so pervasive in late-seventeenth-century drama.

Although *The Royal Mischief* has achieved a certain notoriety, due in part to *The Female Wits*, Manley's second tragedy, *Almyna; or, The Arabian Vow,* has gone virtually unnoticed.[42] Like *The Royal Mischief*, it includes flamboyant spectacles (such as an elaborate Moorish ceremony in the first act) and heroic scope, as well as the familiar Barry/Bracegirdle pairing.[43] Although the play partakes of the (by now) familiar Near Eastern setting with its harems and exotic pageantry, it stands apart from almost all other drama as a protofeminist diatribe. The concern Manley had expressed in the preface to *The Lost Lover* regarding the unfair treatment of women and particularly of women authors[44] comes to the fore in *Almyna*. The play's central action involves the Sultan Almanzor, who, after finding his empress in bed with a slave, has taken a vow to kill any woman he weds (or

42. Hume mentions *Almyna* briefly in *Development of English Drama* (475–76), but Cynthia Lowenthal and Bridget Orr are perhaps the only scholars to take serious notice of the play. See Lowenthal, *Performing Identities on the Restoration Stage* (2002), and Orr, *Empire on the English Stage, 1660–1714* (2001), 131–34.

43. In fact, *Almyna* was Anne Bracegirdle's last performance; Manley suggests that had Bracegirdle not "quit the House" three days before it was due to be revived after the Christmas recess, the play would have had better fortunes ("Preface").

44. "I am satisfied the bare Name of being a Woman's Play damn'd it beyond its own want of Merit." Preface to *The Lost Lover; or, The Jealous Husband* (1696).

beds) after the wedding night. His justification for these actions, drawn from an overblown misreading of the Koran, is that women are soulless beings, no different from cattle or sheep, on earth solely for the purpose of pleasuring men and perpetuating the species:

> For in conjunction with so weak a Sex,
> Who can produce, or hope, a Noble Specie?
> But since, as Man, our Appetities [*sic*] are keen,
> And by our Wants, we feel that we are Mortal:
> Like the other Souless part of the Creation,
> They'r born, and must for our convenience dye,
> As some for Food, these for a softer use.
>
> (12)

Almyna, daughter of the grand vizier, decides to halt the sultan's barbaric practice and convince him that women do indeed have souls, and much of Manley's play revolves around this version of the debate over the character of women. Claiming that "our great Prophet, has enlarg'd my Soul" and that she feels "Sacred Glowings in [her] Bosom" (28), Almyna resolves to marry the sultan in order to reform his philosophy, mentioning in passing that she both loves and admires him. After its sudden addition, this conventional plot twist is never developed; Manley's focus lies squarely on Almyna's conversion of the sultan rather than on any sort of romantic plot. (A more conventional tragic plot appears in the secondary plot, which depicts Almyna's sister, played by Bracegirdle, and her unrequited love for the sultan's brother.)

Manley's feminist argument comes to the fore in the second half of her play. The fourth act begins with an unusual variation on the discovery scene so common in she-tragedy; here the scene opens to reveal a male rather than a female object, one of a small handful of such scenes found in the drama of the period.[45] Although spectacle in general seems to be the emphasis here rather than female voyeurism, as no woman appears to comment on the scene, nonetheless Manley's staging allows the audience to gaze on the male figure:

> *The Curtain rises, and shews the Emperor a Sleep, upon a Sofa, according to the Custom of the East; a she* Moorish *Slave sitting at the Head of the Sofa, upon the Ground, her Face towards the* Sultan*; by her a large white Wax Flambeaux; another she Slave in the same posture sitting at the Door, with another Flambeaux, the Eunuchs waiting in Ranks like Statues, their Knees and Feet close together, and their Arms hanging strait down; the Emperor rises in disorder.* (39)

45. Another such scene appears in Jane Wiseman's *Antiochus the Great; or, The Fatal Relapse* (perf. 1701, pub. 1702) in which Ormades is discovered "*Lying on a Couch*" (23).

The sultan's confusion arises from a dream in which he was confronted with the ghosts of the queens he has murdered and where he cannot enter the promised land because he is "charg'd with the Blood of Innocents" (39). At this point Almyna enters, and having overpowered the sultan with her eyes ("All-seeing, all-commanding; how they pierce me," he exclaims [4:42]), proceeds to overwhelm him with her rhetoric. She begins by observing that women are god's fairest creation and thus must be his "most perfect Creatures." Moreover, because women suffer the same pain when giving birth to a girl as to a boy, and because women die in the same ways as men, they cannot be said to be different from men. She completes her argument by providing a list of noble women: Semiramis, Judith, Virginia, Lucretia, Portia, Clelia, Cleopatra. Placed against the backdrop of Manley's frequently expressed anxiety concerning gender discrimination, Almyna's arguments must be read as directed to a larger audience than the sultan. Just as the sultan succumbs to Almyna's superior reasoning, so too should the men in Manley's audience.

Despite *Almyna*'s heathen setting, Christian imagery and ideology is woven throughout *Almyna*, nowhere more conspicuously than in Manley's representation of her heroine. One of the play's most unusual features is Manley's presentation of Almyna as a female Christ figure, sacrificing herself to save the women who follow her. This motif appears repeatedly throughout the final two acts of the play, as when Almyna tells the sultan that her death will save his soul:

> Yet cou'd I gain but this, to fall the last
> That with my Life, thy cruel Vow might end,
> To save thy precious Soul, so near to ruin,
> And in my Blood, to wash the stains away.
>
> (47)

Like Christ, her blood will redeem him, despite his sins, so that he can enter the promised land from which he is currently barred. Almyna's vision of salvation extends beyond the sultan as she plots to save a future generation of women, exclaiming to her father, "Am I not Ransom for so many Lives? / Was I not born to an exalted End?" (61). In the end, Almyna's blood is not spilled; her faith in female virtue and her courage in the face of death are all that is necessary to convert the sultan. He tests her by staging a mock execution to see if her courage will hold (a ploy that also allowed Manley to design another grand spectacle involving an array of mutes). Almyna remains resolute, and the sultan, entranced by this demonstration of virtue, declares that women have souls, "as divine as wee" (64). After this declaration, the play ends quickly, with Almyna's triumph damped only slightly by the sudden entrance and death of her sister Zoradia and the sultan's brother.

Although *Almyna* is at times more lecture than drama, it represents a fascinating contribution to the ongoing argument for women's moral equality, only slightly veiled by its Moorish setting. This moral equality appears most vividly in Manley's depiction of Almyna as a Christ figure, a tactic that allows Almyna to literally embody the thesis she articulates. With its religious symbolism, *Almyna* represents an unusually feminist vision of Christianity. Ultimately, the play's exotic setting furnishes most of its visual spectacle, for, as with *The Royal Mischief, Almyna* provides the audience with little in the way of female distress. Almyna, a virtuous version of the powerful Homais, prevails over the men around her, including her father and the sultan, the play's two representatives of patriarchal power.

It would be another ten years before Manley wrote her final tragedy. In the meantime, her literary energies were directed toward fiction and political journalism. *Lucius, First Christian King of Britain* (1717) represents a marked divergence from her two earlier tragedies in its avoidance of exoticism and its decorous depiction of noble lovers.[46] Perhaps the most notable change appears in Manley's portrayal of the play's main female character, the virtuous Rosalinda, a conventionally pure heroine who lacks the active energies of Homais and Almyna. Startlingly helpless, Rosalinda's main accomplishment is being the means by which Christianity is brought to Britain. In this she remains largely passive as Lucius falls in love with her and converts out of love; Rosalinda has no need to do anything to effect his conversion. The play's most interesting feature is its political stance, what Melinda A. Rabb describes as a "Tory fantasy" about "true royal bloodlines."[47]

Although Manley's feminist posture eases by the end of her play-writing career, largely, one suspects, because of the changed climate in theater as a whole in the decade that spans the appearance of *The Royal Mischief* in 1696 and *Almyna* in 1706, her often confrontational stance remains unchanged. Although the preface to *Almyna* does not blame the play's lack of success on a sexist audience (as did the preface to *The Lost Lover* and,

---

46. Despite the support of Richard Steele, *Lucius* was not a success, managing a run of only three nights in May 1717, with a single later benefit night for Manley in April 1720.

47. See Rabb's headnote to the play in *The Broadview Anthology of Restoration and Early Eighteenth-Century Drama*, gen. ed. J. Douglas Canfield (2001), 75. I disagree, however, with Rabb's claim that Manley's use of a female character to promote Christianity is unusual. Female characters as proponents of and even martyrs to Christianity were commonplace by the time the play was staged in 1717.

by implication, the preface to *The Royal Mischief*), the play itself, with its feminist polemics, enacts the argument for the equality of women that Manley had presented in her earliest prefaces and poems. Spectacle in her plays does not rely on the suffering of a helpless woman. Instead, her heroines, one good and one evil, not only control their own lives and desires but those of the men around them. Inviting both men and women to participate in voyeurism, Manley delineates her heroines as sexual subjects rather than the objects they represent in conventional she-tragedy.

Viewed as a group, Pix, Trotter, and Manley provide a remarkable example of the diversity of women's writing, employing distinctly different styles and creating dramas that share little in terms of style or content. Mary Pix writes dramas that incorporate female distress and depend on sexual spectacle for their emotional power. Her heroines, particularly in the earlier tragedies written when she-tragedy was at its most sensational, become sexual spectacles presented to an audience's fascinated gaze. Catharine Trotter ignores the voyeurism on which she-tragedy is based, constructing plays that downplay female distress in favor of debates over virtue or the power of friendship. Like Trotter, Delarivier Manley provides little in the way of female distress for her audience, but her two tragedies are full of exotic spectacle and powerful women who control rather than are controlled by the male gaze. If we are searching for a distinctive *écriture féminin,* it is not here.

What sets these three writers apart from their male contemporaries most strongly, however, is their awareness of being women writing in a largely male profession. Each writer confronts this issue in a different way. Pix, the figure who adapted most completely to the literary modes popular at the time, addresses the fact of her sex directly in her prologues and in the dedicatory poems she wrote for her fellow playwrights rather than in her dramas. Catharine Trotter carefully controls demonstrations of sexuality in both her writing and her life itself. Aware of the implications any hint of impropriety could have for herself[48] and for the female characters within her plays, she maintained a stance of rigid chastity for herself and for her characters, something Manley would later mock as her "air of *Virtue pretended.*"[49] Femaleness for Trotter, it seems, required careful self-presentation, otherwise a woman's audience, both male and fe-

---

48. Pix seems to have escaped such rumors, probably because of her much ridiculed obesity. Manley, however, did not, and *The Female Wits* makes several suggestions regarding her less than stellar virtue.

49. *The New Atalantis,* 160.

male, could and would willfully misunderstand her. Manley deals with the issue most directly of all, asserting the fact of her sex and accusing those who opposed her of gender discrimination. The central women in her dramas manifest the same defiant attitude. Unlike Trotter, Manley is less concerned with the evaluation of her character than the potential for a biased assessment of her talent, and she, more than the other two women, constructs an identity for herself and her characters which is conspicuously female.

With their acute awareness of the fact of being female, it is perhaps not surprising that the other trait that the three women share is the vividness and importance of their female characters. Even in an age dominated by female-centered plays, the plays of Pix, Trotter, and Manley stand out. Although their heroines behave in radically different manners, suffering passively, as in the case of Pix's Morena, rather than controlling their passions, as in Trotter's works, or, as in Manley's, controlling the men around them, they are, without question, the focal points of the dramas. More important, each playwright elevates her heroines in a manner unusual in the drama of her male contemporaries: Pix with her ravished but unblemished maidens, Trotter with a series of dignified and patriotic women, and perhaps most notably in Manley's depiction of a female Christ figure. Whether writing she-tragedy or not, these female playwrights do treat "of Heroiens and of sacred things."[50] It is this conviction, that heroines are indeed "sacred things," that finally connects the women playwrights of the early eighteenth century.

50. Pix, prologue to *The Double Distress.*

CHAPTER 5

Nicholas Rowe and the Second Generation of She-Tragedy

Forgive me—but forgive me!

—Jane Shore

Of course, drama did not change suddenly in 1700. She-tragedies were still written, and the spectacle of female suffering continued to dominate the English stage. This continuity with the drama of the late seventeenth century is sometimes overshadowed by the enormous convenience of using the century as scholarly milestone; many studies of drama during this period end abruptly in 1700 and sometimes, as in Derek Hughes's influential book, use that end date to create a sense of closure.[1] Thus, simple chronology is transmuted into literary model. In reality, serious drama in the earliest decades of the eighteenth century was not radically different from that of the late seventeenth century. The first fifteen years of the new century were to produce some of the age's most popular she-tragedies in Rowe's *Fair Penitent* (1703) and *Jane Shore* (1714) and Ambrose Philips's *The Distrest Mother* (1712). The majority of new dramas were still female centered, and revivals of earlier she-tragedies were common. Even a play such as Rowe's *Tamerlane* (1701), with its masculine title and deliberate flattery of William III, relies heavily on the well-established she-tragedy formula for its plot and emotional effect.

Nonetheless, changes were to come in the new century. Although Collier and his followers may have had little actual influence on the content

---

1. Despite the title of his landmark survey, *The Development of English Drama in the Late Seventeenth Century*, Robert D. Hume avoids such a neat conclusion and pushes his analysis well into the first decades of the eighteenth century.

of drama, the antitheatrical movement and its emphasis on morality was indicative of general public sentiment in favor of reform. Popular support for the reform movement was evident in the growth of groups such as the Society for the Reformation of Manners as well as in specific attempts to reform the stage itself.[2] (Maximillian E. Novak notes that promptbooks during these years "reveal the degree to which plays were rewritten to suit the new moral atmosphere.")[3] Politically, this new social dynamic was linked with the growth of a pro-Whig mercantile class that defined itself as pious and ethical, in contrast to what its members saw as the moral bankruptcy of the Restoration court. Even more than the tragedies of the 1690s, the she-tragedies of the new century appealed strongly to the mores of this audience. Whig writers such as Addison and Steele linked domestic virtues to national virtue, a dynamic that played itself out in Nicholas Rowe's tragedies of shattered domesticity and Ambrose Philips's paean to maternity, *The Distrest Mother,* "so often and so highly Applauded by the Ingenious Spectator" as one (Tory) critic wrote ironically. The symbolism of female domesticity intensified with the accession of Queen Anne in 1702. England's new monarch was a strong supporter of moral reform, and Anne took pride in presenting herself to her subjects as a healing, maternal presence, despite the futility of her attempts to produce an heir to the throne. The text chosen for her coronation emphasized the role she wished to assume in her reign: "kings shall be thy nursing Fathers, and queens thy nursing Mothers" (Isaiah, 49:23). After her death, an early biographer memorialized this quality, recording that the English people "ever looked upon her as their common Parent."[4] Although Anne herself displayed little interest in drama and did not attend the theater, as the nation's most prominent woman, the influence of her public image was powerful. Not surprisingly, the more idealized heroines of early-eighteenth-century drama, such as Andromache in *The Distrest Mother,* display domestic and maternal qualities similar to those the queen took care to convey.

In keeping with the conventions established in the 1680s and 1690s, fe-

2. Even Poet Laureate Nahum Tate submitted a proposal recommending "for the Regulating of the Stage & and Stage-Plays" (Lambeth Misc. 933, Art. 57). His letter emphasizes the necessity for reformation of the stage and suggests that the government appoint "supervisors" who would approve all plays, both old and new, which were to appear on the stage.

3. Maximillian E. Novak, "Libertinism and Sexuality," in *A Companion to Restoration Drama,* ed. Susan J. Owen (2001), 66.

4. Abel Boyer, *The History of the Life and Reign of Queen Anne* (1722), 688. For an account of the role Anne sought to assume see Edward Gregg, *Queen Anne* (1980), esp. chap. 5, "The Role of the Monarch."

male suffering and the display of such suffering remained central to the drama of the first two decades of the new century. What did change was the representation of—and response to—female sexuality. Even while female suffering continued to define tragedy, the representation of female sexuality was muted. At the same time, critics defined the plays and their heroines in terms of the actions the heroines take in controlling their own sexual behavior, however small or seemingly innocuous these actions may be. The change is notable in comparison to the tragedies on the 1690s. Recently, Derek Hughes has criticized the tragedies of the 1690s for their lack of subtlety, noting that in contrast to the comedies of the same period, plays such as *The Fatal Marriage* "are formulated with a stark and polarized symmetry" that provides the characters with little in the way of moral choice.[5] With a certain sense of frustration, he concludes his discussion of Restoration tragedy by looking ahead to Ibsen. (Similarly, writing of eighteenth-century tragedy in general, the authors of the *Revels History of Drama in English, 1660–1750* find tragedy "deteriorating" rapidly during the first half of the eighteenth century with the exception of a handful of new plays. They conclude that after the Licensing Act in 1737, "there was nothing to do but stand around and wait for Ibsen.")[6] Hughes's observation is accurate, although his condemnation of the serious drama of the 1690s is harsh and to some extent overlooks the object of these tragedies. Where comedies of the 1690s do indeed focus on characters faced with difficult choices, notably women making difficult choices regarding their sexuality (often involving the conflict between their own desires and social mores), the tragedy of this period is filled with women who have no choices. The illusion of control is absent in these plays. What the tragedies represent, although the comedies do not, are heroines who, inadvertently, overstep the lines of acceptable behavior.[7]

The manner in which heroines step over this line becomes increasingly vexed in the eighteenth century, so that ultimately women cannot violate the codes of chaste behavior and still be considered heroines. One of the most hotly contested developments in serious drama during the first decades of the century was the growing interest in female agency and its

5. Derek Hughes, *English Drama, 1660–1700* (1996), 457.
6. John Loftis, Richard Southern, Marion Jones, and A. H. Scouten, *The Revels History of Drama in English*, vol. 5, *1660–1750* (1976), 285, 287.
7. Characters such as Vanbrugh's Lady Brute in *The Provok'd Wife* and Amanda in *The Relapse* or Southerne's Mrs. Friendall in *The Wives' Excuse* are all trapped in problematic marriages and struggle with the question of whether to commit adultery. They don't, but such questions were enough to make plays such as *The Provok'd Wife* controversial to succeeding generations.

tragic potential. As early as 1701, Charles Gildon spends much of the preface to his tragedy *Love's Victim; or, The Queen of Wales* defending the play's tragic outcome, specifically the death of the heroine Guinoenda; on the one hand, he argues that the play represents the sins of the father being visited on the child, but in addition, he claims that he deliberately created a flaw in his virtuous heroine: "I at the end of the Third Act, took care to let her Love transport her to the Refuge of a Falshood; and that impos'd on Religion, which to make use of on any Account, in that manner may be sufficient Offence, to Justifie her Punishment."[8] While allowing for the vagaries of fate, Gildon also emphasizes the agency of his character; Guinoenda knowingly lied about religious ritual, and it is her conscious performance of this act that comprises her guilt. These issues are relatively minor events in the actual play; only one brief mention in the first act is made of the fact that Guinoenda's "guilty Father's Punishment" might extend to her, and the falsehood that Gildon stresses consists of nothing more than the pretense that her religion requires mourners of shipwreck victims to pay their respects at sea. Nonetheless, Gildon obviously saw the need to defend his play in these terms. The heroine's active volition becomes the rationale for her suffering.

If Gildon felt the need to define his play in terms of his heroine's moral agency, this topic soon dominated critical discussions of serious drama.[9] The easiest way to attack a play's merits seems to have been by censuring the conscious behavior of its heroine. During the first fifteen years of the new century, heroines of serious drama were subjected to a different kind of scrutiny than that given their predecessors. In particular, debates over drama focus on the sexual agency of a play's central female character: to what extent is she culpable for any stain on her honor? In one striking case, an anonymous reviewer takes Ambrose Philips as well as *The Spectator* to task for the chaste behavior of Andromache in Philips's popular *Distrest Mother* (1712). While the grounds for the attack are almost certainly political as the objects were all visible Whigs, Andromache's character becomes the vehicle the author uses to focus his attack. The fact that her sexual honor is never tainted does not signify to the author; instead he concentrates on her attempt to control her sexuality. Assailing Andromache's decision to marry Pyrrhus and then kill herself in order to remain true to her deceased husband Hector, the author claims such a maneuver is immoral and even anti-English:

---

8. Gildon, preface to *Love's Victim; or, The Queen of Wales* (1701).
9. And heroines of comedies, as the responses to Lady Brute suggest.

> All fair and honest Contracts ought to be made in a plain and genuine Sense, equally understood by both Parties; Otherwise 'tis all Trick and Deceit: So that *Andromache*'s engaging to enter into Marriage Bonds with *Pyrrhus;* who undoubtedly expected Marriage Possession too, with a mental Reservation to her self, on her side, of performing only the bare Publick Ceremony, was one of the vilest and most despicable Frauds and Delusions. . . .
>
> Nay, to carry on this Sham Marriage (for such she intends it, a Marriage so like one of our Stage Weddings, that lasts no longer than till the Curtain falls) in a little farther Display of the Merits of her Cause. As after the publick and solemn Seal of Wedlock made by the Priest (whether Christian or Heathen it matters not) the Wife ceases to be *sui juris,* is no more Mistress of her self, the Right and Title to her Person being wholly invested in the Husband; *Andromache*'s intended Tragick Sacrifice of her self to a dead Husband, whose Title to her is wholly expired, in so manifest a wrong to her living Husband's Rightful Claim, is no less than the most flagitious of Robberies.[10]

Having gone through a marriage ceremony, Andromache does not fulfill her share of the "Contract" by giving up the "Right and Title" to her own person as required by English law in which a wife is not sui juris, that is, not capable of managing her own matters. The author's objections center around Andromache's decision to marry and then to kill herself before the marriage can be consummated. In his eyes, even this self-negating example of a woman's attempt to protect her son constitutes a significant social disrupture; maternity ultimately represents a criminal threat to the social and sexual status quo. Using pseudo-Lockean logic, the author demonstrates that Andromache's behavior cannot be defended in terms such as those Locke used to support the Revolution of 1688—or Lady Brute her contemplated adultery; Andromache's planned marriage/suicide does not constitute a "fair and honest Contract." Underlying the mocking of Whig ideology is the author's concern that Andromache's Jesuitical "mental Reservation" undercuts male authority, not simply in the play, but within the larger context of English law. Only then can her decision to maintain a negative sense of autonomy through suicide be seen as the "vil*est*" of frauds and robberies. Denying the husband's "Right and Title" is equivalent to robbery, a crime against property, against society, and implicitly against the integrity of the state.

This passage, with its attempt to bring art into line with the English legal system, asserts the connection spectators and increasingly readers

---

10. *A Modest Survey of that Celebrated Tragedy The Distrest Mother, so often and so highly Applauded by the Ingenious Spectator* (1712), 12–13.

made between artistic representations of a heroine's actions and contemporary society. In his emphasis on the specific illegalities of Andromache's mental reservation, the author locates the issue of female control firmly within current legislation. Even a play such as *The Distrest Mother,* which depends very little on the display of its heroine as a sexual spectacle, can thus be judged in terms of her sexual agency. The result of deliberately identifying the stage with the audience appears in the often explicit lesson attributed to actions, both within the play and on the part of the spectators viewing it. If a heroine's fate can be seen as the result of her conscious actions, then the play itself becomes a moral lesson in a way in which plays such as *The Orphan* or *The Fatal Marriage,* with their innocent but tainted heroines, were not. Increasingly, this new generation of she-tragedies was seen as directed to the female members of the theater audience, a perception perhaps most strongly attached to the works of Nicholas Rowe, whose two great she-tragedies were among the most popular plays of the eighteenth century. In the works of Rowe and his contemporaries, sensation becomes less an end in itself (something which can be said of many of the plays of the late 1690s), and instead pathos becomes the means to an end of moral edification where tableaux of suffering are composed specifically with the goal of uplifting the audience through the process of sympathy or of opening its eyes to the wages of sin.

Chaste Heroines and Chaster Plotting

On the most obvious level, the serious drama of the early eighteenth century is noticeably less lurid than that of the 1690s, especially the final years of the century when she-tragedies proliferated and seemingly every new drama trotted out scenes of incest, rape, murder, and madness. Such changes clearly parallel the increased moral delicacy of early- eighteenth-century comedy, a development widely noted in scholarship on the drama[11] and frequently linked to the attack on the immodesty of the stage launched by Collier in 1698. Although Collier and his followers rarely leveled their attacks on serious drama, playwrights often refer to a reformation of the stage in the prefaces and prologues of their tragedies. As much of the serious drama suggests, in the early eighteenth century playwrights were already engaging in a form of self-cen-

11. See for example Hume, *Development of English Drama,* especially chap. 10, "The Emergence of Augustan Drama, 1697–1710."

sorship, perhaps aware that the sensationalism of previous decades was no longer marketable.

Attempts were even made to purify the playhouses themselves. In 1704, Queen Anne issued an edict prohibiting vizard masks from the theaters. The decree, which also prohibited "person[s] of quality" from going behind the scenes or sitting on the stage specified "that no woman be allowed or presume to wear a vizard mask in either of the Theatres; and that no persons come into either House without paying the price established for their respective places."[12] Clearly directed at the prostitutes who wore masks as the mark of their profession and often sat in the middle gallery looking for trade, the act was apparently hissed when first read in the theaters.[13] But as a prologue notes one year later, as least the portion of the edict directed at "ugly Masks" was adopted fairly readily; "Thanks to good Orders, now that Sport is over."[14] The decorum produced by the absence of these signifiers of prostitution only went so far, and despite such efforts to reform the theaters, they retained their reputation as sites of sexual liaisons.[15] Thus, in *Fantomina* (1725), Eliza Haywood uses a playhouse as the scene of her eponymous heroine's first encounter with the amorous Beauplaisir; in the scene that initiates Fantomina's series of sexual escapades, she dresses and acts like a courtesan—but does not wear a mask.

In serious drama, this increased propriety most often takes the form of deemphasis on overt sexuality, especially that of the plays' female characters. One result of this new restraint is that the chastity of heroines in the plays of the new century more often survives immaculate. Female sexuality remains a contested site, but, when playwrights introduce pathos, they are less likely to accompany it with explicitly sexualized tableaux.

Although, like their predecessors, heroines are still the objects of villainous attacks, they are more like to emerge with their virtue intact. Rape continues to be a popular device and a titillating spectacle, but in these plays the titillation is more likely to stop short, with the virtuous heroine

12. Published in *The Daily Courant*, 24 January 1704.

13. In one antitheatrical pamphlet, Collier reports that the queen's edict, "the Solemn, the Pious Order was read, and both Order, and Actor who read it, hiss'd off the *Stage*." *Mr. Collier's Dissuasive from the Play-House; in a Letter to a Person of Quality, Occasion'd by the late Calamity of the Tempest. To which is added, a Letter written by another Hand; in Answer to some Queries sent by a Person of Quality, Relating to the Irregularities charged upon the Stage* (1704), 21.

14. Prologue to Peter Motteaux, *Farewel Folly* (1705), cited in Leo Hughes, *The Drama's Patrons: A Study of the Eighteenth-Century London Audience* (1971), 166.

15. As Leo Hughes observes, although "Queen Anne was ruling against vizard masks in the original and literal sense . . . masks in the literal sense were all that disappeared from the theater." *The Drama's Patrons*, 166.

saved from her lustful pursuer in the nick of time. With their honor un-sullied, heroines more frequently live to see the end of the play; one re-sult of the refiguring of drama as moral lesson is that an increasing number of tragedies end with virtuous characters rewarded, what Dry-den had described years earlier as "that inferior sort of Tragedies, which end with a prosperous event."[16] Virtuous females may suffer, but if they preserve their chastity, they become exemplary figures, models for the fe-male spectator. This vision of drama as morally illustrative would influ-ence the representation of women in drama, and, ultimately, the form of tragedy in the eighteenth century. In the ideology of early-eighteenth-century she-tragedy, women's tragedies may be sexual, but their triumphs are emphatically chaste.

As sensationalism in drama decreases, the number of new she-tragedies written during the early eighteenth century declines. Success-ful earlier plays, such as *The Orphan* and *The Fatal Marriage* continued to be staged regularly, but new she-tragedies became less and less frequent. Ultimately, critics would look back at the first generation of she-tragedies and find them too often indecent and obscene. They base these judgments on specific examples of impropriety, most often expressions of desire voiced by the heroines. Otway comes in for the most conflicted responses, as critics praise him for writing "more immediately to the heart" than ei-ther his predecessors or his contemporaries, but also find that he is "in many instances indecent, and deficient of moral tendency,"[17] a failing at-tributable to the "licentiousness of the age he wrote in."[18] Most of the comments regarding Otway's "indecency" arise regarding *The Orphan* (by 1718, Gildon could comment that the notorious "Nicky Nacky" scenes in *Venice Preserv'd* "have been left out for many Years").[19] In *The Orphan*, the page's banter with Monimia (1.1.202–79) is singled out for censure, as is Monimia's description of how the supposed Castalio left the marriage bed. This last "conveys no very modest Idea, and such as should not have received utterance from one of her imagined delicacy."[20] In gen-

16. John Dryden, "The Grounds of Criticism in Tragedy" prefixed to his adaptation of *Troilus and Cressida* (1679), in *The Works of John Dryden*, ed. Maximillian E. Novak and George R. Guffey (1984), 13:233. Not surprisingly, in his adaptation, Dryden changes Shakespeare's ending so that the play concludes with more fatalities and thus a "superior" ending.

17. William Hawkins, *Miscellanies in Prose and Verse. Containing Candid and Impartial Ob-servations on the Principal Performers belonging to the Two Theatres-Royal; From January 1773, to May 1775. Likewise Strictures on two favourite Tragedies, viz. The ORPHAN and the FAIR PENI-TENT. Being part of an epistolary Correspondence on those Subjects with a young Lady. With Many other agreeable and interesting Articles, such as Pastoral Songs, Epitaphs, &c. &c.* (1775), 79.

18. Ibid., 80.

19. Charles Gildon, *The Complete Art of Poetry* (1718), 1:237.

20. *The Theatrical Review; or, New Companion to the Play-House: Containing A Critical and*

eral, references to Monimia's bedchamber in words or action are seen as indelicate—a reviewer complains that when Monimia sees Castalio, she retires to her chamber, "for what? Decency denies an answer!"[21] The passages each writer cites are objectionable not simply because of their incorporation of language a newly proper generation found offensive but also because almost every one refers either directly or indirectly to the sexual desire or desirability of the play's main female character.

The movement away from sensationalism and blatantly erotic spectacles began within the first decade of the century in the aftermath of Collier's attacks on the theater. Playwrights quickly discarded their most lurid plots although suggestive and even overtly indecent elements did not vanish completely. In this movement, John Dennis's *Iphigenia* (1700) can be seen as a liminal play. In his third play, Dennis flirts with sensation, in this case brother-sister incest, but ultimately pulls back, resolving the impending disaster without bloodshed or sexual misadventure. Unlike Abel Boyer and Charles Johnson, who also produced versions of Racine's *Iphigenie*,[22] Dennis uses as his general source Euripides' *Iphigenia in Tauris*, in which Orestes, after being pursued by the Furies, encounters his sister Iphigenia. Dennis makes several major alterations to the plot of Euripides' play, some to convey his attack on Catholicism, others to exploit the more lurid possibilities of the classical story. In his version, Orestes is captured and, because he refuses to marry the Scythian queen, condemned to death under the "fatal Image" of Diana. Having become a priestess of Diana, Iphigenia is expected to perform the sacrifice. In the play's opening acts, however, Orestes and Iphigenia have fallen in love and, in the style of 1690s drama, hope to consummate their passion. But before Orestes can marry Iphigenia or be put to the knife, all is revealed and the "tragedy" ends happily, with Orestes switching his affections to the Scythian queen and Iphigenia in turn marrying Orestes' friend. The play thus moves abruptly from overt titillation to strict sexual propriety, a shift that audiences found implausible. As Dennis's preface

---

Historical Account of every Tragedy, Comedy, Opera, Farce, &c. exhibited at the Theatres during the last Season; With Remarks on the Actors who performed the principal Characters. The Whole interspersed with occasional Reflections on Dramatic Poetry in general; the Characters of the best English Dramatic Authors; and Observations on the Conduct of Managers. Calculated for the Entertainment and Instruction of every Lover of Theatrical Amusements. By a Society of Gentlement Independent of Managerial Influence (1772), 1:75.

21. Ibid., 1:76.

22. Boyer's translation, *Achilles; or, Iphigenia in Aulis* (perf. 1699, pub. 1700) competed directly with Dennis's play. Johnson's version, *The Victim* (1714) appeared significantly later and was more successful than either Boyer's or Dennis's. Boyer's play was revised and republished in 1714 with the title *The Victim; or, Achilles and Iphigenia in Aulis*, presumably to cash in on the success of Johnson's play.

indicates, the incongruity struck viewers of the play, and he admits "persons of extraordinary merit" objected to the play's final scene because "*Orestes* upon discovering *Iphigenia* to be his Sister shews too much joy for a Lover."[23]

The reconfiguration of female-centered drama suggested by Dennis's *Iphigenia* can also be seen in the differences between two treatments of what could be described as the imperiled maiden-in-the-harem plot. The first, Mary Pix's *Ibrahim* (1698) was one of the few tragedies of 1698 to be revived, earning high praise from Gildon. The second treatment of the topic, Joseph Trapp's *Abra-Mule; or, Love and Empire* (1704), was even more successful, with a run of fifteen performances when first staged in spring 1704 and numerous revivals throughout the first half of the century.[24] In January 1704, the two plays even appeared at rival theaters, with Drury Lane mounting *Ibrahim* and Lincoln's Inn Fields presenting *Abra-Mule* as its harem play. Trapp's new model of she-tragedy seems to have won this contest; *The London Stage* notes only one additional revival of *Ibrahim* after 1704. The central action in each play is strikingly similar. In each, a beautiful and virtuous maiden loves an equally virtuous and valiant hero. Their love is thwarted when a lustful sultan spies the maiden and instantly desires her. When the heroine refuses the sultan, she is threatened with rape and taken to the harem. Eventually, the tyrannous behavior of the sultan results in his downfall. In *Abra-Mule,* as in *Ibrahim,* the sultan Mahomet even selects Abra-Mule out of a lineup of beauties, although the scene is much more understated than Pix's exotic ceremony of the handkerchief.

Despite such affinities, the plays differ noticeably. Trapp's version of the harem story is significantly chaster in tone and in action. Unlike Pix's Morena, Abra-Mule is never actually raped, and although threatened, there is no real attempt on her virtue. When she first refuses the sultan, he purposely refrains from force, telling her, "Droop not, fair Excellence; your Chastity / Shall not be violated—Holy Rites / Shall make us one and justifie our Pleasures" (40). It is only when he finds her bidding farewell to her lover Pyrrhus that his rage erupts; he sends the lover to the rack and Abra-Mule to the harem, but these grim fates are revoked by the sultan's brother who deposes the sultan. The play's conclusion, like the events throughout the play, is also significantly less lurid. Even though Abra-Mule believes Pyrrhus dead, she refuses to lament her woes,

---

23. John Dennis, preface to *Iphigenia* (1700).

24. *The London Stage* records that *Abra-Mule* was revived in 1710, 1711, 1721, 1722, 1723, 1726, 1735, 1736, 1741, and, for the last time, in 1744.

choosing instead a more stoic response: "Can I think on this, and be content / With Tears and vain Complainings?—Those indeed / Serve to relax less Miseries" (60). Later, her suicide attempt misses its mark and the lovers are reunited. With the exception of two minor characters, no one dies in this tragedy. Even Mahomet survives: "Is not the loss of Empire / Sufficient Punishment?" asks his successor. Trapp avoids conventional scenes of pathos, let alone the spectacle of *Ibrahim*'s gory rape. The result is a play in which sensation plays a minor role and where the central female character, although still passive and subject to the capricious desires of most of the male characters, retains her sexual virtue intact.

A more active display of feminine virtue appears in Ambrose Philips's *The Distrest Mother*, the play so vigorously attacked for its heroine's attempts to control her sexuality. Like Boyer's *Achilles* and Johnson's *The Victim*, *The Distrest Mother* is an adaptation of Racine, this time *Andromaque* (1667). *Andromaque* had already been adapted for the stage in 1675 by John Crowne but made little mark on the London stage.[25] Philips's version of the story of the noble widow and mother, however, was one of the most successful new tragedies, rivaling only Addison's *Cato* and the plays of Rowe in the number of performances staged during the eighteenth century. Despite occasional criticisms, such as that cited earlier, the play was immediately popular, and it was frequently cited in *The Spectator*, with both Addison and Steele writing essays in praise of the play (Steele praised the play extensively even before it premiered). *The Spectator* later returned to the play in two later numbers, one in which Addison describes a visit to the theater with Sir Roger de Coverley, and Steele, writing under the pseudonym "Physibulus," praises the "exalted" emotions generated by Philips's play, emotions "which all generous minds conceive at the sight of virtue in distress" while deploring the ensuing comic epilogue that spoils the purity of these sensations.[26]

The nature of the virtue displayed in *The Distrest Mother* as well as the nature of its heroine's distress is central to *The Spectator*'s approbation. In the first and most comprehensive discussion of the play (No. 290, 1 Feb-

25. Crowne's version was originally acted in the Long Vacation and was obviously less than successful; he remarks, it "deserved a better liking then [*sic*] it found." As Crowne notes in his "Epistle to the Reader," the play was originally translated "by a young Gentleman, who has a great esteem of all *French* plays, and particularly of this," an esteem Crowne himself apparently did not share. He "found neither the Play to answer the Gentleman's Commendation, nor his *Genius* in Verse very fortunate." Crowne did not have time (or, one suspects, the interest) to correct the versification, so he rewrote portions of the play in prose. Claiming, "if the Play be barren of Fancy, you must blame the Original Author," Crowne attempts to distance himself from the final result and from French drama in general.

26. *Spectator*, nos. 335 and 338, Tuesday, 25 March 1712, and Friday, 28 March 1712.

ruary 1 1712), Steele applauds the play's high sentiments and ability to move. He then turns from these conventional topics to the subject of Andromache's particular moral excellences, defining in the process his ideal representation of female virtue:

> We have seldom had any female distress on the stage, which did not, upon cool examination, appear to flow from the weakness rather than the misfortune of the person represented: but in this tragedy you are not entertained with the ungoverned passions of such as are enamoured of each other merely as they are men and women, but their regards are founded upon high conceptions of each other's virtue and merit; and the character which gives name to the play, is one who has behaved herself with heroic virtue in the most important circumstances of a female life, those of a wife, a widow, and a mother. If there be those whose mind have been too attentive upon the affairs of life, to have any notion of the passion of love in such extremes as are known only to particular tempers, yet in the above-mentioned considerations, the sorrow of the heroine will move even the generality of mankind.[27]

Not surprisingly in the age of she-tragedy, Steele's comments focus specifically on "female distress"; however, in his distinction between "weakness" and "misfortune" as the source of this distress, he draws a line between the older, more sensational form of the genre, where heroines suffered for sins, and what he sees as a newer, more morally appropriate mode. Philips's Andromache grieves, but she has done nothing of which she must repent. Steele's comments sound like a rejection of previous modes of she-tragedy, which frequently represented the "ungoverned passions" of its heroines. The implicit reference may be especially directed toward Rowe's *The Fair Penitent,* in which the heroine, in an unguarded moment (literally), gives into her desire for Lothario. By contrast, in *The Distrest Mother* there is no sexual sin, and Steele praises the play's downplaying of sexual desire. By denigrating plays in which the characters are "such as are enamoured of each other merely as they are men and women," Steele seemingly calls for the absence of such desire, finding it a less worthy subject for drama. What tragedy should represent, he suggests, is what he sees in Andromache, love based on more abstract and less physical concepts of merit.

Crucial to Steele's praise of *The Distrest Mother* is his concern that Andromache should be an appropriate role model for English womanhood. He states emphatically,

---

27. *Spectator,* no. 290, Friday, 1 Febuary 1712.

Domestic virtues concern all the world, and there is no one living who is not interested that Andromache should be an imitable figure. The generous affection to the memory of her dead husband, that tender care for her son, which is ever heightened with the consideration of his father, and these regards preserved in spite of being tempted with the possession of the highest greatness, are what cannot but be venerable even to such an audience as at present frequents the English theatre . . . to make a character truly great, this author understands that it should have its foundation in superior thoughts and maxims of conduct. It is very certain, that many an honest woman would make no difficulty, though she had been the wife of Hector, for the sake of a kingdom to marry the enemy of her husband's family and country; and indeed who can deny but she might be still an honest woman, but no heroine?

Everyone, Steele claims, has a stake in Andromache's status as a figure who can *and should* be imitated by women spectators. Her aptness as "imitable figure" derives not from any position of "greatness" but from her "domestic virtues," in particular from the "superior thoughts" she voices regarding her station as wife, mother, and widow. These are the qualities that should animate British women rather than a desire for wealth or power. Andromache's disinterestedness, Steele claims, not only reveals her virtue but also distinguishes between ordinary "honest" women and those appropriate for heroines. Heroines, Steele stipulates, are held to higher "maxims of conduct" than ordinary "honest" (i.e., chaste) women. Immune from temptation, Andromache grieves for her husband and fears for the fate of her son, but she never questions her own decisions or appears to have doubts regarding the propriety or morality of her actions. In her moral certainty, Andromache stands in contrast to Southerne's Isabella, who, like Andromache, is a grieving widow with a small son who marries her husband's rival but does so in order to survive, only to find her life beset with horrors. By Steele's standards, Isabella may be honest, but she could never be heroic.[28]

Addison's and Steele's praise aside, a careful examination of *The Distrest Mother* demonstrates its ties to Racine's *Andromaque* (a point never raised by Philips's contemporaries). For the first three acts of the play,

---

28. In an aside that points to an idealized vision of drama that would later be realized in Steele's own *Conscious Lovers* (1722), he comments, "What is further very extraordinary in this work is, that the persons are all of them laudable, and their misfortunes arise rather from unguarded virtue than propensity to vice. The town has an opportunity of doing itself justice in supporting the representations of passion, sorrow, indignation, even despair itself, within the rule of decency, honour, and good breeding: and since no one can flatter himself his life will be always fortunate, they may here see sorrow, as they would wish to bear it when it arrives."

Philips follows his source closely, often paralleling Racine speech for speech as he represents Orestes' arrival in Epirus, his wooing of Hermione, and Andromache's rejection of Pyrrhus. Only in the play's final two acts does he move away from his source, and even then his changes do not stray far from Racine's play in either plot or sentiment. Philips's alterations take two basic forms, both involving the representation of Andromache. First, he reorders Racine's structure slightly so that the plot, which in Racine's tragedy increasingly focuses on the depiction of Hermione's passion rather than Andromache's virtue, instead remains centered on its title character. Second, he increases the number and intensity of Andromache's references to her son, thus stressing her maternal feelings. These changes, slight though they are, create a heroine expressive of her sorrows, who embodies a new domestic ideal of self-abnegating motherhood. In contrast to Racine's Andromaque, who announces her planned suicide with calm dignity, Philips's heroine is agitated by grief at the thought of parting with her son, grief that takes its shape visibly in the form of almost ever present tears. In an exchange that has no parallel in Racine, Philips presents his heroine awash in tears: Andromache's faithful woman Cephisa asks, "What meant those floods of tears, those warm embraces, / As if you bid your son adieu for ever?" (44). To which Andromache responds,

> Oh, my Cephisa! my swoln heart is full!
> I have a thousand farewells to my son:
> But tears break in! Grief interrupts my speech—
> —My soul overflowes in fondness—let him know
> I died to save him: And would die again.
>
> (46)

Unlike Racine's Andromaque, who conveys her composure through even speech rhythms (in contrast to the more disordered Hermione), Philips's character speaks brokenly, with short phrases and pauses becoming emotional markers which, like her tears, demonstrate her distress.

The play concludes with a scene original to Philips in which Andromache responds to Pyrrhus's death and welcomes her son, now freed from captivity. Where Racine's play concludes with Hermione's death and Orestes' subsequent madness, Philips shifts the focus back once again to Andromache, using the play's concluding lines to emphasize the qualities that have characterized his heroine, her sorrow and her maternal nature. When Cephisa asks, "Alas, then, will your sorrows never end," Andromache replies, in an echo of Southerne's Isabella, "Oh, never, never!—While I live, my tears / Will never cease; for I was born to grieve." But this character-defining grief is lightened by the appearance of her son, and she speaks the concluding lines, providing a moral absent from Racine's starker ending.

> A springing joy, mixt with a soft concern,
> A pleasure which no language can express,
> An extacy that mothers only feel,
> Plays round my heart, and brightens up my sorrow,
> Like gleams of sunshine in a lowering sky.
>   Though plunged in ills, and exercised in care,
> Yet never let the noble mind despair:
> When prest by dangers, and beset with foes,
> The gods their timely succour interpose;
> And when our virtue sinks, o'erwhelmed with grief,
> By unforeseen expedients bring relief.
>
> (57)

Her grief temporarily forgotten, this Andromache's maternal feelings become the means of demonstrating that the gods will reward virtue and "by unforeseen expedients bring relief." Philips's recasting of Racine provides an almost startling contrast to tragedies of the late seventeenth century. His heroine's chastity is unthreatened, and she commits no act for which she must be punished. She suffers, but her distress is a generalized concern at the loss or potential loss of loved ones. Such grief is a very different kind of spectacle from the madness and self-directed anguish that had filled the earlier she-tragedies. Steele's comments on the play provide perhaps the clearest indication of where female-centered drama in the eighteenth century was ultimately headed: toward chaste and less passionate heroines, especially those whose domestic role is something other than simply that of the lover: namely, mothers and daughters, matrons and widows.[29] Increasingly, women in serious drama would diverge from their counterparts in comedy as playwrights emphasized familial rather than romantic ties.

A more problematic heroine, and because of her a more problematic play, can be seen in Edmund Smith's *Phaedra and Hippolitus* (1707), a loose adaptation of Racine's *Phèdre* (1677). Unlike Racine's other female-centered plays, only one version of *Phèdre* appeared on the London stage,

---

29. In Steele's words we also see hints of his own goals in drama; what he praises in Philips's work he would later put into practice himself in *The Conscious Lovers* (1722). In *Steele at Drury Lane* (1952), John Loftis argues that Steele was working on *The Conscious Lovers* long before its premiere. Loftis suggests that Steele began writing *The Conscious Lovers* no later than 1714.

largely, it would seem, because of the nature of the heroine's distress—incestuous love for her stepson. Despite a fine performance by Elizabeth Barry in the title role, *Phaedra and Hippolitus* faltered when first staged, and the tragedy was not acted again until 1722. Even though *The Spectator* cited the failure of the play as an indication of the decay in English taste,[30] critics of the play felt otherwise. In their eyes, the play could never succeed because its heroine was too distasteful and the plays itself "one of the worst that ever appear'd on our Stage":

> [F]or this Reason; *viz.* That the whole Fabrick of it was built on a rotten Foundation, the *Heroine* of the Play being an Incestuous *Phaedra* in the bestial Pursuit of her Husband's Son, a Subject so rank as, (notwithstanding the Wondrous Performance of Mrs. *Barry*) even nauseated the whole, or at least the sober Part of the Audience.[31]

The play's problem, according to critics, lies squarely in its heroine, and more specifically with her aberrant ("bestial") desire. Especially interesting in these accounts of the play's failure is the source of the early-eighteenth-century audience's "nausea," Phaedra's voicing of her unfortunate love.

Taking only the general plot of Racine's play, Smith rewrites it in the form of an English she-tragedy with abundant emotion and, in the pattern of eighteenth-century serious drama, a happy ending for his virtuous characters. In contrast to Racine (and to Greek myth), Smith rewards Hippolitus and his beloved by uniting them in marriage at the end of his play, omitting any reference to Hippolitus's fatal carriage ride. The play's tragedy resides entirely in its discredited heroine and her unnatural desires, which are, as the play's critics observed, broadcast to a surprising number of witnesses. Phaedra's confession of her passion in the opening act constitutes the great weakness of Smith's play; unlike Racine's tragedy, in which Phedre only discloses her feelings under duress to her old nurse, Smith has his character confess not only to her waiting woman, but at the same time to Lycon, minister of state and the play's villain, who uses the knowledge of her doomed passion in an attempt to seize power. If Smith hoped to elevate Phaedra's character by contrasting her with the truly evil Lycon, his gambit appears not to have satisfied his detractors. Instead, critics complained that this heroine was too immodest to appear

30.   "Would one think it was possible (at a time when an author lived that was able to write the Phaedra and Hippolitus) for a people to be so stupidly fond of the Italian opera, as scarce to give a third day's hearing to that admirable tragedy?" *Spectator*, no. 18, 21 March 1711.

31.   *A Modest Survey of that Celebrated Tragedy The Distrest Mother* (1712), 4–5.

on the stage. In the midst of an attack on Nicholas Rowe, Charles Gildon stops to complain that Smith "abominably debas'd" the modesty of his Phaedra and that because of this Smith's character is a travesty of the classical figure. Gildon cautions his reader, "You must not take your Notion of *Phaedra* from that on our Stage by a late Author, where she is Abandon'd enough indeed, to become almost a parallel to *Jane Shore*,"[32] the mistress or "whore" of Edward IV.

The basis of Gildon's distinction between the "modesty" of earlier portrayals of Phaedra and Smith's modern representation is notable; both characters felt the same unnatural desire, but Smith's character, unlike her Greek predecessor, expresses her desire before the dual audience of stage figures and theatergoers. This speech-act verbalizing desire constitutes her greatest sin in the eyes of the eighteenth-century viewer. Speaking desire, rather than simply experiencing it, violates feminine modesty and constitutes an example, however small, of active will. Describing Phaedra as a "monster," one author compares her unfavorably with Dryden's Nourmahal in *Aureng-Zebe*, another woman with incestuous desires, but one who kept "her brutal Passion to her self, and not like the bolder *Phaedra*, making Confidants, and breathing her Incestuous Desires in the Face of a whole Court."[33] Criticism such as this identifies the problem as one of agency. Phaedra may not have been able to control her desires (indeed in Euripides' version of the story they were visited on her by Venus), but she is able to control her speech.

Although his critics focus on Phaedra's speech, Smith frames his play in terms of the perversion of the domestic sphere and on the impact of improper female desire on the public sphere. In *Phaedra and Hippolitus*, Phaedra makes no attempt to involve herself in affairs of state, but the effect of her untoward desire on her relationship with her husband undermines national security. Unlike Racine's character, Smith's Phaedra confesses that not only does she feel an incestuous passion for her stepson but that this infatuation has caused her to reject her own husband.

32. Charles Gildon, *A New Rehearsal; or, Bays the Younger. Containing an Examen of The Ambitious Step-Mother, Tamerlane, The Biter, Fair Penitent, Royal Convert, Ulysses, and Jane Shore. All Written by N. Rowe, Esq. Also a Word or Two upon Mr. Pope's* Rape of the Lock. *To which is prefix'd a Preface in Vindication of Criticism in General, by the Late Earl of Shaftsbury* (1714), 69.

33. Ibid. The play later achieved some degree of popularity, with both critics and playgoers. It was revived over a dozen times between 1720 and 1775. Describing the play as a "consummate Tragedy," William Oldisworth observes in the "Character" of Smith in his *Works*, 4th ed. (1729), that Phaedra "has certainly made a finer Figure under Mr. *Smith's* Conduct, upon the *English* Stage, than either *Rome* or *Athens;* and if she excels the *Greek* and *Latin Phaedra*, I need not say, she surpasses the *French* one, though enbelished [*sic*] withever regular Beauties, and moving Softness, *Racine* himself could give her" (xiv). George Sewell referred to the play as "the incomparable Tragedy of *Phaedra* and *Hippolitus*" (The *Life and Character of Mr. John Philips*, 3d ed. [1720], 9).

> For the Love of thee, of those dear Charms,
> Which now I see are doom'd to be my Ruin,
> I still deny'd my Lord, my Husband *Theseus*,
> The chaste, the modest Joys of spotless Marriage;
> That drove him hence to War, to stormy Seas,
> To Rocks and Waves less cruel than his *Phaedra*.
>   (14)

The sin to which Phaedra confesses here is not unlike the conduct of Andromache, which so incensed the author of *A Modest Survey*, although represented in a far more negative light. Phaedra becomes "monstrous" not only in her incestuous desire but in her attempts to step outside of her proper role in the sexual politics of marriage. Her attempt to control the marriage bed has disastrous results, driving her husband away from his kingdom and thus creating a power vacuum that Lycon hopes to fill. Her rejection of the domestic, of the "modest Joys of spotless Marriage," extends beyond herself to her husband, leading "to War" and "stormy Seas." As the play suggests, just as a woman's chastity can save a nation, even unchaste thoughts can lead to turmoil and bloodshed.

Rowe

The most famed practitioner of she-tragedy and the playwright whose name became almost synonymous with the term (he even coined the phrase)[34] was Nicholas Rowe. During the first fifteen years of the eighteenth century, Rowe wrote three she-tragedies, two of which remained popular throughout the eighteenth century and well into the nineteenth. "Sweet complaining Rowe" quickly became known for his scenes of female pathos; even plays that are not strictly she-tragedies contain extensive representations of female suffering, often brought on by sexual stain.[35] But his two most successful plays, *The Fair Penitent* (1703) and *Jane Shore* (1714), exploit the genre, in the first adhering to and improving on the often hackneyed conventions of she-tragedy and in the

34.   If the reforming Stage shou'd fall to shaming
        Ill-nature, Pride, Hypocrisy, and Gaming;
        The Poets frequently might move Compassion,
        And with *She* Tragedies o'er-run the Nation.
        Then judge the fair Offender, with good Nature;
        And let your Fellow-feeling curb your Satyr.

(Reverse italics, epilogue to *Jane Shore* [1714])

35. See for example Rowe's *Tamerlane* (1701), an overt homage to William III, which nonetheless combines its paean to proper leadership with a subplot featuring the forced marriage and rape of the virtuous Arpasia by the villain Bajazet.

second reconfiguring the form so that pathos overrules passion, creating instead a spectacle of suffering unrivaled in its appeal to the audience's emotions.

From the start, the sexuality of the heroine of each play was a matter of public debate. In both she-tragedies, Rowe's heroines lose their chastity knowingly albeit reluctantly (in *The Fair Penitent* Calista's loss of virtue is presented as an almost involuntary seduction). This representation of sexual agency, muted though it is, incited a flurry of attacks on Rowe's plays. In themselves an indication of Rowe's literary success, the pamphlets' censure of the heroines had little noticeable effect of the success of either work. One of the first such tirades, a satiric prologue written for *The Fair Penitent*, attacks Rowe for his representation of the unchaste Calista:

> Meanly contented with the vulgar Way,
> Some make the Heroine Virtuous in a Play:
> But the bold *Tragic Genius* of our Stage,
> With Novelty resolves t'oblige the Age,
> And with an Heroine PUNK, the Ladies will engage.[36]

By yielding to Lothario, rather than unwittingly losing her virtue as did heroines such as Isabella or Monimia, Calista becomes suspect, more akin to a prostitute or "punk" than a true heroine. Rowe's critics debate whether she repents sufficiently—is she truly penitent or merely ashamed? Samuel Johnson, who later praised *The Fair Penitent* as "one of the most pleasing tragedies on the stage," nonetheless objected that Calista felt "pain from detection rather than from guilt, and expresses more shame than sorrow, and more rage than shame."[37] Although Calista dies at the end of the play and cannot by any logic be perceived as rewarded for her sin, spectators such as Johnson were unsure whether she had suffered enough for having given into passion or that she recognized this act for the sin that it was. Thus, the author of the prologue complains, "She is not sorry that she has play'd the *Whore*, / But that, discover'd, she can do't no more."[38] Such responses reveal the extent to which female sexuality and suffering were linked in the public mind. Female sexual agency immediately established the woman as a "whore" or "punk," and the only way in which a woman who had behaved unchastely could satisfactorily demonstrate her repentance was through prolonged and visible

---

36. Included in *A New Rehearsal*, 59.

37. Samuel Johnson, "Rowe," in *Lives of the English Poets*, ed. George Birkbeck Hill (1905; reprint 1967), 2:68.

38. *A New Rehearsal*, 60.

suffering. Death alone would not suffice. Dramatic representations of such women were not merely unseemly but dangerous, as through them "Ladies [would] engage" with improper sexual role models.

Such objections only intensified after the success of *Jane Shore*, a historical tragedy in which the heroine was the former mistress of a king. One pamphlet lambasts Rowe for choosing such an inappropriate figure as the heroine for a tragedy, complaining "Thy skill Dramatic, unconfin'd, does soar, / Can make a Heroine of a downright Whore."[39] The author suggests that such a literary choice pollutes not only the play but Rowe himself, "Unworthy, boast thy sully'd Wreath no more, / Thy Muse, in Bays, is but a painted Whore."[40] Gildon's burlesque attack on Rowe, *A New Rehearsal; or, Bays the Younger* (1714), explores the issue at greater length, again denouncing Rowe for creating a heroine who is not sufficiently abject. He depicts Rowe as contemplating a feebleminded beggar as the heroine for his next tragedy "because we never had an Ideot professd for a Heroine; so that it wou'd be entirely New, and therefore cannot fail of succeeding, for as no Body before me establish'd Whores for Heroines, so I dare believe, that no Body besides my self ever thought of an Ideot for one."[41] In the pamphlet, "Rowe" ultimately decides against this plan because Granny's idiocy renders her morally innocent:

> Whoring in her can scarce be call'd a Crime: But that is no Heroine for me, who does not play the whore knowingly, wittingly, and of choice. The Critics may talk of Art and Rules, and I know not what, but I am for Nature; I hate Art and Rule— (81)

The core of Gildon's complaint is the active carnality of Rowe's heroines, who, by deliberately acting unchastely, "play the whore knowingly, wittingly, and of choice." Art, Gildon suggests, must incorporate morality as well as decorum, qualities in which he finds Rowe's plays and their heroines lack. For Gildon, as for Steele, a woman's sexual behavior determines her role in literature, thus "*Incontinency* in [a] Woman"[42] renders her unfit to be a heroine. Female sexuality constitutes a woman's worth in art as it had routinely in life, something that had not necessarily been true of tragedy in the 1680s and 1690s.

Rowe's two major she-tragedies center not simply on a woman's sex-

---

39. *A Lash for the Laureat; or, An Address by way of Satyr; Most Humbly Inscrib'd to the Unparallel'd Mr. Row, On Occasion of a late insolent Prologue to the Non-Juror* (1718), 4.

40. Ibid., 5.

41. Gildon, *New Rehearsal*, 80–81

42. Ibid., 69.

ual virtue, but on the moral implications of a fall from purity. In *The Fair Penitent*, Rowe turned to an earlier age to find a tantalizing story of female cupidity around which he could build what he termed "a melancholy tale of private woes" ("Prologue"). He found what he needed in Philip Massinger and Nathan Field's *The Fatal Dowry* (1632), but the qualities in which Calista is closest to her seventeenth-century source are those that made her most problematic to eighteenth-century audiences. For Rowe, earlier ages might provide fertile subjects for she-tragedy, but the elements he drew from English history and English drama needed to be re-created within a different understanding of female sexuality and its ramifications. In its original state, Renaissance drama could not satisfy the theatrical conventions involving the display both of female sexuality and the suffering that such sexuality (ideally) engendered. One of Rowe's greatest talents lay in his ability to reimagine older plots within a distinctly eighteenth-century framework. To this end, he emphasized the domestic setting of his tragedy, where audiences would "meet with Sorrows like [their] own" ("Prologue") rather than the more distant catastrophes of empire. "Private woes" such as those depicted in *The Fair Penitent* are connected to female sexuality, and all can be traced to Calista; she is the source of desire within the play, her own and that which other characters project onto her, and these conflicting desires result in calamity.

Private woes become public matters onstage, and the extent to which Rowe strove to satisfy contemporary concerns can be seen in the manner in which he adapted his source.[43] By no stretch of imagination can Massinger and Field's play be considered a she-tragedy. Not only does it contain no pathos, but its main female figure, Beaumelle, is openly desirous and eager to commit adultery. She asserts her claim to sexual liberty:

> Though a thousand watches were set on mee,
>   . . . I yet would vse
> The Liberty that best likes mee. I will reuell,
> Feast, Kisse, imbreace, perhaps grant larger fauours:
> Yet such as liue vpon my meanes, shall know
> They must not murmur at it.[44]

43. While Rowe never acknowledged his source, it appears to have been recognized by at least some of his contemporaries. Gildon comments on the connection in *The New Rehearsal*, predictably finding Massinger's tragedy "a much better Play." Massinger and Rowe "are equally guilty of making their Heroine a *Whore*; but the latter Poet has made her more unpardonable and obstinate, and still less worthy of Pity" (57).

44. 3.1.196–201. This reference and all others are taken from *The Plays and Poems of Philip Massinger*, ed. Philip Edwards and Colin Gibson (1976), vol. 1.

Early on she is shown kissing her lover onstage, unlike Calista who shuns her seducer and exclaims, "How didst thou dare to think that I wou'd lie / A Slave to base Desire, and brutal Pleasures (4.1). Even more explicitly, in act 4, scene 2 Beaumelle's lewd laughter is heard clearly by her husband and the audience. (Comments the keeper of the "music-house" where she is found, "Ah! / That women, when they are well pleas'd, cannot hold, / But must laugh out" [4.2.89–91].) Although the nature of her sin is made clear, Beaumelle herself is never made the centerpiece of an erotic tableau, not surprising considering that her role would have been played by a boy rather than a woman, nor does she display "distress." Instead, the focus of the scene quickly shifts to the struggle between the husband and the lover. In a subsequent scene, she repents and is executed by her cuckolded husband after a mock trial. Massinger's play may be sensational, but it is never sentimental. There is no seduction (Beaumelle's lover displays relatively little agency throughout the play), and the whole affair is seemingly masterminded by Beaumelle's lady-in-waiting, Bellapert. The play ends with male friendship exalted even in death and Beaumelle largely forgotten.[45]

While keeping the basic outlines of Massinger and Field's plot (a woman in love with one man marries another chosen by her father and tragedy results), Rowe changes the entire tenor of the play. Where *The Fatal Dowry* concentrates largely on the legal and political affairs of the cuckolded husband and only occasionally on Beaumelle, the issue of Calista's chastity lies at the heart of Rowe's tragedy. Calista does not appear in the opening scenes of the play, but the importance of her sexual body is firmly established by the end of the first act. The play begins with a scene of homosocial bonding as Sciolto embraces Altamont as his son, a bond that is made possible by the exchange of Calista in marriage. This pattern of male connection over the female body is repeated later in the act when we learn that Lothario intends to use evidence of his relationship with Calista to revenge himself on Altamont, his political rival. In each case, the body of the woman is the medium through which men establish relationships with one another.[46] With the entrance of Lothario, we learn that Calista has lost her virginity; at some time in the past he "stole unheeded" into her bed chamber, finding "the Fond, Believing, Love-sick Maid, / Loose, unattir'd, warm, tender, full of Wishes." Although Lothario admits "I snatch'd the glorious, golden Opportunity, / and with pre-

---

45. See J. Douglas Canfield, *Nicholas Rowe and Christian Tragedy* (1977), 111–12, for a discussion of the thematic differences between the two tragedies.

46. In yet another example of homosocial bonding, Horatio's friendship with Altamont is cemented by his marriage to Altamont's sister Lavinia.

vailing, youthful Ardour prest her,"[47] an act of seduction that seemingly borders on rape, his account is more than balanced by Horatio's insistence on Calista's guilt. (Horatio envisions how "her Hot Imagination wanders, / Contriving Riot, and loose scapes of Love; / And while she clasps thee close makes thee a Monster" [1.1.176]). Although today we may see Horatio's obsession with Calista's corrupt sexuality as evidence of his own latent desire, within the context of the play his comments draw attention not only to her tainted sexuality but to the fact of her desire. And it was precisely the existence of this desire that alarmed Rowe's critics, prompting them to question the sincerity of Calista's contrition.

Passion and repentance are the two axes of Calista's character. "Ruin'd" before the play begins, Calista has experienced desire (as Lothario graphically describes in the opening act), but in contrast to Smith's Phaedra, she never voices these longings. Instead, she expresses her sense of betrayal with her lover and, perhaps most vividly, her sense of frustration with her lot as a woman in a man's world. Fully conscious of her "undoing," her "Lab'ring Heart . . . swells with Indignation" (2.1.182), unlike the plaints of more passive heroines, such as Isabella's "born to suffer" or Andromache's "born to grieve." Defined by passionate intensity, the character was among the most demanding female roles, and decades later, Susanna Cibber, often named as the best actress of her generation, would be thought to be too "languid" to represent Calista properly.[48] Calista's numerous expressions of misery, coupled with repeated requests for death amply express her regret, and in the play's final act she rejects the "Art" of penitence taught by scholars, claiming that she has "more real Anguish in my Heart / Than all their Pedant Discipline e'er knew" (5.1.233). The play's detractors may have had an earlier speech in mind when they complained that Calista's repentance was no more than regret for being found out, as, in the second act, she explains her desire for exile or death as a means to escape publicity for her shame:

> There I fain wou'd hide me,
> From the base World, from Malice, and from Shame;
> For 'tis the solemn Counsel of my Soul,
> Never to live with publick Loss of Honour:

---

47. Act 1, scene 1, page 169. This and all further references to *The Fair Penitent* and *Jane Shore* are taken from Nicholas Rowe, *Three Plays*, ed. J. R. Sutherland (1929). Because this edition does not provide line numbers, I have used page numbers in order to avoid confusion.

48. Owing, as Samuel Foote suggests, "to the natural Weakness of her Constitution" (she has weak lungs, he theorizes). *The Roman and English Comedy Consider'd and Compar'd. With Remarks on the Suspicious Husband. And an Examen into the Merits of the present Comic Actors* (1747), 35–36.

> 'Tis fix'd to die, rather than bear the Insolence
> Of each affected She that tells my Story,
> And blesses her good Stars that she is virtuous.
>
> (2.1.181)

For the woman who would later describe herself as an "imperfect Copy" of her father (act 5), loss of honor is a central concern that reinforces her impression, common to many she-tragedy heroines, of being a "publick" spectacle. By the end of the fourth act, she has already become, in the eyes of the play's one virtuous woman, a synonym for "faithless Woman . . . false and fair" (4.1.231).[49]

Rowe juxtaposes Calista's passionate and flawed character with that virtuous "She," Horatio's wife Lavinia, a model woman depicted as constitutionally chaste. Lavinia cannot even comprehend sexual duplicity, telling Horatio,

> My little Heart is satisfy'd with you,
> You take up all her room: as in a Cottage
> Which harbours some Benighted Princely Stranger,
> Where the good Man, proud of his Hospitality,
> Yields all his homely Dwelling to his Guest,
> And Hardly keeps a Corner for himself.
>
> (1.1.178)

The domestic image and depiction of female love as self-abnegation provides a pattern of sexual virtue. By contrast, Calista laments the woman's lot, "thro' ev'ry State of Life the Slaves of Man"; woman is first subjected to a father and then to the "Tyrant Husband" who "holds Domestick Bus'ness and Devotion / All we are capable to know." She rejects such notions, demanding an "equal Empire o'er the World" (3.1, pp. 196–97), a proposal, which, although compelling, runs directly counter to contemporary views of women's role. Betrayed by her position as a woman, Calista attempts to usurp male authority; after Horatio confronts her with evidence of her sin, she calls for a sword so that she can "urge her Vengeance" (3.1.201). The phallic image and unfeminine desire for vengeance compound her sin of unchasteness and further distance her from

49. The extent of the play's influence can be seen by the role it plays in popular culture. By 1730, the characters had come to represent the archetypal figures of the seducer, the betrayed woman, and her hapless husband (today Lothario's name still connotes a womanizer). Some items expand on the premise of the play, but often these pieces have no direct link to the play aside from borrowing names. One such publication, *The Forsaken Fair. An Epistle from Calista in her Late Illness at Bath, to Lothario on his Approaching Nuptials* (1736), has no connection to the play, and instead refers to a contemporary scandal.

Frontispiece to *The Fair Penitent* from *The Dramatick Works of Nicholas Rowe* (1728).

the feminine ideal of a character such as Lavinia or Philips's maternal Andromache.

It is not until the final act that the spectacle of Calista's sexuality—and the suffering it has caused her—is exhibited; until then it is the central topic of discourse, discussed, debated, but not displayed. The act begins with a discovery scene that Rowe exploits to great effect:

> Scene *is a Room hung with Black; on one side, Lothario's Body on a Bier; on the other, a Table with a Skull and other Bones, a Book, and a Lamp on it*
>
> CALISTA *is discover'd on a Couch in Black, her Hair hanging loose and disordered: After Musick and a Song, she rises and comes forward* (5.1.232)

Reclining in an attitude suggestive of Lothario's earlier description of her seduction, she becomes an erotic spectacle, spied on by her father and by the audience. In the posture of humility that Edward Young found so fascinating, Calista enacts Mulvey's principle of "looked-at-ness,"[50] presented to the audience's gaze in a sexually coded attitude marked by disordered clothing and in particular by loosened hair, a symbol of sexual experience, especially of violated chastity. The setting, with its book, lamp, and skull, evokes the popular image of the penitent Magdalene, an allusion particularly appropriate for Rowe's dishonored heroine.[51]

If Calista is the object of the audience's gaze throughout the scene, the horrible object of her gaze is the corpse of Lothario, and Rowe, like Southerne and Congreve before him, reiterates the impotence of the female gaze. Although Rowe does not introduce a male figure to threaten the recumbent Calista, when Sciolto enters, he points directly to the evils of the female gaze, describing his daughter as "Spectatress of the Mischief which she made" (5.1.234). In contrast to his daughter, whose gaze is expressly masochistic—she stares on the gory corpse of her seducer or on herself ("I've turn'd my Eyes inward upon my self, / where foul Offence, and Shame have laid all waste" [5.1.235])—Sciolto voices a traditional masculine dynamic of sight and desire. As he continues to berate his daughter, his words betray an obsessive and even incestuous scrutiny: "I

---

50. "In their traditional exhibitionist role, women are simultaneously looked at and displayed, with their appearance coded for strong visual and erotic impact so that they can be said to connote *to-be-looked-at-ness*. Woman displayed as sexual object is the leit motif of erotic spectacle: from pin-ups to strip-tease, from Ziegfield to Busby Berkeley, she holds the look, plays to and signifies male desire." Laura Mulvey, "Visual Pleasure and Narrative Cinema," in *The Sexual Subject: A Screen Reader in Sexuality* (1992), 27.

51. See for example Georges de la Tour's famous (and often reproduced) representations of the penitent Magdalene. El Greco and Titian, among many others, also painted the subject multiple times.

Georges de la Tour, *The Repentant Magdalene* (ca. 1635). National Gallery of Art, Washington, D.C.

thought the Day too short to gaze upon thee," "How I have stood, and fed my Eyes upon these" (5.1.334).[52] Because of this impassioned exchange between parent and child, the act's emotional center, and thus that of the play itself, shifts to the father-daughter relationship. Only after word arrives of Sciolto's imminent death does Calista describe herself as "all Contagion, Death, and Ruin" (5.1.241). It is Sciolto's death, not the consciousness of her sexual crime, that drives her to suicide; labeling herself a "Parricide," she stabs herself. This heroine defines herself in terms of her father, not her lover or husband, and Sciolto's blessing is the "celestial" sound that grants Calista final peace.

The focus on a father-daughter bond rather than on lovers' passion that characterizes the final acts of *The Fair Penitent* was to intensify as the eighteenth century progressed; ultimately it would represent a major shift in the emotional dynamic of almost all forms of literature.[53] The passionate leave-taking between father and daughter sets the tone for the play's final scene in which both Sciolto and Calista—although not Altamont— die. Remarkably for the genre, Calista dies in a scene almost devoid of pathos. Rowe bows to the proprieties by having his heroine ask Altamont for pity as she dies (a response she had dismissed as "insupportable" earlier in the play), but the effect is minimal. Although an erotic spectacle for much of the play, Calista lacks the yielding and self-denying nature of most she-tragedy heroines. Regretful of her sin and aware of her loss of honor, she suffers without the scenes of madness or visible anguish so characteristic of earlier she-tragedies. Such spectacle, however, would become the centerpiece of Rowe's next she-tragedy.

Over a decade after *The Fair Penitent*, Rowe wrote his most popular play, *The Tragedy of Jane Shore* (1714), a work unparalleled for its prolonged representation of pathos. Based on the historic figure of the mistress of Edward IV, the play incited complaints regarding the sins of its heroine, but despite its supposedly inappropriate subject matter, the play was immensely successful. It ran for eighteen nights in February and March

52. This fascination with gazing on the beloved object is absent in the language of Altamont, Calista's lovelorn husband.

53. Later readings of the play cited the relationship between father and daughter as central. At mid century William Hawkins dedicates much of his interpretation of *The Fair Penitent* to Sciolto's failings, reading the play as a tragic enactment of a failed father-daughter relationship. He declares openly that "the subject of this play is an excellent moral; it shews in an eminent degree, the dangerous consequence of parents forcing their children into marriage against their own inclinations" (81). He later comments that while he feels compassion toward most of the characters, Sciolto deserves none, adding "I sincerely wish every parent whom providence has endued with a family of children, would take warning by Sciolto's misconduct, and not force them into marriage against their own consent" (87).

and constituted the only major success of the 1714 theater season. The popularity of the play spawned an explosion of publications related to the topic; as discussed earlier, opponents of Rowe chided him for using a "whore" as his heroine (nonetheless using the popularity of his tragedy as a mechanism to sell their own writings) while printers scrambled to publish accounts of Jane's life. Several major booksellers in London produced competing versions of Jane's life, more evidence of the fascination with Rowe's heroine and in particular with her sexuality. The pamphlets range from historical accounts that draw heavily on Sir Thomas More's life of Jane Shore[54] to erotic fiction that creates an elaborate narrative of Jane's early life, a near rape or two, and her seduction by the king. They share two obsessions: one, Jane's sexual sins; and two, the spectacle of her penance. In the eyes of the early eighteenth-century reader, Jane becomes a symbol of carnality, characterized exclusively by her adultery with a royal lover. The spectacle of her penance, depicted extensively in each account, becomes a scene of humiliation deliberately eroticized for the reader. Typically, the narratives use this moment to illustrate the intersection of sensuality and shame:

> Since [*Richard*] cou'd not prove her a Witch, [he] was satisfy'd with proving her a Whore, a thing as well known as what Sex she was of. The Crime being thus easily prov'd upon her, she was Sentenc'd to do Pennance [*sic*] upon a *Sunday*, at *Paul*'s Cross; accordingly she walk'd round it in a Procession, with a Modest look and Sober Pace, holding a Torch in her Hand; her Dress was what became a Penitent, very plain and White; The emblem of her Contrition, which however was more in Shew than Reality. She had nothing of her usual Attire on, but her Kirtle, yet her natural Beauty made her look lovely in the Eyes of the Spectators, whose pity for her Misfortunes, prepar'd them to receive the stronger Impression of her Charms. The gazing of the Multitude gave a Blush to her Cheeks, which she wanted before, her Complexion being of the Palest, and her decent Behaviour render'd her so amiable that People did not think so much of her Penitence as of her Person.[55]

The author emphasizes the scene's importance as visual spectacle, describing the procession and detailing Jane's appearance in the plain white

---

54. As, for example, the anonymous pamphlet *The Life and Character of Jane Shore. Collected from our best Historians, chiefly from the Writings of Sir Thomas More; Who was her Cotemporary, and Personally knew Her* (1714).

55. *The Life and Death of Jane Shore; Containing the whole Account of her Amorous Intrigues with King Edward the IV. and the Lord Hastings: Her Penitence, Punishment and Poverty. To which are added, Other Amours of that King and his Courtiers; with Several Antient Love Poems, Written by the Wits of those Times. Also An Heroick Epistle from King Edward IV to Jane Shore, with her Answer* (1714), 14–15. This passage is a close paraphrase of Sir Thomas More's account of Jane Shore in his *History of Richard III*.

dress, the "emblem" or physical marker of her contrition, and her equally white skin which becomes tinged with a sexually suggestive blush. The author even suggests in his narrative that the entire event is spectacle, the penance "Shew than Reality." By the end of the passage, the eroticism of the spectacle dominates, graphically illustrating the interconnected nature of sexuality and pathos as the pity of the spectators makes them more alert to Jane's physical allure, preparing them "to receive the stronger Impression of her Charms." Not only does the gaze of the multitude make Jane more attractive by making her blush, but ultimately pity becomes a conduit for desire.

As the pamphlet writers suggest, Rowe's play takes the spectacle of Jane's contrition as its subject, and, while the play elaborates on the image of the fallen woman as erotic object *and* as moral lesson, the pamphlets' emphasis on the physical nature of Jane's penance demonstrates the visual power of the play's final scenes. In *Jane Shore*, Rowe virtually ignores his heroine's past sins, leaving them to the (apparently) well-primed imagination of his audience. Although the play opens with a passing reference to Jane's "light Wantonness" (1.1.258), such immorality is set firmly in the past; the Jane whom Rowe presents is a figure of unrelenting pathos, a woman "sunk in Grief" who "never sees the Sun, but thro' her Tears" (1.1.258). Indeed, Jane is overcome by tears throughout the play, apologizing on her first appearance, "Oh, forgive my Tears! / They fall for my Offences—and must fall / Long, Long e'er they shall wash my Stains away" (1.2.262). As Jane's words suggest, her tears serve as a physical sign both of her repentance and of her impure past. In the semiotics of eighteenth-century theater, they are also an appropriate feminine response to affliction, operating to dramatize a woman's defenselessness and increase her pathos. As Jones DeRitter notes, Rowe's passive, domesticated heroine stands in stark contrast to accounts of Jane from an earlier era.[56] Tearful and helpless, Jane's figure embodies her sins and her repentance in a very real sense. As she enters the stage in the second scene, Bellmour comments, "Sure, or I read her Visage much amiss, / Or Grief besets her hard" (1.2.260). As later reviews of the play would indicate, an actress's success in the role would depend on her ability to make the signs of Jane's distress abundantly clear to the audience.[57]

Even more than Calista, Jane has sinned and sinned knowingly by be-

---

56. "The play attempts to substitute a passive, highly domesticated exemplar of feminine virtue for the more activist public heroine of the chronicles and the history plays." Jones DeRitter, "'Wonder not, princely Gloster, at the notice this paper brings you': Women, Writing, and Politics in Rowe's *Jane Shore*," *Comparative Drama* 31, no. 1 (spring 1997): 87.

57. Sarah Siddons was especially renowned for this quality, even causing some reviewers to believe she and not only the character she played was on the brink of death.

coming the mistress of Edward IV, but, as if in response to the criticism of *The Fair Penitent,* in this play Rowe makes his heroine's repentance both overt and continual. From the opening scenes we are presented with the spectacle of a woman overwhelmed with guilt who accepts all misery as punishment for her sins. She "look[s] with Horror back" on her "past polluted Life,"

> And for those foolish Days of wanton Pride,
> My Soul is justly humbled to the Dust:
> All Tongues, like yours, are licens'd to upbraid me,
> Still to repeat my Guilt, to urge my Infamy,
> And treat me like that abject Thing I have been.
>
> (2.1.277)

The moral erotics of the tragedy hinges on Jane's misery, graphically depicted every time she appears onstage and narrated by other characters when she is absent. Through her humiliation, and the passiveness on which it depends, Rowe transforms his heroine from sinner into victim. Whether threatened with rape or left to starve in the streets of London, Rowe's Jane is helpless to prevent her own destruction. Throughout the play she suffers not merely the pangs of remorse (brought on by her own wrongdoing), but miseries inflicted by others for "crimes" she did not commit; she is thus paradoxically more sinned against than sinning.

An essential component of her role as suffering heroine is her viability as spectacle, and despite Jane's putative plainness, Rowe quickly establishes her as a captivating object in the audience's eyes. Although Hastings describes Jane in the first scene as "sunk" and "pining," a mere shadow of her former voluptuous self, claiming that "Her waining Form no longer shall incite / Envy in Woman, or Desire in Man" (1.1.258), the play quickly contradicts this assertion. Jane's form may indeed be waning, but the sight of it is still capable of inciting both desire in men and envy in women, as Hastings's attempt to rape Jane and Alicia's subsequent jealousy demonstrate. In his pursuit of Jane, Hastings demonstrates to the audience that she is now, as she has been in the past, an object of desire and, at the same time, paradoxically acts to reestablish Jane's sexual virtue. As Susan Staves has argued, in literature although not in actuality, the very act of rape conveys virtue, even in the act of taking it away because stage rapists are not interested in violating the unchaste.[58] By attempting to force Jane, Hastings restores sexual virtue to a woman who has seemingly lost it.

---

58. Susan Staves, "Fielding and the Comedy of Attempted Rape," Unpublished paper delivered at the Houghton Library, Harvard University, February 1988.

The play's secondary female character, Alicia, is another fallen woman, but one whose angry passion neatly offsets Jane's meek remorse. Alicia has allowed herself to become Hastings's mistress, and her love for him has "set at nought [her] noble birth" and "spotless Fame" (2.1.272). Like Jane, she has knowingly transgressed to become in the eyes of society no better than a whore, but unlike Jane, she regrets only the fact that her lover's affections have cooled. Although Alicia is cognizant of her fallen nature and her debasement in the eyes of men, she blames her lover, not herself, attacking Hastings for his neglect:

> Art thou not false?
> Am I not scorn'd, forsaken and abandon'd,
> Left, like a common Wretch, to Shame and Infamy;
> Giv'n up to be the Sport of Villains' Tongues,
> Of Laughing Parasites, and Lewd Buffoons;
> And all because my Soul has doated on thee
> With Love, with Truth, and Tenderness unutterable?
> (2.1.271)

Unlike Jane, who embraces such mortifications as penance for her sins ("my Soul is justly humbled to the Dirt"), Alicia is resentful and unrepentant. She may regret her fall, but only because, as critics of Calista had argued, "she can do't no more." Notably, Alicia considers Jane's past as "golden," when Jane could "behold a Monarch, / Lovely, Renown'd, a Conqueror, and Young, / Bound in our Chains, and sighing at our Feet" (1.2.264); Jane rejects this image of female power, instead describing Edward's passion as "fatal."

The contrast between Jane and Alicia constitutes an important part of the play's "technology of gender" in which Jane's penance represents proper feminine comportment within a moral, patriarchal society. Jane repents her sexual incontinence but most especially her betrayal of her husband and the bond of marriage; her submission to fate exemplifies a larger pattern of womanly compliance. In stark contrast to Catharine Trotter's plays of female friendship, *Jane Shore* represents female bonds as hollow as Alicia betrays her friend to Gloster and later refuses to aid her as she expires. Jane's true friend is her forgiving husband who supports her throughout the play and who risks his life to save her. By contrast, Alicia's self-centered obsession with Hastings highlights the play's lesson about the sanctity of the marriage bond and the evils that come to those (women) who break it. Typically uncontrolled and passionate, Alicia ends the play frenzied, unable to repent her sin. Her madness, like that of Trotter's Elvira rather than Belvidera or Isabella, operates as moral lesson rather than as tableau of pathos: thus ends the truly sinful woman.

Rowe reserves his pathos for the play's final act, which incorporates a tableau of misery unequaled on the British stage. The act is dedicated to Jane's final humiliation as Rowe provides his audience with an uninterrupted display of the pathetic, sustaining the pathos until the play's final moralistic lines. The entire act centers on the punishment exacted on Jane by that favorite stage villain, Richard of Gloster. Unlike the penance described in the historical accounts, in which Jane Shore was simply made to humble herself by walking through London on a single given day, Rowe's Jane is turned into the streets, "to rot upon a dunghill." Although Gloster officially damns Jane for her refusal to support his claim to the throne, in the larger morality of the play Jane is punished for her earlier adultery with Edward IV. The political framework of the play offers a rationale for Gloster's actions as well as providing a suggestive portrayal of a man who would do anything to gain the throne, from breaking the law to inciting civil war. By supporting the legitimate line, Jane is established as an appropriately Whig heroine at a time when Queen Anne was near death and the succession was a contested issue.[59]

The act begins with Bellmour and Dumont/Shore discussing Jane's misery as she helplessly wanders the streets of London. In direct contrast to the accounts given by Jane's biographers, Rowe describes the witnesses of this spectacle as heartless and cruel, thus heightening the pathos of his own theatrical spectacle. Instead of sympathetic observers, Jane is surrounded by a "Rabble," who "crowd for a View, / Gaping and Gazing, Taunting and Reviling; / Some Pitying, but those, alas! how few!" (5.1.314). Bellmour's description of Jane's forlorn figure urges the theater audience to reject the "rabble" and themselves become the missing pitying onlookers.

> Submissive, sad, and lowly was her Look;
> A burning Taper in her Hand she bore,
> And on her Shoulders carelessly confus'd
> With loose Neglect her lovely Tresses hung;
> Upon her Cheek a faintish flush was spread,
> Feeble she seem'd, and sorely smit with Pain,
> While bare-foot as she trod the flinty Pavement,
> Her Footsteps all along were mark'd with Blood.
> Yet silent still she pass'd and unrepining;
> Her streaming Eyes bent ever on the Earth,
> Except when in some bitter Pang of Sorrow,

---

59. Lisa A. Freeman provides an insightful reading of the play in terms of its bourgeois political ideology. *Character's Theater: Genre and Identity on the Eighteenth-Century English Stage* (2002), 134–43.

> To Heav'n she seem'd in fervent Zeal to raise them,
> And beg that Mercy Man deny'd her here.
> (5.1.315)

All that remains of the historical account is Jane's blush and the taper she bears in her hand. Rowe enhances that image with the familiar sexual signifier of the tresses hanging with "loose Neglect." In this final representation of Jane, however, Rowe complicates any erotic implications by an emphasis on physical and emotional pain. Unlike the calm figure described in the pamphlets who made her penance with "a Modest look and Sober Pace," Rowe's Jane suffers visibly and with exquisite pathos. As always, the marks of her anguish are written on her body; "feeble" and "sorely smit with Pain," she leaves behind her a trail of tears and of bloody footprints, the horrifying physical emblem of her distress. In her passive, silent suffering Jane is the ideal object of all eyes, those of the "Rabble," of Bellmour, and ultimately of the audience. Like Young's ideal woman with her posture of humiliation, Jane's own gaze, downcast and veiled with tears, allows and even encourages her multiple audiences to witness the corporeality of her suffering.

And corporeal it certainly is, as Bellmour's description of Jane acts as an extensive stage direction for Jane's final entrance. Rowe's own stage direction, "*Enter* JANE SHORE, *her Hair hanging loose on her Shoulders, and bare-footed*" (5.1.319), links Jane's appearance firmly with Bellmour's description. Her entrance initiates a scene of graphic physical and emotional misery unequaled in English drama; Jane's death scene is both prolonged and an overt spectacle. Reminding herself that humiliation is a righteous punishment for her sins ("Yet, yet endure, nor murmur, Oh! my Soul!"), Jane creeps painfully about the stage, enduring rejection from the by now crazed Alicia, the discovery/shock of her husband's presence, and ultimately death from starvation and exposure. The extremity of Jane's suffering, which far exceeds anything in Rowe's sources, clearly constitutes the scene's raison d'être, and the play frankly emphasizes, perversely to a modern audience, the pleasure of watching a helpless woman's painful decline. The thrill of the scene is indelibly tied to the physical suffering of its heroine. The play ends with Bellmour's pious exhortation, "Let those, who view this sad Example, know, / What Fate attends the broken Marriage Vow" (5.1.333), but more memorable is Jane's final plea to her husband, "forgive me—but forgive me" (5.1.332), a plea that in its emphasis on culpability encapsulates the early eighteenth-century's moral agenda.

In the intensity of the pain portrayed in this final scene, visual spectacle becomes moral message so that the extraordinary graphic nature of

Jane's suffering serves a dual purpose: first, as vivid theatrical spectacle; and, second, as the prompt for an explicitly gendered response to the play. At the same time that they were stirred by Jane's adversity, women in the audience were expected to read her as a warning. *The Dramatic Censor* lauds the play and the theaters that produced it for "the wholesome lesson it inculcates to the fairer half of the rising generation."[60] Even Jane's "incontinency" can be tolerated because of her usefulness as an example of the woes that befall women who stray. Contemplating the effect the spectacle of Jane's suffering should have on women, one author exclaims:

> If we look round and view the House all o'er
> Shall we not find, at least one modern Shore? . . .
> Ye faithless Fair that stain the Marriage Bed
> Like wretched Shore from virtuous Husbands fled!
> Avoid these Scenes with most industrious Care,
> Least sudden Horror, seize you with Despair.

He expresses an unusually graphic vision of the lesson women can learn from Jane's suffering, speculating that the very sight will:

> Inflect a Dagger in your guilty Breast,
> Poison your Joys, deprive your Soul of Rest:
> Haunt you all Day in ev'ry Place and Hour,
> Prey on your Vitals, ev'ry Hope Devour.
> Make you with Grief your hapless State deplore
> Curse the bright Day, and wish you were no more![61]

By emphasizing the horrors that await the fallen women, the stage can be a "school" of virtue for women, teaching an explicitly sexual concept of virtue.

In this most visual of she-tragedies, the spectacle of Jane's suffering epitomizes the ambivalent moral aesthetics of female suffering as well as the effort made to separate male and female response to theater. Ultimately, arguments regarding serious drama often become arguments involving women: in the audience and on the stage. As Steele writes in *Spectator* 446,

> It is to be hoped, that some time or other we may be at leisure to restrain the licentiousness of the theatre, and make it contribute its assistance to

60. [Francis Gentleman], *The Dramatic Censor; or, Critical Companion* (1770), 1:9.
61. *The Theatrical Portrait, A Poem on the Celebrated Mrs. Siddons, in the Characters of Calista, Jane Shore, Belvidera, and Isabella* (1783), ll.92–93, 96–107.

the advancement of morality and to the reformation of the age. As matters stand, multitudes are shut out from this noble diversion, by reason of those abuses and corruptions that accompany it. A father is often afraid his daughter should be ruined by those entertainments, which were invented for the accomplishment and refining of human nature.[62]

Through the examples, both good and bad, presented in plays such as *The Distrest Mother* and *Jane Shore*, the drama of the early eighteenth century does "advance morality." As Steele's argument makes clear, however, the "reformation of the age" to be brought about by this newer generation of tragedy is profoundly feminine: fathers fear for their daughter's virtue, not for that of their sons. In this sense, the "ruin" Steele evokes implies a sexual fall, a point reiterated in William Whitehead's remark regarding women spectators. Whitehead exhorts the young women in theater audiences to remember that England's literary and sexual purity is riding on their shoulders, "A Nation's Taste Depends on you. / —Perhaps a Nation's Virtue too." His words make explicit the link his contemporaries saw between sexuality on the stage and female sexuality in general. Women, both fictional and real, represent a conduit for national virtue through their personal chastity, and their actions carry a symbolic value as the embodiment of a distinctly English virtue linking domestic and national concerns. This connection between sexual and political virtue was to find its ultimate expression in the subject of the next chapter, Nicholas Rowe's final she-tragedy, *The Tragedy of Lady Jane Gray*.

62. *Spectator*, no. 446, 1 August 1712.

CHAPTER 6

Sex, Politics, and the Hanoverian Succession: Refiguring Lady Jane Grey

On August 1, 1714, Queen Anne died, leaving the English throne to her distant relative, George Lewis, Elector of Hanover. Although precautions for a peaceful transfer of the crown had been established since the Act of Settlement in 1701, tensions mounted across the country, dividing public opinion along political and religious lines. Party politics were in a state of turmoil; parliamentary elections early in the year had transformed Tory dominance into a Whig majority. Supporters of Anne's half brother, James Francis Edward Stuart, had declared him king of England on her death, and some Tories, dismayed by the prospect of a foreign ruler (and an increasingly powerful Whig leadership), had fled to James's support in France while his Scottish followers raised an army and threatened to invade England.[1] Although the 1715 Jacobite rebellion never posed a serious threat to the throne or to the Anglican church, the specter of Catholic absolutism was a powerful political scare tactic used by Whig writers, and in the years immediately surrounding the succession it was invoked routinely in support of George I.

Women were an important part of this political unrest. Not only were they (notoriously) part of the "rage of party" that had infected the nation over the past decade,[2] but they were frequently used by writers as polit-

---

1. Henry St. John, viscount Bolingbroke, and James Butler, duke of Ormonde, both fled to France following George I's purge of Tory ministers. For discussions of Jacobitism in England both before and after the Hanoverian succession, see Paul Kleber Monod, *Jacobitism and the English People, 1688–1788* (1989); also Kathleen Wilson, *The Sense of the People: Politics, Culture, and Imperialism in England, 1715–1785* (1995).

2. See for example *Spectator* no. 81, in which women demonstrate party loyalty through the placement of patches, 2 June 1711.

ical emblems in the war of words that stirred England. This appropriation of the woman as symbol was most prevalent among Whigs who supported the Hanoverian succession. Not surprisingly, Jacobite propaganda tended to focus on male figures, notably on the absence of a rightful king (i.e., James Stuart) and on the flaws of George I.[3] Although James's refusal to convert to Protestantism meant that he had no realistic chance of gaining the throne of England, to disaffected High Church Tories he was still a powerful symbol of England's values—and George I an example of the downfall of these values.[4] By contrast, Whig propaganda called on female symbols in support of its agenda, contrasting the virtuous Protestant women of England with the supposedly corrupt opponents of George I.

The political representation of women was to have unusual implications. One of the most basic assumptions promulgated by Whig writers was that a woman's sexual virtue was linked necessarily to her political views. Thus, Addison represents prostitutes flocking to the Jacobite cause; in *The Freeholder* No. 3, he imagines a Jacobite soldier receiving the enthusiastic support of whores. As the supporters of the Pretender head toward their defeat at Preston, they are cheered on by the dregs of society, "particularly in two or three Balconies, which were filled with several tawdry Females, who are known in that Country by the ancient Name of *Harlots*. This Sort of Ladies received us every where with great Demonstrations of Joy, and promised to assist us with their Prayers."[5] By contrast, women who possess proper (sexual) virtue support the Whig cause. Addison continues the topic of female sexual virtue and political affiliation in his next issue, where he writes,

> It is with great Satisfaction I observe, that the Women of our Island, who are the most eminent for Virtue and good Sense, are in the Interest of the

3. Favorite Tory or Jacobite emblems were horns, referring to George I's cuckoldry by his wife Sophia Dorothea, and turnips, alluding to the story that he was hoeing turnips when he received the news of Anne's death. See Monod, *Jacobitism*, 57–58 passim.

4. The point of view is graphically expressed in pamphlets such as *British Wonders; or, A Poetical Description of the Several Prodigies and the Most Remarkable Accidents that have happen'd in Britain since the Death of Queen Anne* (1717) which describes the destruction of English glory (the cows are dying, signaling the destruction of the English diet, for example). It traces these ominous portents to the absence of a rightful king:

> No Wonder, since there's no such thing
> As Honour, where there is no King;
> For Honour, every Body knows,
> From Crowns originally flows:
> And where there's no Crown'd-Head to give it,
> No Man can merit or receive it.
>
> (25)

5. Joseph Addison, *The Freeholder*, no. 3 (Friday, 30 December 1715). Defoe makes a similar connection between prostitutes and high-church Tories (see *Review*, 11 May 1710).

present Government. . . . It is indeed remarkable that the Inferiour Tribe of common Women, who are a Dishonour to their Sex, have in most Reigns, been the profest Sticklers for such as have acted in Opposition to the true Interest of the Nation.[6]

Addison makes his distinction clear: virtuous women support the "present" (i.e., Whig) government. To do otherwise would immediately label them as sexually as well as politically impure, "common Women" who are a "Dishonour to their Sex," the one improper impulse being a metonymy for the other.

This argument was supported by the long line of anti-Catholic literature, which had represented Catholicism as the source of perverse sexuality—especially perverse female sexuality. In Protestant parlance, the Catholic church was the "whore of Rome," an entire religion feminized and sexually impugned. Moreover, in the eyes of English Protestants, Catholicism encouraged women to become nuns, keeping them from their natural roles as wives and mothers. The result of such "unnatural" celibacy was to create women who were either sex-starved virgins or lesbians.[7] If Catholicism were let loose on England, Whig rhetoric argued, the effects were liable to be sexually catastrophic. "The Explanation," a virulently anti-Catholic broadside, details the sexual improprieties that Catholicism could inflict on England:

> The Jesui'ts [*sic*] shall your Wives keep Chaste,
>   Each Fryer confess his Nun:
>   The Men shall Shrive,
>   The Women Sw—ve
> So all shall be forgiven,
>   Your Daughters Whore,
>   Then quite their Score
> And make 'em fit for Heaven[8]

Although men as well as well as women copulate in this verse, the broadside's emphasis here as elsewhere falls squarely on female carnality: men "shrive," but women "swive," and the end result is that England's daughters become whores. A later broadside makes a similar equation of Catholicism and lubricious female sexuality.

---

6. Addison, *The Freeholder,* no. 4 (Monday, 2 January 1716).

7. My thanks to Jenny Spinner for sharing her extensive information on anti-Catholic propaganda with me.

8. "The Explanation" (1685).

> In such a free licentious State [France],
>   What Merit can hope Praise?
> Where Men Reform'd Religion hate,
>   And Women wear no *Stays*.[9]

France's Catholicism, its hatred of "Reform'd Religion," is the root of its evil; the effect of such a religion is licentiousness. In an unreformed land, women "wear no *Stays*"; in other words, they are not only licentious in their behavior, but they are *visibly* so (the absence of stays was one sign of a prostitute).

As such examples indicate, women functioned as symbols, both figurative and actual. To be a standard-bearer for the proper Protestant cause, a woman had to be in Addison's words "eminent for Virtue" in her private as well as her public life. If previously the worst character a woman could have was "of being an ill Woman," one who had transgressed sexually, by professing the wrong political views "she may *likewise* deserve the Character of an ill Subject"[10] (emphasis mine). The two qualities, it seems, cannot be separated, at least for the Whig writer. Any semblance of impurity in a woman calls into question her politics, a crucial issue when the woman is being used as a representative of specific political views. These factors were to influence the representation of women, especially in a medium as strongly linked to the visual as drama. At a time when a woman's political significance was figured from her sexual virtue and specifically from the physical portrayal of this virtue, details of characterization and performance could be provocative, especially in a genre as dependent on displays of female sexuality as she-tragedy.

ONE of the more unusual outgrowths of the Hanoverian succession was the brief but intense obsession with Lady Jane Grey that swept the British nation. The erudite girl who was pushed onto the throne after the death of Edward VI was one of England's favorite Protestant martyrs, and she took on a symbolic meaning for writers on both sides of the debate. For Nicholas Rowe and other Whig supporters of the new regime, Lady Jane Grey provided an ideal representation of Protestant virtue besieged by Catholic vice. She was the focus of a flurry of publication in 1714 and 1715 that culminated in the public performance of her story in Rowe's final play, *The Tragedy of Lady Jane Gray*. In 1715, with the Hanoverian succes-

---

9. "A New Ballad" (1728). The tune for this ballad was used earlier for an explicitly anti-Jacobite broadside, "Ye weavers all of Spittle Fields."
10. Addison, *The Freeholder*, no. 26 (Monday, 19 March 1716).

sion the subject of public protests and a Jacobite rebellion imminent, a figure such as Rowe's devout but indomitable Jane represented an idealized picture of British national character juxtaposed against the potential evils that could accompany Catholic rule. With her patriotic outbursts and final refusal to convert in the face of death, Jane embodied Rowe's Whig sympathies and, in the context of contemporary politics, represented a strong statement in favor of George I.

The history of Lady Jane Grey, the sixteen-year-old girl who was placed on the throne as a Protestant alternative to Mary I and who was deposed and later executed for her faith, presented a ready-made example of Protestant virtue and Catholic tyranny. Rowe was not the only writer to sense the timeliness of Lady Jane's story. By the time Rowe's play appeared on the stage at Drury Lane, the figure of Lady Jane Grey had already been used repeatedly in political debate. Long associated with England's Protestant heritage, she was popularly perceived as a type of English religious virtue. (Jacobite sympathizers turned to another emblem of afflicted womanhood, using Mary, Queen of Scots, as their political icon and describing her suffering and death in terms almost identical to those used by the Whigs when discussing Lady Jane.)[11] Lady Jane's story had been made popular in the previous century by John Foxe, whose *Book of Martyrs* heralded her virtue, focusing in particular on her refusal to violate her faith and on the details of her subsequent execution. In addition to her potential as political figurehead, the very image of indomitable virtue in the form of a young girl provided vivid dramatic possibilities, and at least two playwrights before Rowe had dramatized her story. In 1694, John Banks published *The Innocent Usurper; or, The Death of Lady Jane Gray*, a play which Banks claimed was written "ten years since," but whose depiction of a sympathetic usurper rendered it unstageable. Banks presents Jane as a conventional she-tragedy heroine, passionately in love with her new husband and full of details about their connubial exchanges. Despite the play's troubled history, it is largely devoid of overt political commentary, focusing instead on the passions and pathos of its heroine, traits characteristic of Banks's tragedies. A second

---

11. See for example *The Fate of Majesty, Exemplified in the Barbarous and Disloyal Treatment (by Traiterous [sic] and Undutiful Subjects) of the Kings and Queens of the Royal House of the Stuarts. From the Reign of* ROBERT, *the first Monarch of that Name, to the last of the most August Princes of that unhappy Family. To which is added, a Vindication of* MARY, *Queen of Scots, who was (contrary to the Laws of God, Nations and Nature) put to Death in the Days of Queen Elizabeth; from the scandalous and vile Aspersion of Buchanan, the Scotch Historian. As also a Preface in Defence of the Solemn Observation of the Anniversaries of King* CHARLES *the First's Martyrdom, King* CHARLES *the Second's Restoration, and Queen ANNE's Birth, Accession, and Coronation* (1715).

play, based largely on *The Innocent Usurper,* was written, although never published or performed, by Edmund Smith. Rowe admitted that Smith's manuscript was a source for his own play, although he stressed that the final product was entirely his own, claiming "the manner and Turn of his Fable was so different from mine, that I could not take above five and twenty or thirty Lines at the most; and even in those I was oblig'd to make some Alteration."[12] The only point where Rowe claimed to agree with Smith was in the earlier playwright's anti-Catholicism, applauding his representation of the "Persecuting Spirit by which the Clergy were then animated."

Rowe's play is only the best remembered part of a near obsessive interest in Lady Jane Grey during the years 1714 and 1715. During this time of perceived political and religious threat, her figure appears again and again onstage and in print. One of the earliest and most elaborate of these works was Edward Young's poem, *The Force of* RELIGION; *or, Vanquish'd Love. (Illustrated in the Story of Lady Jane Gray).* Published first in 1714 before Queen Anne's death, Young's poem celebrates female virtue, which he sees both in Lady Jane and in Queen Anne. The poem is set after Jane has been deposed and imprisoned, much of it after she has been sentenced to death; it focuses on Jane's beauty and piety, and the effect these qualities have on those around her. Buoyed by its applicability to current events, the poem went through three editions in less than two years and was so popular that one bookseller (J. Roberts) rushed out a biography of Lady Jane and advertised it on the title page as "Very proper to be bound up with Mr. Young's excellent Poem, founded upon this Noble History."[13]

The biographies of Lady Jane Grey that appeared shortly after Young's poem clearly participated in the politicized interpretation of her story, which intensified after the death of Queen Anne. Roberts's publication makes its stance evident in its detailed title: *The Life, Character, and Death of the most Illustrious Pattern of Female Vertue, The Lady* Jane Gray, *who was Beheaded in the* Tower *at 16 Years of Age, for her stedfast Adherence to the Protestant Religion.* Sentiment obviously ran high over Jane's political import; the British Library copy of *The Life* contains the words "a damned Lye" written beneath the last words of the title.[14] Although, like Young,

---

12. Nicholas Rowe, preface to *The Tragedy of Lady Jane Gray* (1715), ed. Richard James Sherry (1980), 5. All further references to *Lady Jane Gray* will be taken from this text and noted parenthetically.

13. *The Life, Character, and Death of the most Illustrious Pattern of Female Vertue, The Lady* Jane Gray, *who was Beheaded in the* Tower *at 16 Years of Age, for her stedfast Adherence to the Protestant Religion* (1714).

The Life focuses on Jane's piety, it casts her as an actor in a tragedy with national implications. Describing Jane's demeanor at execution as "unconcern'd," "as she had acted the former Part of her Tragedy," the author sets Jane on an imaginary stage, the object of all eyes as her "mournful Spectators were drown'd in Floods of Tears."[15] In presenting Jane as spectacle and her death as political theater, the author identifies the appeal of her story as inextricably visual:

> There was no Doubt but the Death of this innocent Lady would excite the highest Degrees of Compassion and Regret; therefore, since the World could not bear so moving a Sight, a Scaffold was erected with in the Verge of the *Tower*, where she might satisfy the Severity of the law, without any Danger to the State.[16]

As the author suggests, the power of Jane's story derives from the "Sight" of both her virtue and her suffering. This combination creates a spectacle so potent it threatens national security and must be hidden away from the eyes of "the World," from the public, whose "compassion and Regret" might undermine the state.[17] The power of this spectacle was perceived to operate on the individual as well as the collective level and was not to be taken lightly; the author notes that Jane's death "had a most violent Operation on Judge *Morgan* . . . for shortly after he fell mad, and in all his Ravings, still call'd to take away the Lady JANE from him."[18]

A tragedy with these elements, performed against a backdrop rife with political significance, could hardly fail to succeed, and *The Tragedy of Lady Jane Gray* was easily the most successful play of the 1714–1715 theater season.[19] Its popularity spawned a host of rival publications: Banks's play was republished after being out of print for over a decade, and two pamphlets appeared attacking both the play and its author (*Lady Jane Gray* was the only play of the season to be so honored). The first, *Remarks on the*

14. Shelfmark 1103.c.18(6).

15. *Life, Character, and Death of Lady Jane Gray*, 26.

16. Ibid., 24–25.

17. The author credits the power of her death scene with changing national policy; emotions ran so high after her death that Bishop Gardiner "became hateful to the Nation," 27.

18. Ibid., 26–27. These lines are almost identical to those in Foxe's *Book of Martyrs* describing the effect of Jane's execution: "It is to be noted, that Judge *Morgan*, who gave the Sentence of Condemnation against her, soon after he had condemned her, fell Mad, and in his raving cried out continually, to have the Lady *Jane* taken away from him, and so ended his Life." John Foxe, *Acts and Monuments of Matters most Special and Memorable, Happening in the Church: with an Universal History of the same* . . . , 9th ed. (1684), 3:30.

19. The play ran for ten nights in April and May 1715 and was staged again in October, two days before the anniversary of George I's coronation.

Tragedy of the Lady Jane Gray; In a Letter to Mr. Rowe attacks the play for its political lesson, discrediting Rowe and his politics by denigrating the character of Jane. The author argues that not only is the character merely a sop to the actress Anne Oldfield, but that Jane's highly touted virtue is mere treason. He complains that in the play "a *Protestant* Princess is clapp'd on the Throne, in Prejudice to the Right Heir to the Crown . . . *Jane* is no Rightful *Parliamentary* Monarch; but a Princess basely substituted by the Will of a deceas'd Predecessor."[20] The complaint accurately reads Jane's relevance to the current political situation, and in attacking the glorification of her character, the author reveals his own Jacobite views. George I, like Jane, was a ruler "substituted by the Will of a deceas'd Predecessor," and the author's emphasis on the prejudice against the "Right Heir to the Crown" represents a thinly veiled appeal for Anne's nearest relative, James Edward Stuart.

The author of the second pamphlet, Charles Gildon, used *Lady Jane Gray* largely as a marketing ploy, reprinting an older attack on Rowe under a new title and adding a few quick pages of negative commentary on the play.[21] Gildon compares Rowe's play unfavorably with Banks's earlier tragedy, complaining that Rowe's character is a picture of flat virtue and commenting disparagingly that "[he] seems to be afraid, that a Connubial Love in a young Lady of 15, should lessen her Character, but certainly without the least Reason; for that is not a Blemish, but a Beauty."[22] Finding fault with Rowe's avoidance of Jane's sexuality, Gildon suggests that representing her as a political martyr detracts from her "beauties" as a woman. The issues raised in both pamphlets bear on more than Rowe's characterization of Lady Jane Grey, questioning the literary representation of women and their intrusion into the political sphere. The difficulty lies not in the woman herself, but in the popular representation of that woman. At its core, the debate over Lady Jane Grey centers on her position in the public eye: should she be presented as lover or as martyr, as woman or as political icon—and are the terms mutually exclusive. Rowe's emphasis on the latter gave his play topical appeal in 1715 and again in 1745,[23] but not after the perceived threat of Catholic invasion dissipated. Later readers, unswayed by such fears, found Jane's character

20. *Remarks on the Tragedy of The Lady Jane Gray; in a Letter to Mr. Rowe* (1715), 6.

21. Aside from his comments on *Lady Jane Gray*, Gildon's pamphlet, *Remarks on Mr. Rowe's Tragedy of the Lady Jane Gray, and all his other plays"* (1715) is a reissue of an earlier attack on Rowe, entitled *A New Rehearsal; or, Bays the Younger*.

22. Gildon, *Remarks*, 11.

23. *Lady Jane Gray* was revived in 1745 at the time of the second Jacobite rebellion as well as during the 1730s, perhaps due to increased tensions between England and France when France and Spain attacked English ally Austria in the war of the Polish succession.

cold and unsympathetic. These shortcomings are perhaps best articulated by Elizabeth Inchbald:

> The heroine of this drama possessed every grace of person, every adornment of mind, the attraction of youth, and the dignity of royalty.— She was hurled from a throne to mount upon a scaffold; and this lamentable story is here told by one of our most pathetic dramatists; and yet neither reader nor auditor ever sheds a tear for the unhappy fate of Lady Jane Grey!
>
> All surprise will cease, that this illustrious female wants power to move the passions, when it is recollected, that she had no passions of her own with which to affect those of mankind.
>
> The very virtues of Lady Jane seal up the heart against pity. Perfection must be admired, not undervalued by compassion.[24]

In creating such a vision of perfection, Rowe erases the possibility of sympathetic engagement with the heroine of the play, a problem exacerbated when theater managers in the later eighteenth century pruned the play, omitting the political rhetoric and leaving the woman. The furor over Lady Jane Grey raises questions regarding the conflicts inherent in making a woman a political symbol. Can she be both symbol and woman? In the end, how is such a public figure to be read?

> As long as we have Passions, as well as Reason, we shall own the Force of outward Appearances.
>
> EDWARD YOUNG, dedication to *The Force of* RELIGION; *or, Vanquish'd Love* (1715)

Edward Young provides one answer to this problem of interpretation in *The Force of* RELIGION; *or, Vanquish'd Love*.[25] Written before Queen Anne's death, at the very beginning of the Lady Jane vogue, the poem appeared before the events of 1715 had made Lady Jane controversial, so that Young could focus his poem on individual piety rather than national politics. Much less overtly political than the works that were to follow it, Young's poem is instead concerned with Jane as object of a frankly libidinous male gaze. Set in the days following Jane's capture by Mary I,

24. Elizabeth Inchbald, headnote to *Lady Jane Gray*, in *The British Theatre*, 10:3.
25. In Two Books, 2d ed. (1715). The epitaph reads "Gratior and pulchro veniens in Corpore Virtus." Virgil. All further references will be made to this edition and cited parenthetically.

the poem discusses Jane's love for her husband, and in more detail, his passion for her. It concludes as Mary's emissaries offer to remit the death sentence on Jane, her husband, and her father if she converts to Catholicism. The two men plead with her, but Jane's faith remains strong and she refuses to convert, thus, as the title indicates, "vanquishing love." Jane's convictions are only one part of the poem. Equally important to Young is describing the effect that the sight of such virtue has on others. The operation of faith is to a large extent determined by the gender of the believer; even though Jane's desires come in conflict with religion and must be subdued, the desire of the men who gaze on her beauty and witness her virtue ultimately increases their faith.

Before his poem even begins, Young provides a detailed explanation of the mechanics of vision and virtue, exploring not only the piety of the Protestant martyr but detailing the peculiar pleasure men take in watching a virtuous woman. He attempts to reconcile the sexual and the spiritual in the form of a heroine who renounces love yet is at the same time adored by all men, including, by implication, the male readers of Young's poem. The subject of Young's poem is the spectacle of the virtuous woman, a topic that Young details in his dedication, in the passage quoted at length in chapter 3. Such a spectacle is important, for "when that which is Lovely joins with [Good], the latter makes Interest with our Senses for the Admission of the former." Provided with a beautiful, and thus sensually gratifying, object, Young explains, men "fix our Eyes on a fair Example of Piety . . . and Gaze our selves into a Newness of Life." His words outline a process in which the male subject gazes on the female object ("fair Example"), in the process inciting desire in the subject, a sensation that Young attempts to sublimate into religious ecstasy. (Young was not alone in drawing connections between lovely righteousness, male desire, and virtuous response. Addison describes a similar process, although in his paradigm, male desire leads to political rather than religious virtue.)[26]

Young finds his epitome of lovely virtue in Lady Jane Grey whose beauty, he explains, increased because she was virtuous while "her Religion it self admitted of Advantage, and receiv'd Prevalency, as well as Lustre, from the Elegance of her Mien, and the Gracefulness of her Person" ("dedication"). Using the model of scopic pleasure discussed earlier

26. See *Freeholder*, no. 11 (Friday, 27 January 1716): "*A Lady of the Association*, who bears this Badge of Allegiance upon her Breast, naturally produces a Desire in every Male-Beholder, of gaining a Place in a Heart which carries on it such a visible Mark of its Fidelity. When the Beauties of our Island are thus industrious to shew their Principles, as well as their Charms, they raise the Sentiments of their Country-men, and inspire 'em at the same Time both with Loyalty and Love."

(see chapter 3), he explains why men find the story of Lady Jane Grey so titillating: she was both beautiful and good, so her story is doubly captivating. The desire and virtue that represent Jane's central conflict work in tandem for the men in Young's poem as they do for the speaker in the dedication. Jane's husband Guildford, described as weaker in virtue than Jane, by watching her not only excites his desire but ultimately strengthens his moral fortitude. Jane's virtue thus stands in contrast to male virtue; the dedication tells readers how to interpret the poem by acting as witnesses of Jane's merit, and ultimately how to interpret the figure of the woman, whose role in this system is defined by her status as object. In keeping with the emphasis on voyeurism in the dedication, Young enumerates the sublime delights of gazing throughout the poem. The narrator repeatedly acts as spectator, vividly describing what he "sees" and focusing the imaginary gaze of the reader inexorably on the figure of Lady Jane Grey. In doing so, he even brings himself and his readers directly into the visual world of the poem, noting, "We, Disbelieving our own Senses, Gaze [at Jane] . . . We gaze; and as we gaze, Wealth, Fame, decay, / And all the World's vain Glories fade away" (8). Young's Jane is surrounded by watching eyes: her husband's and her father's as well as those of Young and his readers. (The poem's frontispiece highlights Jane's role as object of the male gaze, as did the poem's other highly touted illustration.

Moral perfection and sexuality coexist neatly in Young's paradigm of virtue. He begins his poem with a highly suggestive variation of the conventional invocation to the muse, beseeching her to "indulge my fond Desire" and to inspire his "melting Soul" (1). Likewise, his portrait of Jane stresses her lovely appearance and her very physical allure, a quality emphasized by the important role of Guildford, through whose desirous eyes the narrator often gazes. Importantly, Jane's status as a sexually experienced woman is made clear early in the poem as Young describes Guildford's fond memories of his wedding night:

> Now on the Bridal Bed his Eyes were cast
> And Anguish fed on his Enjoyments past;
> Each recollected Pleasure made him smart,
> And ev'ry Transport stabb'd him to the Heart.
> That happy Moon, which summon'd to Delight;
> That Moon which shone on his dear nuptial Night,
> Which saw him fold her yet untasted Charms
> (Deny'd to Princes) in his longing Arms;
> Now sees the transient Blessing fleet away.
>
> (6–7)

Lady Jane Grey before her execution. Illustration from *The Force of Religion* by Edward Young, 1715.

Through the mechanism of Guildford's memory, Young hints at Jane's sexual "charms" and invites the reader to imagine these nuptial "Enjoyments." This Jane is clearly no virgin. Later in the poem, the reader again looks through Guildford's eyes as he gazes at Jane, detailing her every beauty and, rather horribly, imagining her coming execution:

> But all her Charms in Silence traces o'er;
> Her Lip, her Cheek, and Eye, to Wonder wrought,
> And wond'ring sees in sad presaging Thought,
> From that fair neck, that World of Beauty fall,
> And rowl along the Dust, a ghastly Ball.
>
> (27)

Examples such as these establish Jane as object of the reader's eye, a role that she plays through the poem. The inclusion of Guildford's uxorious thoughts makes certain that Jane's virtue cannot be divorced from her desirability. At every turn, her virtue is conflated with her physical beauty, thus Young describes Jane swooning halfway through the poem after hearing that Guildford may die; she strikes "her lovely Breast," "staggers with the Wound" and sinks "a breathless Image to the Ground" (17). As senseless "Image," she is the object of all eyes, a role, Young implies, men expect women to play.

As Young's dedication has already suggested, men cannot help but respond to women sexually; these sexual urges, however, should be diverted into religious impulses, and the physical act of seeing is the means to this end. In this way, the titillation of envisioning Jane's sexual beauty and virtuous suffering should stir male readers to greater heights of religious fervor. The poem concludes with a practical example of how the sight of such virtue should work when Jane proclaims her desire to die rather than turn apostate:

> Her Lord and Father view, with Transport fill'd,
> Their utmost Efforts to her Virtue yield;
> Her firm Resistence, flush'd with Shame, approve,
> With Joy exulting, while they die with Love.
>
> (37)

Here again are the male gaze and the female object as Jane's husband and father *watch* this virtuous image. Despite the religious context (a woman's embrace of martyrdom for the sake of her faith), the language used to describe this avowal of faith has decidedly sexual overtones. The two men are filled with "transport" by the scene and "die with Love" while the object of their gaze is "flush'd with Shame"; taken out of context, the lines suggest an attempted seduction. As with the voyeur watching the beautiful woman at her devotions, the observer's religious response is inextricable from his sexual response.

WHEN the venue for such images shifted from the privacy of the reader in the closet to the public forum of the stage, the representation of the female object became more problematic. As discussed earlier, writers of she-tragedy were accustomed to using the titillating sight of womanhood as the play's central dramatic spectacle, not worrying, as Young did, about its role as a catalyst for male virtue. However, whereas in earlier plays the suffering of the doomed heroine had facilitated the plays' political message, in a political climate where overt female sexuality was linked to Jacobite sentiments, the conventional she-tragedy, with its emphasis on polluted female sexuality, could become a liability. Political ideology had been commonplace in drama before the unrest that surrounded the Hanoverian succession, and Rowe himself had famously stated his allegiance to William III and the Whigs in *Tamerlane*—a play revived several times in the years after Anne's death. But never before had the specific characterization of a play's female protagonist carried so much figurative significance.

An early example of how anti-Jacobite rhetoric affected the dramatic representation of female figures can be seen in an adaptation of Massinger and Dekker's tragedy, *The Virgin Martyr* (1622), staged as the political tensions were beginning to mount. The first play by actor and playwright Benjamin Griffin, *Injured Virtue*, links the martyrdom of a chaste woman with a lurid representation of the evils of Catholicism. Recognizing the potential of Massinger's play as well as the political capital to be reaped from representing the Whig heroine, Griffin rushed the play into production in the summer of 1714, near the time of Anne's death, staging the play originally in Richmond and later in the year at the King's Arms Tavern in Southwark.[27] *The Virgin Martyr* provided the basic ingredients Griffin needed: a virtuous, Protestant female character and a vigorous attack on Catholicism transparently signified by worship of pagan gods with incense and censers. As originally written, *The Virgin Martyr* provides a clear condemnation of heretical "Roman" religion; Griffin takes this foun-

27. Although the play bears the date 1715, it was evidently published late in 1714. For details on the productions of *Injured Virtue*, see Sybil Rosenfeld, *Strolling Players and Drama in the Provinces, 1660–1765* (1939), 274–75.

dation and exaggerates the anti-Catholic message, using the play's main female figure as his emblem of true (Protestant) Christianity.

In *The Virgin Martyr*, Massinger and Dekker present an almost Manichean struggle between good and evil, embodied in the contrast between Christianity and Roman paganism. Dorothea, the title character, is opposed by Theophilus, a "Persecutor of the Christians" so zealous that he tortures and later puts to death his own daughters when they adopt Christianity. Where Dorothea is supported through her eventual trials by a good spirit (Angelo) disguised as a page, Theophilus's perfidy is accomplished through the urging of an evil spirit, Harpax. Theophilus has Dorothea executed (her head is struck off onstage), but even this act is not enough to condemn him, and he converts after a visit from Angelo. Although Griffin keeps the basic plot line of his source, he simplifies the action and focuses attention more directly on Dorothea by minimizing the importance of other characters. Angelo and Harpax are omitted as is the low humor provided by Dorothea's servants. Only aspects of the plot that directly relate to Dorothea and her pious faith appear onstage; even the conversion of Theophilus's two daughters is curtailed. What does survive from *The Virgin Martyr* is the emphasis on debauched female sexuality as a result of the Roman religion so that the play echoes the familiar emphasis on debased female sexuality found so often in early eighteenth-century anti-Catholic propaganda. When Dorothea converts the daughters of Theophilus, she emphasizes the degradation of the Roman church, exclaiming "Your gods! your temples! brothel-houses rather," and detailing the sexual perversions of the Roman gods. Not only is the religion itself corrupt, but it has an inevitable corrupting influence on those women who practice it, perverting chastity into prostitution. Thus, Dorothea asks if the girls intend to "give [their] chast Body up to the Embraces / of Wantonness and Lust? have it said of you, / This is the common Prostitute to Man, / A Mistress in the Arts of Wickedness, / Who knows all Tricks and Labarynths [*sic*] of Desire / That are unchaste and foul?" (36).

Throughout his adaptation, Griffin establishes woman's symbolic role as protector of the faith, as well as her position as object of the gaze, keeping these two functions inextricably connected. Because Dorothea is the object of the male gaze, she can be the representative of the true faith and an emblem of Whig values. She is the central object of the play, but the effect of the scrutiny directed toward her is strictly evangelical as men who gaze on her find their hearts stirred by heavenly love. Although the source play is relatively chaste, with its most titillating scenes appearing when Dorothea is threatened with a rape that never occurs, Griffin contains any possibility of the erotic by expunging all references to

Dorothea's sexuality. Instead, characters describe her in terms of her virtue and the effect this virtue has on those who witness it. Thus her death scene (moved offstage, in contrast to *The Virgin Martyr*), like the execution of Lady Jane Grey, is described in terms of its effect on viewers:

> I went, and saw the dreadful Scene of Death;
> She kneel'd before the Block, her Arms extended,
> And eyes erect to Heaven, devoutly Praying
> For all Mankind, for those that sought her Death,
> With so sedate a Consistency of Mind,
> That it drew Tears from every Eye that saw her.
>
> (60)

For honorable characters, witnessing the execution has near miraculous effects, as with one figure who claims, "'tis this Sight alone must work my Cure" (55). Conversely, the evil Theophilus, like the judge who condemned Lady Jane Grey, is driven to near madness by the sight of Dorothea's righteousness, unmoved by threats of torture or death. But the greatest ocular proof of Dorothea's virtue occurs after her death, in the form of a stunning vision. In the final act, Griffin's Theophilus enumerates his slaughter of Christians (1,400 in Britain, 2,000 in Gallia, 8,000 in Asia, 2,000 in Greece, 200 in Italy—an astounding 13,600 in all). As the play demonstrates, however, even this man can be saved through the intervention of the virtuous Dorothea. In contrast to Massinger and Dekker, Griffin presents Theophilus's conversion as the result of a vision of Dorothea, not a visit from a spirit. Sexuality is never an issue in the play's relatively simplistic model of vision in which sight of female excellence leads directly to male virtue.

For Nicholas Rowe, the connection between woman as symbol and woman as object was more problematic. In dramatizing the story of Lady Jane Grey, Rowe drew on the familiar dramatic form for which he had become famous. Yet, despite the seemingly ready-made template of the suffering heroine, it is precisely this tradition of she-tragedy that ultimately results in *Lady Jane Gray*'s deficiencies, as the play was the only one of Rowe's she-tragedies not to become part of the standard eighteenth-century theatrical repertoire.[28] The problems inherent in Rowe's representation of Lady Jane Grey arose from the collision of his political propaganda

28. Despite its popularity when first staged, *Lady Jane Gray* was revived only sporadically, usually during times when anti-Catholic sentiments ran high. Unlike both *The Fair Penitent* and *Jane Shore*, it never became a vehicle for great actresses; both of Rowe's other she-tragedies appeared on a nearly yearly basis in one or sometimes both of the patent houses.

with a dramatic tradition in which the female figures suffer not for their virtue but for their sins. These female figures are spectacles with one specific and noninterchangeable function: either model of virtue or fallen heroine.

Jane's multiple functions are apparent from the play's opening words as the prologue announces: "To-night the Noblest Subject Swells our Scene, / A Heroine, a Martyr, and a Queen." Jane does embody the three roles promised in the prologue: she ascends the English throne, ultimately dies for the Protestant cause, and suffers in the manner appropriate to a "heroine." Although this tripartite focus was enough to assure the success of Rowe's tragedy when first staged, the three female roles Rowe mapped out in his prologue coexist uneasily. In order to maintain the status of political symbol, Rowe's Jane Grey must be a figure of strong and unsullied virtue; any smirch on her character represents a flaw in the political agenda and religious faith she embodies. In her purity, however, she differs notably from other heroines of she-tragedy who, however virtuous they may be, are quickly established as both desirable and desiring and frequently, especially in the tragedies of writers such as Southerne and Rowe, transgress sexually: falling, suffering, and repenting for their sin. Rowe's political program has a profound effect on the form and content of the she-tragedy and its heroine; no longer a fallen woman, the title figure has become a symbol of virtue whose own desires are sublimated for a higher political good. His play presents a new heroine, as political propaganda requires the erasure of female desire and overt sexuality—although not the woman's role as object of desire—qualities that until then had been hallmarks of she-tragedy.

For Rowe's audience, this change in the representation was problematic. They expected to see a typical she-tragedy with its characteristically titillating spectacle of a fallen woman, and even Rowe has difficulty evading the constraints of the dramatic form for which he had become famous. Tragedy, especially the she-tragedy of Rowe and his predecessors, rests on a well-defined division between male and female, in this case the actor and the sufferer. A drama's success depended on the skillful manipulation of its central female character, an image customarily presented to the audience in the form of a sexual spectacle of feminized suffering. Rowe's tragedy, and the general fascination with the figure of Lady Jane Grey that surrounded its production, presents an image of womanhood constructed in a political arena. Deliberately designed as both an icon of political virtue and a spectacle of female suffering, Rowe's Lady Jane is, in a sense, both hero and heroine, an active model of virtue and a passive image of distress. Rowe's play demonstrates what happens to the heroine when she is refigured as political symbol but also reveals that even changes to the heroine's character cannot remove her from her position as object of the gaze. The problem of Lady Jane Grey becomes the problem of whether virtue can coexist with the representation of the woman as spectacle.

But what happens if a tragedy's heroine is designed to be something other than simply the beautiful object of all these gazing eyes? As the preface and prologues to Rowe's final tragedy emphasize, Lady Jane Grey was to be a different kind of heroine, a character whom audiences should not confuse with the titillating sexual transgressors of earlier she-tragedies. The anonymous prologue, for example, focuses on the new nature of Rowe's heroine, even arguing that Rowe was atoning for the corrupt nature of earlier characters such as Calista and Jane Shore:

> No soft Enchantments languish in her Eye,
> No Blossoms fade, nor sick'ning Roses die:
> A nobler Passion ev'ry Breast must move,
> Than youthful Raptures, or the Joys of Love.[29]

These lines herald the presence of this new heroine, warning viewers not to expect the "languishing" beauties of previous she-tragedies. The author centers his discussion on the singular nature of this heroine and on the response she should prompt in the male theater audience: the spectator should feel no lustful "raptures" but a "nobler Passion" not dependent on a display of sexuality. In this way, Rowe's use of Jane as spectacle should operate very differently from that of writers such as Young. Rowe even admitted that in the depiction of his title character he altered history in favor of political expediency. "If, in the Poetical Colouring, I have aim'd at heightening and improving some of the Features, it was only to make her more worthy of those Illustrious hands to which I always intended to present her."[30] As the play itself indicates, these "Poetical Colourings" were necessary in order to present a character who could incite passion without "soft Enchantments," one who could uphold a political ideal and articulate the Whig party line without the distractions of "rapture."

In his own prologue, Rowe stresses the chasteness of his heroine, signaling a break with the sexually tainted heroines of his earlier tragedies. In contrast to these experienced women, Lady Jane is emphatically pure:

---

29. Prologue to *The Tragedy of Lady Jane Gray.*
30. Dedication, "To Her Royal Highness THE PRINCESS of *Wales,*" *The Tragedy of Lady Jane Gray,* ed. Sherry.

> No wandring Glance one wanton Thought confess'd,
> No guilty Wish inflam'd her spotless Breast:
> The only Love that warm'd her blooming Youth,
> Was, Husband, England, Liberty, and Truth.

Jane's love for "*England*, Liberty, and Truth" is certainly strong through-out the play; however, unlike the Jane depicted by Banks and Young, her feelings for her husband seem lukewarm at best. Unlike the men around her on the stage and in the audience, Jane's "glance" neither wanders nor stimulates her own desire, and she actively discourages the gaze of oth-ers, as Rowe suggests, in contrast to Young, that the erotic is a distraction rather than an enticement to virtue. When Guildford begs at the end of act 1, "Allow me but to look on you and sigh" (1.1.283), she reproves him and counters his desirous gaze with a vision of the terrors of death:

> Still wilt thou frame thy Speech to this vain Purpose . . .
>   Are we not,
> Like Wretches in a Storm, whom ev'ry Moment,
> The greedy deep is gaping to devour?
> Around us see the pale despairing Crew,
> Wring their sad Hands and give their Labour over;
> The Hope of Life has ev'ry Heart forsook,
> The Horror sits on each distracted Look,
> One solemn Thought of Death does all employ.
>   (1.1.285–95)

As Gildon's pamphlet complained, Rowe's Jane is indeed possessed by "Gloominess and Despondence,"[31] resolutely resisting her role as object of desire within the context of the play and deflecting the male gaze onto political and religious abstractions such as the "pale despairing crew" who watch in horror as the ship of state sinks beneath them.

Rowe's insistence on redefining the heroine, especially the visual spec-tacle of the heroine familiar to earlier eighteenth-century theatergoers suggests that only when made virtually asexual, when recreated as saint and "*England*'s better Angel" (3.376), can a woman be placed in the pub-lic sphere and used as the vessel for political ideology. In direct contrast to Young's poem, sexual love barely "warms" this "blooming Youth." Jane mentions her love for Guildford briefly and even then in dispas-sionate terms, remarking only that "my heart has fondly lean'd toward thee" (2.1.145). Although agreeing to marry Guildford, she insists that

---

31. Gildon, *Remarks*, 11.

they postpone the wedding night, an interdiction to which Guildford readily agrees, "I will forego a Bridegroom's sacred Right, / And sleep far from thee, on the unwholesom Earth" (2.161–62). Unlike Young's poem, in Rowe's play the marriage is never consummated, thus ensuring that Jane remains virginal, untainted by the filth of human sexuality. Her whole heart remains consecrated to England as, even when accepting Guildford's proposal of marriage, she can think only of "sinking Altars, and the falling State" (2.226). At the end of the play, when her martyrdom is assured, she rejects passion, sharply reproving Guildford when he seeks to embrace her: "Here break we off at once; and let us now, / Forgetting Ceremony, like two Friends / That have a little Bus'ness to be done, / Take a short Leave" (5.290–93).

This seeming coldness has an important, if dampening, rhetorical purpose. Jane may reject attempts to fix her as conventional object of desire because she must prove herself to be without sexual—or political—appetites. The question of Jane's desires is essential to the success of Rowe's moral. Any impropriety would discredit Rowe's message, thus Jane can neither appear interested in pleasure of the flesh nor express unwomanly ambitions. She must be at the same time completely pure, untouched by a woman's fears and yet unwilling to take on too masculine a role. Rowe attempts to sidestep potential improprieties by centering his play on Jane's impersonal love for abstractions such as God and country. Thus, the play's first two acts focus on her pious reverence for Edward VI and her concern for the religious threat facing her country, and the final acts explore her accession to the throne and its grave consequences. Unlike Banks's play where Jane accepts the throne out of love for her husband, Jane's "cold Heart kindles" (3.353) only when confronted with the threat English liberty faces from "Hair-brain'd Zeal, and Cruel Coward Priests" (3.350). Told by her father that only she can save England, she reluctantly accepts the crown and death at the same moment:

> Take me, Crown me;
> Invest me with this Royal wretchedness;
> Let me not know one happy Minute more,
> Let all my sleepless Nights be spent in Care,
> My Days be vex'd with Tumults and Alarms,
> If only I can save you; if my fate
> Has mark'd me out to be the Publick Victim,
> I take the Lot with Joy. Yes, I will Die
> For that Eternal Truth my Faith is fix'd on,
> And that dear Native Land which gave me Birth.
> (3.397–406)

No personal ambitions taint this unwilling queen; her desire for power is no greater than her desire for Guildford, and she acts only out of an abstract yearning for England's greater good. By linking misery to power, Rowe makes the political female more palatable; a proper woman suffers when forced against her will into the public realm. Jane herself describes desire for power in the same language Rowe uses in his prologue to denote sexual desire, claiming "Ambition's guilty Fires have [not] warm'd me" (4.327) as she joyfully gives up the crown (4.321–33).

Only when cleansed of desires inappropriate for a woman and for an ideal can Jane articulate Rowe's propaganda, and the final scenes of the play depict Jane as captive and martyr. Imprisoned by Queen Mary's more powerful forces, she is given the choice of renouncing her faith or death. Her scornful rejection of this offer and the subsequent scaffold scene provide Rowe with the opportunity for a blatantly partisan commentary on contemporary politics. A "Divine Example" (5.265) of piety and fortitude, Jane gives her (Protestant) prayer book to her maid and mounts the scaffold, calling on Heaven to

> Raise up a Monarch of the Royal Blood,
> Brave, Pious, Equitable, Wise, and Good:
> In thy due Season let the Hero come,
> To save thy Altars from the Rage of *Rome:*
> Long let him reign, to bless the rescu'd Land
> And deal out Justice with a righteous Hand.
> And when he fails, Oh may he leave a Son,
> With equal Vertues to adorn his Throne;
> To latest Times the Blessing to convey,
> And guard the Faith for which I die to-day.
> *Lady* Jane *goes up to the Scaffold, the Scene closes.*
>   (5.342–52)

A paean clearly addressed to George I (the Protestant monarch who replaced Mary was, after all, Elizabeth I), Rowe's words exaggerate the political crisis England faced into a religious cataclysm. In 1715, while James Edward Stuart had declared himself king, his forces were weak and England's altars were hardly in danger of being commandeered by Catholic priests. By conflating present-day politics with earlier atrocities, Rowe not only presents George I as leader of the faith but as a national savior heralded by a genuine English saint. For this legerdemain to work smoothly, Rowe's mouthpiece must be disinterested, unconflicted, and divorced from personal desire, ultimately inhuman.

If Rowe's Lady Jane Grey is inhuman, she is also, of necessity, a heroine—
the primary dramatic object in the play that bears her name. As discussed
earlier, the heroine fulfilled a very specific function in the tragedies of the
late seventeenth and early eighteenth century. She was designed to be the
central object of the audience's gaze, an effect accomplished through the
use of tableaux such as so-called discovery scenes in which the scene
draws and reveals the heroine to the audience, often while a male character narrates her beauties. The heroine's suffering was a necessary part
of visual appeal; in plays such as Southerne's *Fatal Marriage* and Rowe's
own *Jane Shore* it constitutes the bulk of the play. In the serious drama of
this era, the heroine is beautiful, distressed, and ultimately passive. No
more active than her more amorous counterparts in *The Fatal Marriage,
The Fair Penitent,* or *Jane Shore,* Jane accepts her function as "Publick Victim," but, by stressing that it is fate that has "mark'd [her] out" for this
role, she remains ultimately passive.[32] Even though she lacks the open
sensuality that characterizes earlier she-tragedy heroines, Jane nonetheless fulfills the heroine's most basic function as the suffering object of the
male gaze. But is it possible to have a heroine designed to be the object of
all these eyes and yet avoid the visual erotic component of the gaze? In
order to satisfy his audience's expectations, Rowe strives to preserve
Jane's position as the central focus of all eyes, onstage and off, maintaining control of the gaze while draining it of its erotic elements by purify-
ing Jane's character. The resulting uneasy alliance between stoic Christian
virtue and theatrical display is ultimately unsuccessful as Rowe cannot
circumvent completely the explicitly visual demands of his genre.

   Although Rowe tries to avoid making Jane a sexual object, his play
shares Young's intense focus on Jane's role as image. *The Force of Religion*
emphasized Jane's sexuality rather than her political symbolism, but it
did establish Jane as a visual icon. Although Rowe eschews sexuality,
fearing it will obscure his political message, his play nonetheless depends
on the visual display of Jane's virtue. This link between the two works is
literally emblematic; later editions of Rowe's play used an illustration
from Young's poem as a frontispiece, not, as was usual, the portrait of a
contemporary actress in the title role. Like Young's poem, the play's
power also derives from its ability to show Jane as a living "image." A
self-professed "Publick" victim, Jane's efficacy as a heroine depends on
her ability to become the object of all eyes, an attribute that was even more
crucial in the theater than on the printed page. The climax of *Lady Jane*

---

32. For a discussion of Jane's Christian heroism, see Canfield, *Nicholas Rowe and Christian
Tragedy* (1977), chap. 3.

Gray represents the realization of these features, like so many she-tragedies in previous decades.

The play's final act builds on the idea of Jane as public spectacle, from the accounts of her trial to the two tableaux with which the play concludes. The act begins ominously, with the evil priest Gardiner making preparations for Jane's execution; care must be taken, he warns, that "No Crouds may be let in, no maudlin Gazers" (5.24) because the power of Jane's virtuous image may induce civil revolt (the same concern voiced in the various biographies of Lady Jane Grey). Gardiner's fear that Jane's physical presence could have potent effects is borne out by Pembroke's comment that the sight of Jane's "sacred Form" (a phrase which in itself is both religiously and sexually suggestive) "mov'd the Hearts of a rude ruthless Crowd" (5.99). Describing Jane as a "beauteous Traitress," Gardiner's description of the trial reinforces her visual impact as he relates that

> With silent Grief the mournful Audience sat,
> Fix'd on her Face, and list'ning to her Pleading.
> Her very Judges wrung their Hands for Pity;
> Their old Hearts melted in 'em as she spoke,
> And Tears ran down upon their silver Beards.
>   (5.83–87)

Gardiner's chronicle of Jane as object of a universal male gaze negates his claim that Pembroke overestimates the power and virtue of her image because he "look[s] upon her with Lovers Eyes" (5.101). With their eyes "fix'd upon her Face," Jane's very judges share Pembroke's response; seemingly, the entire courtroom looked upon Jane with "Lovers Eyes."

The account of Jane's trial is followed almost immediately by a tableau that enacts exactly Young's rapt vision and which is the scene chosen for the play's—and the poem's—frontispiece. The scene draws, and *"discovers the Lady* Jane *Kneeling, as at her Devotion; a Light and a Book plac'd on a Table before her."* All the components of Young's fantasy are present: the young, beautiful, and great lady; the humble position; and the deflected gaze, fixed as her woman informs Guildford, "upon the sacred Page before her, / Or lifted with her rising Hopes to Heaven" (5.146–47). Guildford acts as voyeur in this scene, savoring the image and directing the audience to "Mark her Vermilion Lip with Fervour trembling! / Her spotless Bosom swells with sacred Ardour, / And burns with Extasy and strong Devotion" (5.149–51). Piety may be present, but to the male observer it is mingled inextricably with the erotic details of vermilion lips and swelling bosom. No matter how hard Rowe may try to escape from eroticizing his heroine, in the end he cannot.

The play ends with Jane as public victim, again set as tableau as *"The Scene draws, and discovers a Scaffold hung with Black, Executioner and Guards."* Against this backdrop, Jane bids farewell to the world and makes her speech foretelling a Protestant hero; the scene projects no pathos, but in its representation of "how like a Saint she ended" (5.26) it defines the audience as those "maudlin Gazers" Gardiner had sought to avoid. Jane ends, then, as sanctified object of a communal gaze and for all her ideological rhetoric remains object rather than subject and image rather than actor. Although Rowe attempted to transform the genre of she-tragedy, he could not alter his audience's expectation of what his heroine should represent and how she should behave. As responses to his representation of Lady Jane Grey demonstrate, the heroine, no matter how virtuous or politically commendable, when held up as a theatrical spectacle remains coded as a sexual object. Although the political text might require an erasure of female desire, male desire remained. As long as sexual spectacle was a necessary part of drama, the woman, whether erotic or not, icon or whore, would be interpreted within a sexual context. Only by removing the woman as spectacle can this cycle be broken.

Afterword

The plays that have been the focus of this book were a mainstay of the stage not only in London but in the English-speaking world. For more than a century the tragedies of Congreve, Southerne, and Rowe dominated the stage, remaining second in popularity only to the tragedies of Shakespeare. They represent an era in which women were a dominant presence on the stage, both as actresses and as the centerpieces of dramas in which these actresses performed. For the four decades between 1680 and 1720, these characters, their passions, and their sorrows defined tragedy as drama turned away from the masculine heroics of an earlier age. Only when female sexuality became increasingly risky to stage did this pattern begin to shift. In the early years of the eighteenth century, women continued to dominate the stage, but their distress provided an increasingly moral message of the wages of sin.

I chose to title these final pages an afterword because in them I glance literally at what comes after *The Tragedy of Lady Jane Gray*, to consider both the fate of she-tragedy and its influence on the British stage. On the one hand, the dilemma represented by Rowe's final play heralded the death of a genre; after 1715, very few new plays were written in the mode of the she-tragedy. Moreover, the actresses who helped popularize the genre were themselves gone from the stage: Anne Bracegirdle retired from the stage in 1709 and Elizabeth Barry, the greatest actress of the age, died in 1713. Although the tragedies of Otway, Southerne, Congreve, and Rowe continued to dominate the stage, after 1715 playwrights rarely wrote in the mode that Barry, Bracegirdle, and later Anne Oldfield had made popular. On the other hand, the most successful she-tragedies remained a standard part of the English repertoire; roles such as Monimia, Calista, Isabella, and Jane Shore became the benchmark of an actress's abilities as a tragedian.

Even when she-tragedies were no longer being written, audiences continued to take pleasure in watching distress, specifically the tableau of the suffering woman. Thus it is perhaps not surprising that when Adam Smith wrote his immensely influential *Theory of Moral Sentiments* (1759), his favorite examples of the moral power of human sympathy were not only drawn from drama but from the she-tragedies of Southerne and Otway. (Shakespeare, by contrast, receives but a single reference). Perhaps the greatest proof of the influence of she-tragedy is the broadening representation of pathos in drama. By the mid eighteenth century, women were no longer the sole embodiments of suffering. As seen perhaps most famously in George Lillo's *The London Merchant* (1731), the depiction of male suffering becomes central to a play's moral and emotional impact, and by mid century pathos in drama is largely ungendered. A function in part of the dominance of actors such as David Garrick and Spranger Barry, male pathos—of humble men and even of kings—becomes a common part of tragedy.

During this time, the performance of pathos also becomes increasingly moral. The emotions such scenes were designed to evoke in theater audiences were seen as the prelude to moral virtue; in this way, Jane Shore's anguish represents a useful lesson for her female audience. Through this process, she-tragedy becomes not simply a form of titillation but an active social good. With moral implications to be drawn from the performance of pathos, attacks on the theater dwindle. The antitheatrical pamphlets that had proliferated in the years around the turn of the century subside almost completely by the middle of the century. The majority of these attacks can be traced to a group of Scottish clergymen who considered plays and diversions un-Christian in and of themselves. Unlike Collier and his followers, they rarely decry the sexual immorality of the stage, and never debate the pernicious effects that spectators, especially female spectators, might suffer by watching immoral images. The concern with the effect of spectatorship on women that had so obsessed Collier and his followers never emerges in these works. Women as spectators excite no more anxiety than do than men in the theaters.

The theater of the Restoration and early eighteenth century represents a pivotal moment not only in theater history but in English social history. As the time when women were first embodied by women on the public stage, it represented not only an era of literary discovery but of anxiety. Women functioned as symbols of both domestic and imperial propriety, and their chastity was a paradigm for stability within the family and the nation. With theater presenting an open display of women and their behavior, these fictitious representations were assumed to have a significance that reached far beyond the theater walls. The representation of improper desire, even within the legitimate bounds of marriage, suggested social disintegration and inappropriate political alliances. Playwrights and their audiences grappled with the implications not only of staging women but of watching them. As the often-heated responses to female characters indicate, these stage women were more than simply actresses; because they stood before the public eye, they represented an age's view of the proper codes of feminine behavior. In the feminization of serious drama, we see the intersection of the literary and cultural functions of theater as female suffering allayed these anxieties while providing the authenticity that the fate of kings and empires no longer possessed.

Bibliography

Primary Works

Addison, Joseph. *The Freeholder.* Ed. James Leheny. Oxford: Clarendon Press, 1979.
Addison, Joseph, and Richard Steele. *The Spectator.* 5 vols. Ed. Donald F. Bond. Oxford: Clarendon Press, 1965.
An Address to the Ladies on the indecency of Appearing at Immodest Plays. London, 1756.
Astell, Mary. *The First Feminist: Reflections upon Marriage and Other Writings by Mary Astell.* Ed. Bridget Hill. New York: St. Martin's Press, 1986.
Austen, Jane. *Northanger Abbey.* Ed. R. W. Chapman. London: Oxford University Press, 1933.
Baker, Richard. *Theatrum Redivivum; or, The Theatre Vindicated, in Answer to Mr. Pryn's Histrio-mastix: Wherein his groundless Assertions against Stage Plays are discovered, his miss-taken Allegations of the Fathers manifested, as also what he calls his Reasons, to be nothing but his Passions.* London, 1662.
Banks, John. *The Innocent Usurper; or, The Death of Lady Jane Gray.* London, 1694.
——. *The Island Queens; or, The Death of Mary Queen of Scotland* (1684). Ed. Jayne Elizabeth Lewis. Reprinted for the Augustan Reprint Society. New York: AMS Press, 1995.
——. *The Unhappy Favourite; or, The Earl of Essex.* London, 1682.
——. *Vertue Betray'd; or, Anna Bullen* (1682). Ed. Diane Dreher. Reprinted for the Augustan Reprint Society. Los Angeles: William Andrews Clark Memorial Library, 1981.
Behn, Aphra. *The Works of Aphra Behn.* 6 vols. Ed. Montague Summers. London, 1915. Reprint, New York: Phaeton Press, 1967.
Betterton, Thomas [compiled by William Oldys and Edmund Curll]. *The History of the English Stage, from the Restauration to the Present Time Including the Lives, Characters and Amours, of the most Eminent Actors and Actresses. With Instructions for Public Speaking; Wherein the action and Utterance of the Bar, Stage, and Pulpit are Distinctly considered.* London, 1741.
Bickerstaffe, Isaac. *The Plain Dealer: A Comedy, with Alterations from Wycherly.* London, 1766.

Blackmore, Sir Richard. Preface to *King Arthur. An Heroick Poem. In Twelve Books.* London, 1697.

Bonduca; or, The British Heroine. London, 1695.

Bossuet, Jacques Benigne. *Maximes et réflexions sur la comédie.* 1694.

Boyer, Abel. *Achilles; or, Iphigenia in Aulis.* Perf. 1699, pub. London, 1700.

———. *The History of the Life and Reign of Queen Anne.* London, 1722.

Brady, Nicholas. *The Rape; or, The Innocent Imposters.* London, 1692.

British Wonders; or, A Poetical Description of the Several Prodigies and the Most Remarkable Accidents that have happen'd in Britain *since the Death of Queen Anne.* London, 1717.

Cibber, Colley. *An Apology for the Life of Colley Cibber.* Ed. B. R. S. Fone. Ann Arbor: University of Michigan Press, 1968.

Cobb, Samuel. *Poems on Several Occasions.* London, 1707.

Collier, Jeremy. *A Defence of the Short View of the Profaness and Immorality of the English* STAGE, &c. Being a REPLY to Mr. Congreve's *Amendments, &c. And to the Vindication of the Author of the Relapse.* London, 1699.

———. *A Farther Vindication of the Short View of the Profaneness and Immorality of the En-*glish Stage. *In which the Objections of a late Book, Entitled,* A Defence of Plays, *are Consider'd.* London, 1708.

———. *Mr. Collier's Dissuasive from the Play-House; In a Letter to a Person of Quality; Occasion'd By the late Calamity of the Tempest.* London, 1703.

———. *Mr. Collier's Dissuasive from the Play-House; In a Letter to a Person of Quality: Occasion'd By the late Calamity of the Tempest. To which is added, a Letter written by another Hand; in Answer to some Queries sent by a Person of Quality, Relating to the Irregularities charged upon the Stage.* London, 1704.

———. *A Second Defence of the Short View of the Profaneness and Immorality of the Egnlish Stage &c. Being a reply to a book, entituled, the Ancient and Modern Stages Surveyed, &c.* London, 1700.

———. *A Short View of the Immorality, and Profaneness of the English Stage, together With the Sense of Antiquity upont his Argument.* London, 1698.

The Conduct of the Stage Consider'd. Being a Short Historical Account of its Original, Progress, various Aspects, and Treatment in the Pagan, Jewish and Christian World. Together with the Arguments urg'd against it, by Learned Heathens, and by Christians, both Antient and Modern. With Short Remarks upon the Original and Pernicious Consequences of Masquerades. London, 1721.

Congreve, William. *Amendments of Mr. Collier's False and Imperfect Citations, &c.* London, 1698.

———. *The Complete Plays of Congreve.* Ed. Herbert Davis. Chicago: University of Chicago Press, 1967.

Crowne, John. *Andromache.* London, 1675.

The Daily Courant.

Defoe, Daniel. *A Review of the State of the British Nation.* Facsimile reprint, New York: AMS Press, 1965.

Dennis, John. *The Critical Works of John Dennis.* 2 vols. Ed. Edward Niles Hooker. Baltimore: Johns Hopkins University Press, 1943.

———. *Iphigenia.* Perf. 1699, pub. London, 1700.

D[orrington], T[heophilus]. *The Excellent Woman Described by her True Characters and Their Opposites.* London, 1692.

Downes, John. *Roscius Anglicanus* (1708). Introduction by John Loftis. London, 1708. Reprint, Los Angeles: William Clark Memorial Library, 1969.

[Drake, James]. *The Antient and Modern Stages Survey'd; or, Mr. Collier's View of the Immorality and Profaneness of the English Stage set in a true light. Wherein some of Mr. Collier's mistakes are rectified, and the comparative Morality of the English Stage is asserted upon the Parallel.* London, 1699.

Dryden, John. *To My Dear Friend Mr. Congreve.* London, 1694.

———. *Works of John Dryden.* Ed. Edward Niles Hooker, H. T. Swedenberg, Jr., et al. 20 vols.; in progress. Berkeley: University of California Press, 1956–.

Duffett, Thomas. *The Amorous Old Woman; or, 'Tis Well if It Take.* London, 1674.

D'Urfey, Thomas. *The Campaigners; or, The Pleasant Adventures at Brussels. A Comedy. With a Familiar Preface upon a Late Reformer of the Stage. Ending with a Satyrical Fable of the Dog and the Ottor.* London, 1698.

"The Explanation." 1685.

The Fatal Discovery; or, Love in Ruines. Perf. 1697, pub. London, 1698.

The Fate of Majesty, Exemplified in the Barbarous and Disloyal Treatment (by Traiterous and Undutiful Subjects) of the Kings and Queens of the Royal House of the Stuarts. From the Reign of ROBERT, the first Monarch of that Name, to the last of the most August Princes of that unhappy Family. To which is added, a Vindication of MARY, *Queen of Scots, who was (contrary to the Laws of God, Nations and Nature) put to Death in the Days of Queen Elizabeth; from the scandalous and vile Aspersion of Buchanan, the Scotch Historian. As also a Preface in Defence of the Solemn Observation of the Anniversaries of King* CHARLES *the First's Martyrdom, King* CHARLES *the Second's Restoration, and Queen* ANNE's *Birth, Accession, and Coronation.* London, 1715.

The Female Wits; or, The Triumvirate of Poets at Rehearsal (perf. 1697, pub. 1704). Ed. Lucyle Hook. Reprinted by the Augustan Reprint Society. Los Angeles: William Clark Library, 1967.

Filmer, Edward. *A defence of Plays; or, The Stage Vindicated, From several Passages in Mr. Collier's Short View, &c. Wherein is offer'd The most Probable Method of Reforming our PLAYS. With a Consideration How far Vicious Characters may be allow'd on the STAGE.* London, 1707.

Foote, Samuel. *The Roman and English Comedy Consider'd and Compar'd. With Remarks on the Suspicious Husband. And an Examen into the Merits of the present Comic Actors.* London, 1747.

The Forsaken Fair. An Epistle from Calista in her Late Illness at Bath, to Lothario on his Approaching Nuptials. London, 1736.

Foxe, John. *Acts and Monuments of Matters most Special and Memorable, Happening in the Church: with an Universal History of the same: Wherein is set forth at large, the whole race and course of the Church, from the Primitive Age to these later Times of Ours, with the bloody times, horrible troubles, and great persecutions against the true martyrs of Christ, sought and wrought as well by heathen emperors, as now lately practiced by Romish Prelates, especially in this realm of England and Scotland: now again as it was recognized, perused, and recommended to the studious reader by the Author, John Foxe; whereunto are annexed certain additions of like persecutions which have happened in these later times; to which also is added the Life of the Author both in Latine and English.* 9th ed. Vol. 3. London, 1684.

[Gentleman, Francis]. *The Dramatic Censor; or, Critical Companion.* 2 vols. London, 1770.

Gildon, Charles. *A Comparison Between the Two Stages.* Ed. Staring B. Wells. Princeton: Princeton University Press, 1942.

———. *The Complete Art of Poetry.* 2 vols. London, 1718.

———. *The Lives and Characters of the English Dramatick Poets. Also an Exact Account of all the Plays that were ever yet printed in the English Tongue; their Double Titles, the Places where Acted, the Dates when printed, and the Persons to whom Dedicated; with Remarks and Observations on most of the said Plays. First begun by Mr.* Langbain, *improv'd and continued down to this Time, by a Careful Hand.* London, 1699.

——. *Love's Victim; or, The Queen of Wales.* London, 1701.

——. *A New Rehearsal; or, Bays the Younger. Containing an Examen of The Ambitious Step-Mother, Tamerlane, The Biter, Fair Penitent, Royal Convert, Ulysses, and Jane Shore. All Written by N. Rowe, Esq. Also a Word or Two upon Mr. Pope's* Rape of the Lock. *To which is prefix'd a Preface in Vindication of Criticism in General, by the Late Earl of Shaftsbury.* London, 1714.

——. Preface to *Phaeton; or, The Fatal Divorce.* London, 1698.

——. *Remarks on Mr. Rowe's Tragedy of the Lady* Jane Gray, *and all his other plays . . . With Some Observations upon, I. Mr. Smith's* Phaedra and Hippolytus. *II. Mr. Philips's* Distress'd Mother. *III. Mr. Addison's* Cato. *IV. Mr. Pope's* Rape of the Lock, &c. *To which is prefix'd, a prefatory discourse in defence of criticism. Collected from the works of the late Earl of Shaftsbury.* London, 1715.

——. *The Roman Bride's Revenge.* London, 1697.

Gosson, Stephen. *Plays Confuted in Five Actions.* London, 1582.

Griffin, Benjamin. *Injured Virtue; or, The Virgin Martyr.* London, 1714.

Halifax, George Savile, Marquis of. *The Lady's New Years Gift; or, Advice to a Daughter.* London, 1688.

Hawkins, William. *Miscellanies in Prose and Verse. Containing Candid and Impartial Observations on the Principal Performers belonging to the Two Theatres-Royal; From January 1773, to May 1775. Likewise Strictures on two favourite Tragedies, viz. The* ORPHAN *and the* FAIR PENITENT. *Being part of an epistolary Correspondence on those Subjects with a young Lady. With Many other agreeable and interesting Articles, such as Pastoral Songs, Epitaphs, &c. &c.* London, 1775.

Hill, Aaron. *Elfrid; or, The Fair Inconstant.* London, 1710.

Hopkins, Charles. *Boadicea, Queen of Britain.* London, 1697.

——. *Friendship Improved; or, The Female Warrior.* London, 1700.

Horneck, Anthony. *Delight and Judgment; or, A Prospect of the Great Day of Judgment, and its power to damp, and imbitter Sensual Delights, Sports and Recreations.* London, 1684.

Inchbald, Elizabeth. *The British Theatre; or, A Collection of Plays which are acted at the Theatres Royal, Drury Lane, Covent Garden, Haymarket, and Lyceum. Printed under the Authority of the Managers, from the Prompt Books. With Biographical and Critical Remarks by Mrs. Inchbald.* 20 vols. London, 1824.

Johnson, Charles. *The Victim.* London, 1714.

Johnson, Samuel. *Lives of the English Poets.* 3 vols. Ed. George Birkbeck Hill. Oxford: Clarendon Press, 1905. Reprint, New York: Octagon Books, 1967.

Jordan, Thomas. Prologue to *Othello* in *A Nursery of Novelties in Variety of Poetry. Planted for the delightful leisures of Nobility and Ingenuity.* London, 1665.

Knolles, Richard. *The Turkish History from the Original of that Nation to the Growth of the Ottoman Empire with the Lives and Conquests of their Princes and Emperors. By Richard Knolles . . . with a Continuation to this Present Year MDCLXXXVII, whereunto is added, the Present State of the Ottoman Empire by Sir Paul Rycaut. The Sixth Edition, with the Effigies of all the Kings and Emperors, newly engraven at large on copper.* 3 vols. London, 1687.

A Lash for the Laureat; or, An Address by way of Satyr; Most Humbly Inscrib'd to the Unparallel'd Mr. Row, On Occasion of a late insolent Prologue to the Non-Juror. London, 1718.

Lee, Nathaniel. *Works.* 2 vols. Ed. Thomas B. Stroup and Arthur L. Cooke. New Brunswick, NJ: Scarecrow Press, 1954.

A Letter to a Noble Lord, To whom alone it Belongs. Occasioned by a Representation at the Theatre Royal in Drury-Lane of a Farce, called Miss Lucy in Town. London, 1742.

The Life and Character of Jane Shore. Collected from our best Historians, chiefly from the Writings of Sir Thomas More; Who was her Cotemporary, and Personally knew Her. London, 1714.

The Life and Death of Jane Shore; Containing the whole Account of her Amorous Intrigues with King Edward the IV. and the Lord Hastings: Her Penitence, Punishment and Poverty. To which are added, Other Amours of that King and his Courtiers; with Several Antient Love Poems, Written by the Wits of those Times. Also An Heroick Epistle from King Edward IV to Jane Shore, with her Answer. London, 1714.

The Life, Character, and Death of the most Illustrious Pattern of Female Vertue, The Lady Jane Gray, who was Beheaded in the Tower at 16 Years of Age, for her stedfast Adherence to the Protestant Religion. London, 1714.

Lillo, George. *The Dramatic Works of George Lillo.* Ed. James L. Steffensen. Oxford: Clarendon Press, 1993.

Manley, Delarivier. *The Adventures of Rivella.* Ed. Katherine Zelinsky. Toronto: Broadview Press, 1999.

———. *Almyna; or, The Arabian Vow.* London, 1707.

———. *The Lost Lover; or, The Jealous Husband.* London, 1696.

———. *The New Atalantis.* Ed. Rosalind Ballaster. London: Pickering and Chatto, 1991.

———. *The Royal Mischief.* London, 1696.

Massinger, Philip. *The Plays and Poems of Philip Massinger.* 5 vols. Ed. Philip Edwards and Colin Gibson. Oxford: Clarendon Press, 1976.

Memoirs of the Life, Writings, and Amours of William Congreve Esq; Interspersed with Miscellaneous Essays, Letters, and Characters Written by Him. Also some very Curious Memoirs of Mr. Dryden and his Family, with a Character of Him and his Writings by Mr. Congreve. Compiled from their respective Originals, by Charles Wilson, Esq. London, 1730.

Milton, John. *Complete Poems and Major Prose.* Ed. Merritt Y. Hughes. Indianapolis: Odyssey Press, 1957.

A Modest Survey of that Celebrated Tragedy The Distrest Mother, so often and so highly Applauded by the Ingenious Spectator. London, 1712.

Moliere. *The Misanthrope, Tartuffe, and Other Plays.* Trans. Maya Slater. Oxford: Oxford University Press, 2001.

More, Sir Thomas. *The History of Richard III and Selections from the English and Latin Poems.* Ed. Richard S. Sylvester. New Haven: Yale University Press, 1976.

Motteux, Peter. *Farewel Folly.* London, 1705.

Mountfort, William. *Zelmane; or, The Corinthian Queen.* London, 1705.

Mr. Collier's Dissuasive from the Play-House; in a Letter to a Person of Quality, Occasion'd by the late Calamity of the Tempest. To which is added, a Letter written by another Hand; in Answer to some Queries sent by a Person of Quality, Relating to the Irregularities charged upon the Stage. London, 1704.

"A New Ballad." 1728.

Oldisworth, William. "A Character of Mr. Smith," prefixed to *The Works of Mr. Edmund Smith Late of Christ-Church, Oxford: Containing, I. Phaedra and Hippolitus. II. A poem on the Death of Mr. Philips. III. Bodleian Speech. IV. Pococrius, &c.* London, 1729.

Oldmixon, John. *Reflections on the Stage, and Mr. Collyer's Defence of the Short View. In Four Dialogues.* London, 1699.

Otway, Thomas. *The Works of Thomas Otway.* 2 vols. Ed. J. C. Ghosh. Oxford: Clarendon Press, 1932.

Philips, Ambrose. *The Distrest Mother.* London, 1712.

Pix, Mary. *The Conquest of Spain.* London, 1705.

———. *The Double Distress.* London, 1701.

———. *Ibrahim, the Thirteenth Emperour of the Turks.* London, 1696.

———. *Queen Catharine; or, The Ruines of Love.* London, 1698.

Prynne, William. *Histrio-Mastix, the Players Scovrge; or, Actors Tragaedy.* London, 1633.

Racine, Jean. *Complete Plays.* 2 vols. Trans. Samuel Solomon. New York: Random
House, 1967.

Remarks on the Tragedy of The Lady Jane Gray; in a Letter to Mr. Rowe. London, 1715.

*A Representation of the Impiety and Immorality of the English Stage, With Reasons for
putting a Stop thereto: and some Questions Addrest to those who frequent the Play-
Houses.* London, 1704.

Rochester, John Wilmot, Earl of. *Valentinian.* London, 1685.

Rowe, Nicholas. *Three Plays.* Ed. J. R. Sutherland. London: The Scholartis Press, 1929.

———. *The Tragedy of Lady Jane Gray.* 1715. Ed. Richard James Sherry. Salzburg:
Salzburg Studies in English Literature #59, 1980.

Rycaut, Sir Paul. *The History of the Turkish Empire, from the Year 1623, to the Year 1677.
Containing the Reigns of the Three last Emperors, viz. Sultan Morat, or Amurat IV.
Sultan Ibrahim, and Sultan Mahomet III, his Son, the Thirteenth Emperor, now Reigning.*
6th ed. London, 1687.

———. *The Present State of the Ottoman Empire. Containing the Maxims of the Turkish
Polity; the most Material Points of the Mahometan Religion; Their Sects and Heresies;
Their Convents and Religious Votaries; Their Military Discipline; With an exact
Computation of their Forces both by Sea and Land. In Three Books.* London, 1687.

Rymer, Thomas. *Critical Works.* Ed. Curt A. Zimansky. New Haven: Yale University
Press, 1956.

*A Seasonal Examination of the Pleas and Pretensions of the Proprietors of, and Subscribers
to, Play-Houses, Erected in Defiance of the Royal Licence. With Some Brief Observations
on the Printed Case of the Players belonging to Drury-Lane and Covent-Garden
Theatres.* London, 1735.

Sewell, George. *The Life and Character of Mr. John Philips.* 3rd ed. London, 1720.

Shadwell, Thomas. *The Complete Works of Thomas Shadwell.* 5 vols. Ed. Montague
Summers. London: Fortune Press, 1927.

Smith, Adam. *The Theory of Moral Sentiments.* Ed. D. D. Raphael and A. L. Macfie.
Oxford: Clarendon Press, 1976.

Smith, Charlotte. *The Old Manor House.* London, 1793.

Smith, Edmund. *Phaedra and Hippolitus.* London, 1707.

Smith, Henry. *The Princess of Parma.* London, 1699.

Southerne, Thomas. *The Works of Thomas Southerne.* 2 vols. Ed. Robert Jordan and
Harold Love. Oxford: Clarendon Press, 1988.

*The Stage Acquitted. Being a Full Answer to Mr. Collier, and the other Enemies of the
Drama. With a Vindication of King Charles the Martyr, and The Clergy of the Church of
England, From the Abuses of a Scurrilous Book, Called,* The Stage Condemned. *To which
is added, the Character of the Animadverter, and the Animadversions on Mr. Congreve's
Answer to Mr. Collier.* London, 1699.

*The Stage Condemn'd, and The Encouragement given to the Immoralities and Profaneness
of the Theatre, by the English Schools, Universitys and Pulpits, Censur'd. King Charles
I. Sundays Mask and Declaration for Sports and Pastimes on the Sabbath, Largely Related
and Animadvertsed upon. The Arguments of all the Authors that have Writ in Defence of*

the Stage against Mr. Collier, Consider'd. And the Sense of the Fathers, Councils, Antient Philosophers and Poets, and of the Greek and Roman Stages, and of the First Christian Emperours concerning the DRAMA *Faithfully Deliver'd.* Together with the Censure of the English State and of several Antient and Modern Divines of the Church of England upon the STAGE. And Remarks on diverse late Plays, as also on those presented by the two UNIVERSITIES to King Charles I. London, 1698.

Steele, Richard. *The Conscious Lovers.* London, 1722.

Swift, Jonathan. *Journal to Stella.* Ed. Harold Williams. Oxford: Clarendon Press, 1948.

The Theatrical Portrait, A Poem on the Celebrated Mrs. Siddons, in the Characters of Calista, Jane Shore, Belvidera, and Isabella. London, 1783.

The Theatrical Review; or, New Companion to the Play-House: Containing A Critical and Historical Account of every Tragedy, Comedy, Opera, Farce, &c. exhibited at the Theatres during the last Season; With Remarks on the Actors who performed the principal Characters. The Whole interspersed with occasional Reflections on Dramatic Poetry in general; the Characters of the best English Dramatic Authors; and Observations on the Conduct of Managers. Calculated for the Entertainment and Instruction of every Lover of Theatrical Amusements. 2 vols. By a Society of Gentlemen Independent of Managerial Influence. London, 1772.

Trapp, Joseph. *Abra-Mule; or, Love and Empire.* London, 1704.

Trotter, Catharine. *Agnes de Castro; or, The Force of Generous Love.* London, 1688.

———. *The Fatal Friendship.* London, 1698.

———. *Love at a Loss; or, Most Votes Carry It.* London, 1700.

———. *The Revolution in Sweden.* London, 1706.

———. *The Unhappy Penitant.* London, 1701.

Vanbrugh, John. *Complete Works.* 4 vols. Ed. Bonamy Dobree and Geoffrey Webb. London: Nonesuch Press, 1927–28.

Wiseman, Jane. *Antiochus the Great; or, The Fatal Relapse.* Perf. 1701, pub. London, 1702.

Wycherley, William. *The Plays of William Wycherley.* Ed. Arthur Friedman. Oxford: Clarendon Press, 1979.

Young, Edward. *The Force of* RELIGION; *or, Vanquish'd Love. (Illustrated in the Story of Lady Jane Gray).* In Two Books. 2d ed. London, 1715.

Young Lady. *The Unnatural Mother.* London, 1698.

Secondary Works

Adams, Percy G. "What Happened in Olivia's Bedroom? or, Ambiguity in *The Plain Dealer.*" In *Essays in Honor of Esmond Linworth Marilla,* ed. Thomas Austin Kirby and William John Olive, 174–87. Baton Rouge: Louisiana State University Press, 1970.

Anthony, Sister Rose. *The Jeremy Collier Stage Controversy, 1698–1726.* New York: Benjamin Blom, 1937.

Armstrong, Nancy. *Desire and Domestic Fiction: A Political History of the Novel.* Oxford: Oxford University Press, 1987.

Backscheider, Paula. *Spectacular Politics: Theatrical Power and Mass Culture in Early Modern England.* Baltimore: Johns Hopkins University Press, 1993.

Ballaster, Ros. "The First Female Dramatists." In *Women and Literature in Britain, 1500–1700,* ed. Helen Wilcox, 267–90. Cambridge: Cambridge University Press, 1996.

Bamford, Karen. *Sexual Violence on the Jacobean Stage.* New York: St. Martin's Press, 2000.

Barish, Jonas. *The Antitheatrical Prejudice.* Berkeley: University of California Press, 1981.

Braverman, Richard. *Plots and Counterplots: Sexual Politics and the Body Politic in English Literature, 1660–1730.* Cambridge: Cambridge University Press, 1993.

The Broadview Anthology of Restoration and Early Eighteenth-Century Drama. Gen. ed. J. Douglas Canfield. Toronto: Broadview Press, 2001.

Brown, Laura. "The Defenseless Woman and the Development of English Tragedy." *SEL* 22 (1982): 429–43.

Bull, John. *Vanbrugh and Farquhar.* Basingstoke: Macmillan, 1998.

Burke, Helen. "'Law Suits,' 'Love Suits,' and the Family Property in Wycherley's *The Plain Dealer.*" In *Cultural Readings of Restoration and Eighteenth-Century Theater,* ed. J. Douglas Canfield and Deborah C. Payne, 89–113. Athens: University of Georgia Press, 1995.

Camera Obscura 20/21, 1989.

Canfield, J. Douglas. *Heroes and States: On the Ideology of Restoration Tragedy.* Lexington: University Press of Kentucky, 2000.

———. *Nicholas Rowe and Christian Tragedy.* Gainesville: University Presses of Florida, 1977.

———. *Tricksters and Estates: On the Ideology of Restoration Comedy.* Lexington: University Press of Kentucky, 1997.

Clark, Constance. *Three Augustan Women Playwrights.* New York: Peter Lang, 1986.

de Lauretis, Teresa. *Technologies of Gender: Essays on Theory, Film, and Fiction.* Bloomington: Indiana University Press, 1987.

DeRitter, Jones. "'Wonder not, princely Gloster, at the notice this paper brings you': Women, Writing, and Politics in Rowe's *Jane Shore.*" *Comparative Drama* 31, no.1 (spring 1997): 86–104.

Doane, Mary Ann. *The Desire to Desire: The Woman's Film of the 1940s.* Bloomington: Indiana University Press, 1987.

———. *Femmes Fatales: Feminism, Film Theory, Psychoanalysis.* New York: Routledge, 1991.

———. "Film and Masquerade: Theorizing the Female Spectator." *Screen* 23, nos. 3–4 (1982): 74–87.

———. "Masquerade Reconsidered: Further Thoughts on the Female Spectator." *Discourse* 11, no. 1 (1988–89): 42–54.

Donoghue, Emma. *Passions between Women: British Lesbian Culture 1669–1801.* New York: HarperCollins, 1995.

Ezell, Margaret. *Writing Women's Literary History.* Baltimore: Johns Hopkins University Press, 1993.

Fisk, Deborah Payne. "Reified Object or Emergent Professional? Retheorizing the Restoration Actress." In *Cultural Readings of Restoration and Eighteenth-Century Theater,* ed. J. Douglas Canfield and Deborah Payne, 13–38. Athens: University of Georgia Press, 1995.

Foucault, Michel. *History of Sexuality.* Vol. 1. *An Introduction.* Trans. Robert Hurley. New York: Vintage-Random House, 1976.

Freeman, Lisa A. *Character's Theatre: Genre and Identity on the Eighteenth-Century English Stage.* Philadelphia: University of Pennsylvania Press, 2002.

Gallagher, Catherine. "Who Was That Masked Woman? The Prostitute and the Playwright in the Comedies of Aphra Behn." *Women's Studies* 15 (1988): 23–42.

Genest, John. *Some Account of the English Stage: From the Restoration to the Present.* 10 vols. Bath: H. E. Carrington, 1832.

Gill, Pat. *Interpreting Ladies: Women, Wit, and Morality in the Restoration Comedy of Manners.* Athens: University of Georgia Press, 1994.

Gregg, Edward. *Queen Anne.* London: Routledge & Kegan Paul, 1980.

Haggerty, George E. *Men in Love: Masculinity and Sexuality in the Eighteenth Century.* New York: Columbia University Press, 1999.

Hagstrum, Jean. *Sex and Sensibility: Ideal and Erotic Love from Milton to Mozart.* Chicago: University of Chicago Press, 1980.

Holland, Peter. *The Ornament of Action: Text and Performance in Restoration Comedy.* Cambridge: Cambridge University Press, 1979.

Howe, Elizabeth. *The First English Actresses: Women and Drama, 1660–1700.* Cambridge: Cambridge University Press, 1992.

Hughes, Derek. *English Drama, 1660–1700.* Oxford: Clarendon Press, 1996.

———. "*The Plain Dealer*: A Reappraisal." *Modern Language Quarterly* 43, no. 4 (1982): 323–24.

Hughes, Leo. *The Drama's Patrons: A Study of the Eighteenth-Century London Audience.* Austin: University of Texas Press, 1971.

Hume, Robert D. *The Development of English Drama in the Late Seventeenth Century.* Oxford: Clarendon Press, 1976.

———. "Jeremy Collier and the Future of the London Theater in 1698." *Studies in Philology* 96, no. 4 (fall 1999): 480–511.

Jardine, Lisa. *Still Harping on Daughters: Women and Drama in the Age of Shakespeare.* Brighton: Harvester Press, 1983.

Kendall, Kathryn. "Catharine Trotter Cockburn and Me: A Duography." In *The Intimate Critique: Autobiographical Literary Criticism,* ed. Diane P. Freedman, Olivia Frey, and Frances Murphy Zauhar, 273–82. Durham, NC: Duke University Press, 1993.

———. "Finding the Good Parts: Sexuality in Women's Tragedies in the Time of Queen Anne." In *Curtain Calls: British and American Women and the Theater, 1660–1820,* ed. Mary Anne Schofield and Cecilia Macheski, 165–76. Athens: Ohio University Press, 1991.

———. "From Lesbian Heroine to Devoted Wife; or, What the Stage Would Allow." *Journal of Homosexuality* 12 (May 1986): 9–21.

Lock, F. P. "Astraea's 'Vacant Throne': The Successors of Aphra Behn." In *Women in the Eighteenth Century and Other Essays,* ed. Paul Fritz and Richard Morton, 25–36. Toronto: Hakkert, 1976.

Loftis, John. *Steele at Drury Lane.* Westport, CT: Greenwood Press, 1952.

Loftis, John, Richard Southern, Marion Jones, and A. H. Souten. *The Revels History of Drama in English.* Vol. 5. *1660–1750.* London: Methuen, 1976.

The London Stage 1660–1800: A Calendar of Plays, Entertainments, and Afterpieces Together with Casts, Box-receipts, and Contemporary Comment Compiled from the Playbills, Newspapers, and Theatrical Diaries of the Period. 5 parts. Ed. Emmett L. Avery et al. Carbondale: Southern Illinois University Press, 1962–1968.

Love, Harold. "Who Were the Restoration Audience?" *The Yearbook of English Studies* 10 (1980): 21–44.

Lowenthal, Cynthia. *Performing Identities on the Restoration Stage.* Carbondale: Southern Illinois University Press, 2002.

Markley, Robert. *Two-Edg'd Weapons: Style and Ideology in the Comedies of Etherege, Wycherley, and Congreve.* Oxford: Clarendon Press, 1988.

Marsden, Jean I. "Mary Pix: The Woman Writer as Commercial Playwright." *Studies in the Literary Imagination* 32, no. 2 (fall 1999): 33–44.

———. "Rape, Voyeurism, and the Restoration Stage." In *Broken Boundaries: Women and Feminism in Restoration Drama*, ed. Katherine M. Quinsey, 185–200. Lexington: University Press of Kentucky, 1998.

Monod, Paul Kleber. *Jacobitism and the English People, 1688–1788*. Cambridge: Cambridge University Press, 1989.

Mulvey, Laura. "Afterthoughts on 'Visual Pleasure and Narrative Cinema' inspired by *Duel in the Sun*." *Framework* 6 nos. 15–17 (1981): 12–15. Reprinted in *Feminism and Film Theory*, ed. Constance Penley, 69–79. New York: Routledge, 1988.

———. "Visual Pleasure and Narrative Cinema." *Screen* 16, no. 3 (autumn 1975): 6–18. Reprinted in *The Sexual Subject: A Screen Reader in Sexuality*, ed. John Caughie and Annette Kuhn, 22–34. London: Routledge, 1992.

Mulvihill, Maureen E. "A Feminist Link in the Old Boys' Network: The Cosseting of Katherine Philips." In *Curtain Calls: British and American Women and the Theater, 1660–1820*, ed. Mary Anne Schofield and Cecilia Macheski, 71–104. Athens: Ohio University Press, 1991,

Munns, Jessica. *Restoration Politics and Drama: The Plays of Thomas Otway, 1675–1683*. Newark: University of Delaware Press, 1995.

Nicoll, Allardyce. *History of English Drama, 1660–1900*. 6 vols. Cambridge: Cambridge University Press, 1952–59.

Novak, Maximillian E. "Libertinism and Sexuality." In *A Companion to Restoration Drama*, ed. Susan J. Owen, 53–68. Oxford: Blackwell, 2001.

Orgel, Stephen. *Impersonations: The Performance of Gender in Shakespeare's England*. Cambridge: Cambridge University Press, 1996.

———. "Nobody's Perfect; or, Why Did the English Stage Take Boys for Women." *Southern Atlantic Quarterly* 88 (1989): 7–30.

Orr, Bridget. *Empire on the English Stage, 1660–1714*. Cambridge: Cambridge University Press, 2001.

Pateman, Carole. *The Disorder of Women: Democracy, Feminism, and Political Theory*. Palo Alto, CA: Stanford University Press, 1989.

———. *The Sexual Contract*. Palo Alto, CA: Stanford University Press, 1988.

Pearson, Jacqueline. *The Prostituted Muse: Images of Women and Women Dramatists, 1642–1737*. New York: St. Martin's Press, 1988.

Quinsey, Katherine M., ed. *Broken Boundaries: Women and Feminism in Restoration Drama*. Lexington: University Press of Kentucky, 1996.

Roberts, David. *The Ladies: Female Patronage of Restoration Drama, 1660–1700*. Oxford: Clarendon Press, 1989.

Rosenfeld, Sybil. *Strolling Players and Drama in the Provinces, 1660–1765*. Cambridge: Cambridge University Press, 1939.

Rosenthal, Laura. "'Counterfeith Scrubbado': Women Actors in the Restoration." *Eighteenth Century: Theory and Interpretation* 34, no. 1 (1993): 3–22.

———. *Playwrights and Plagiargists in Early Modern England: Gender, Authorship, Literary Property*. Ithaca: Cornell University Press, 1996.

Rothstein, Eric. *Restoration Tragedy: Form and the Process of Change*. Madison: University of Wisconsin Press, 1967.

Salkeld, Duncan. *Madness and Drama in the Age of Shakespeare*. Manchester: Manchester University Press, 1993.

Scouten, Arthur H., and Robert D. Hume. "'Restoration Comedy' and its Audiences, 1660–1776." *Yearbook of English Studies* 10 (1980): 45–69.

Sedgwick, Eve K. *Between Men: English Literature and Male Homosocial Desire*. New York: Columbia University Press, 1985.

Shanley, Mary Landon. "Marriage Contract and Social Contract in Seventeenth-Century Political Thought." *Western Political Quarterly* 32, no. 1 (1979): 79–91.

Shapiro, Michael. *Gender in Play on the Shakespearean Stage: Boy Heroines and Female Pages*. Ann Arbor: University of Michigan Press, 1994.

Smith, James L. Introduction to *The Plain Dealer*. New York: W. W. Norton, 1979.

Stacey, Jackie. *Star Gazing: Hollywood Cinema and Female Spectatorship*. London: Routledge, 1994.

Staves, Susan. "Fielding and the Comedy of Attempted Rape." Unpublished paper delivered at the Houghton Library, Harvard University, February 1988.

Straub, Kristina. *Sexual Suspects: Eighteenth-Century Players and Sexual Ideology*. Princeton: Princeton University Press, 1992.

Straznicky, Marta. "Restoration Women Playwrights and the Limits of Professionalism." *ELH* 64 (1997): 703–26.

Wilson, Kathleen. *The Sense of the People: Politics, Culture, and Imperialism in England, 1715–1785*. Cambridge: Cambridge University Press, 1995.

Index of Plays Cited

Index of Plays Cited

General Index